Josh McDowell

365 Devotions for Teens
Connecting LIFE *and* FAITH

SHILOH RUN PRESS
An Imprint of Barbour Publishing, Inc.

JANUARY

An Awesome God

First Things First

My Bible Reading:
In the beginning God created the
heavens and the earth. (Genesis 1:1)

How about those New Year's resolutions? At the beginning of the year some students might resolve to make better grades, work out more, eat healthier, play less video games, etc. The idea of a new year naturally leads to thinking of a fresh start, a new beginning.

The first verse of the Bible starts off with a new beginning when it says "In the beginning God. . ." (Genesis 1:1). Everything in the universe had its beginning with God. That's the best way to start a new year—beginning with God first.

Jesus talked about putting God first and how everything else would be taken care of in your life. He said not to worry about material things like what you're going to eat or drink or wear. He said, "Your heavenly Father already knows all your needs. Seek the Kingdom of God [first] above all else, and live righteously, and he will give you everything you need" (Matthew 6:32–33).

Truth is, that's an awesome New Year's promise: put God first in your life and God will take care of you. And you can count on it, because "the LORD always keeps his promises; he is gracious in all he does" (Psalm 145:13).

My Prayer: God, You are the new beginning to everything. Thank You for all that You created and all that You provide. Help me put You first and keep You first in my life this year, starting today. You are an awesome God! Amen.

Totally Awesome

My Bible Reading:
"Do not forget the things I have done throughout
history. For I am God—I alone! I am God,
and there is no one else like me." (Isaiah 46:9 NLT)

What does "totally awesome" mean? Words like *truly impressive, absolutely astonishing, incredibly amazing, mind-blowing, breathtaking, magnificent, stunning*—those are some words that define totally awesome.

Yet the meaning of the word *awesome* goes deeper than thinking of something being terrific. The idea of awesome can also represent a feeling of fear and wonder; it is that sense of awe and amazement of the truly extraordinary. And it is this total sense of awesomeness that best expresses the view of the Almighty God of the universe.

Truth is, the prophet Isaiah went on to explain that God never had a beginning nor will He have an ending. He is all-powerful, everywhere-present, all-knowing, and unchanging. That is really a totally awesome God!

*My Prayer: I am in awe of You, God. You are beyond awesome.
And what is so mind-blowing and beyond my comprehension
is that even though You are so great and beyond me—You have
chosen to love the likes of me. Thank You! That is awesome! Amen.*

Who Is Forever?

My Bible Reading:

Before the mountains were born,
before you gave birth to the earth and the world,
from beginning to end, you are God. (Psalm 90:2)

Did you have a goldfish when you were really young? Where is it now? What's your first memory of the car your parents owned? What happened to that car? Remember the burning candles on your last birthday cake? How long did the flames last?

If you had a goldfish, it has long passed away. The car your parents had when you were born is probably on the junk heap. And the burning candles on your birthday cake? They have long been snuffed out. Everything in this world and everything you experience has an end. But not so of God. He has no beginning and has no end. "You are always the same"—the Bible says of God—"you will live forever" (Psalm 102:27).

Truth is, the idea of a forever—someone who had no beginning and has no ending—stretches the mind. But that is part of who God is, an everlasting, eternal, and forever God. But as difficult as that is to grasp, here is the amazing thing. You are a forever person too if you have placed your trust in Jesus.

My Prayer: *I am so thankful that You are forever. While I can't comprehend the idea of a never-ending life, I am so glad You offer me life eternal with You. You are an awesome God. I love that You are forever, and I am thankful I know You as my eternal God. Amen.*

A Real Superhero

My Bible Reading:
"O Sovereign LORD! You made the heavens and
earth by your strong hand and powerful arm.
Nothing is too hard for you!" (Jeremiah 32:17)

Superheroes: Superman, Superwoman, Iron Man, Wonder Woman,
Wolverine, Storm, Batman, Raven, the list goes on. Wouldn't it be
great to personally know one of these characters? What would it be
like to hang out with Superman, Wolverine, Storm, or Raven? Having
a superhero as a friend could feel quite prestigious and would pretty
much guarantee you a lot of "friends."

Superheroes are fictional, of course. But in their world they all
have some weaknesses or limitations. Not so with the God of the
Bible. " 'I know that you [God] can do anything,' " Job said, " 'and no
one can stop you' " (Job 42:2). God doesn't tire out. There is no limit
to His power. No one can defeat Him. He may give people freedom
to do what they want for a time, but eventually, in the end, God wins
out. Think of the advantage of knowing a superhero winner like that.

Truth is, God is a powerful God who is there to strengthen and
guide you. He wants you to rely on Him every day as your friend and
superhero.

*My Prayer: You are the Almighty God who can accomplish anything.
Help me today to rely on You and tap into Your strength for what I
need. Thank You that You are powerful and that You love me. Amen.*

January 5

Your Image

My Bible Reading:
Then God said, "Let us make human beings
in our image, to be like us." (Genesis 1:26)

Before the sun ever shone, before the rain ever fell, before there was air to breathe. . .there was relationship. Think about it. The eternal God of the universe has always existed as relationship. God the Father has always loved His Son; God the Son has always loved His Father; and God the Holy Spirit has always loved both the Father and the Son. In this cycle of perfect relationship God created you. Why? He created you in His relational image so you could experience and enjoy all the benefits relationships offer.

Truth is, God didn't create you because He needed relationships—He already existed as relationship. He created you because by nature He has a relational heart and He wants you to enjoy the goodness of life in relationship with Him and others. That's a great image to live out!

*My Prayer: Thank You for creating me in Your relational image.
I want to experience relationship like You. In this New Year
teach me to have a compassionate and loving heart like You.
Help me express that to someone today. Amen.*

Hide & Seek

My Bible Reading:
"If you look for me wholeheartedly, you will find me.
I will be found by you," says the LORD. (Jeremiah 29:13–14)

Who hasn't played hide-and-seek at one time or another? "1, 2, 3, 4. . .10. Ready or not, here I come!" The idea, of course, was to find your friends and tag them before they touched home base and became safe. You may have outgrown the hide-and-seek game, but God still wants you to "play" a version of that game with Him.

In many respects God is hidden from you because He is not a *material* being. The Bible says, "'God is Spirit, so those who worship him must worship in spirit and in truth'" (John 4:24). Even though He is invisible to you, He wants you to seek Him so you will experience His spiritual presence every day in your life.

Truth is, Jesus said to seek and "keep on seeking, and you will find" (Matthew 7:7). He really wants to be found so you can feel Him close to you, like a best friend. Keep seeking Him because He's the best thing in life!

My Prayer: *Thank You that You want me to find You and know You as my best friend. Give me more of a desire to seek You out in Your Word and in prayer. And let me find all that I need in You today. Amen.*

Count on It

My Bible Reading:
"Be sure of this: I am with you always,
even to the end of the age." (Matthew 28:20)

There aren't a lot of things you can count on in life. But there are some. Try this out on a friend. Ask someone to:

1. Choose a number—any number.
2. Double it.
3. Add twelve to that number.
4. Divide the new number by two, then subtract the original number.
5. Now add one.

Then tell the person the number he or she has is seven! It will surprise your friend because you will be right. The answer will always be seven. Test it out yourself. If you followed the instructions exactly, your answer will always come out to seven. Whether you start with five or fifty billion, the final number will be seven. That is a mathematical truth you can count on.

Truth is, at times people and situations in life can be disappointing and you may wish you could have someone to count on. And you do! Jesus will always be there for you—always, every time. It is in God's nature to always be true. He never changes. "Jesus Christ is the same yesterday, today, and forever" (Hebrews 13:8).

My Prayer: Thank You that You were there for me yesterday, that I can count on You to be there for me today, and that You will be there for me for the rest of my life and beyond. Help me share this truth with a friend today. Amen.

Worries?

My Bible Reading:
Give all your worries and cares to God,
for he cares about you. (1 Peter 5:7)

D o you ever worry? Do you sometimes worry you won't make a good enough score on a test? What about sports? There are always worries about not doing enough to win or helping the team win. There are relationship worries like, "Am I likable enough or will the people I care about remain my friends for very long?" There are home-life worries like, "Will my family always be a safe and peaceful place where I can relax and be accepted for just being myself?"

Now use your imagination. Imagine Jesus materializing and visiting you in a quiet place. He places a hand on your shoulder and in a soft voice says, "I really care what is happening to you right now. It hurts Me that you hurt. I want you to know that I'm here for you, no matter what."

You begin to open up and share with Jesus the details of your struggle. He leans forward and says in a caring voice, "I'm really sorry you're going through all this." You look closer and see tears of compassion filling His eyes.

Then just as you are about to get up, Jesus reaches out and touches your arm. In a tender voice, He says, "I want you to know that I'm your safe place. You can always come to Me without fear of rejection or ridicule. I'll be your closest friend."

Truth is, Jesus isn't an imaginary friend. He is real and He cares about everything that is happening to you. He says, " 'Be sure of this: I am with you always, even to the end of the age' " (Matthew 28:20).

My Prayer*: Thank You, Jesus, that You care about me and all that is happening in my life. Help me accept that and bring my worries and cares to You each day. I know You are with me and You do care. Amen.*

Ultimate Goodness

My Bible Reading:
"He is the Rock; his deeds are perfect. Everything he does is just and fair. He is a faithful God who does no wrong; how just and upright he is!" (Deuteronomy 32:4)

Think about your happiest moment in life. What was your best meal ever? Where was your best vacation? Remember the most beautiful sight you ever saw? As you think about those, you are recalling moments of joy, contentment, beauty, and goodness. Now, where did all those good things come from?

The Bible says, "Whatever is good and perfect is a gift coming down to us from God our Father" (James 1:17). He is the originator of all that is good. It's not that God just does things that are perfectly good. He is perfectly good by His very nature. He is " 'the one who is holy and true' " (Revelation 3:7). " 'The LORD is just! He is my rock! There is no evil in him!' " (Psalm 92:15).

Truth is, the reason you can count on God to do good and honor what He says He will do is that, by His very nature, He is true and holy and right. God will not and cannot go against His goodness and do wrong. There is absolutely no evil in His character and "it is impossible for God to lie" (Hebrews 6:18). "He remains faithful, for he cannot deny who he is" (2 Timothy 2:13).

My Prayer: Thank You, God, for Your goodness. I want to reflect Your goodness in my own life. Help me show some goodness to others today. Maybe as a result, someone will see a little of Your goodness in me. Amen.

He Knows It All!

My Bible Reading:

O LORD, you have examined my heart and know everything about me. You know when I sit down or stand up. You know my thoughts even when I'm far away. You see me when I travel and when I rest at home. You know everything I do. You know what I am going to say even before I say it, LORD. . . . Such knowledge is too wonderful for me, too great for me to understand! (Psalm 139:1–6)

God knows a lot! He knows everything about your past. He knows everything about who you are right now. And He knows every thought, motive, and deed you'll ever have and do in your future. That may seem a little scary at first, but since God is all-knowing it means He has all the answers to life as well.

Truth is, relying on such an all-knowing God would make sense, and that is precisely what He wants you to do. "Trust in the LORD with all your heart; do not depend on your own understanding. Seek his will in all you do, and he will show you which path to take" (Proverbs 3:5–6).

My Prayer: I am so thankful that You are all-knowing. I don't want to rely on my own knowledge to plan my today or tomorrows. Help me know Your will for my life. Show me the paths I should take. You are an awesome God who cares about me and my future. I want to follow Your ways. Amen.

Faith Plus

My Bible Reading:
It is impossible to please God without faith. Anyone who
wants to come to him must believe that God exists and that
he rewards those who sincerely seek him. (Hebrews 11:6)

Doesn't everything we believe about God, the Bible, and the
Christian religion boil down to faith—sincerely believing? A lot
of people will say that, but that's not what the Bible says or what God
expects. The Bible says, "Faith is the assurance of things hoped for,
the conviction of things not seen" (Hebrews 11:1 NASB). So where do
the *assurance* and *conviction* of your faith come from? They actually
come from a "faith plus"—a faith plus evidence or knowledge of the
things not seen.

Have you ever flown in a plane? You exercise faith when you do.
You believe the pilot can fly the plane safely even though you don't
generally see him. You probably have never seen the expert engineers
and machinists who built the plane, but you believe the aircraft is
safe. Your assurance of safety comes from your knowledge that the
airline company has a good track record and the evidence of expert
pilots. You put your faith in the plane and pilot plus the evidence that
airplanes are a safe form of travel. It's faith plus evidence that gives
assurance and conviction to your belief.

Truth is, Jesus doesn't want you to blindly believe in Him and His
Word. He wants you to explore the evidence that God is real, that
His Word is reliable, that Jesus is the Son of God, that He died and
rose from the dead to purchase your salvation. Jesus wants you to
have a faith plus—a belief that is backed up with evidence. That will
give your faith assurance and conviction.

My Prayer: *Jesus, thank You that You want me to examine
who You are, how Your Word is reliable, and why Your
truths are in my best interest to follow. You want my faith
to be full of assurance and confidence and I want that too.
Help me grow each day in my faith in You. Amen.*

Faith & Doubt

My Bible Reading:
When Jesus woke up, he rebuked the wind and the raging
waves. Suddenly the storm stopped and all was calm.
Then he asked them, "Where is your faith?" (Luke 8:24–25)

Jesus was once taking a nap on a boat that was crossing the Sea of Galilee. His disciples were with Him. It wasn't uncommon in the area for storm clouds to gather quickly and make boating hazardous. That's what happened. The storm was so fierce that the disciples thought they were going to drown. They yelled to Jesus that the boat was about to go down.

After Jesus stopped the storm with His mere words, He asked the disciples, " 'Where is your faith?' " (Luke 8:25). Instead of trusting in what Jesus could do, Jesus' followers had doubts. Jesus' followers had doubts because they concentrated more on their problems than looking to the Problem-Solver.

Truth is, doubts seem to melt away when you focus on God's caring heart to protect you. The Bible says, "God's way is perfect. All the LORD's promises prove true. He is a shield for all who look to him for protection" (Psalm 18:30).

My Prayer: *Help me look to You, O God, as my caring protector when times get tough. I don't want to doubt Your caring heart. I want to get to know You better and understand how much You really care about me and everything that is going on in my life. Help me trust You more today. Amen.*

Proud of It

My Bible Reading:

I know the greatness of the LORD—that our Lord is greater than
any other god. The LORD does whatever pleases him throughout all
heaven and earth, and on the seas and in their depths. (Psalm 135:5-6)

How do you feel when you ace a test? What about when you win
at a sporting event or even win at a video game—how does
that make you feel? It's natural to have a sense of pride when you
accomplish something. You inherited that quality from God Himself.

After each creative act God sort of stepped back, looked at it,
stuck out His chest and said, "That's good!" He declared His creative
work "good" seven times in Genesis. He was proud of what He
had done. But He was really proud on the day He created humans.
Because on that day the Bible says, "He saw that it was *very* good"
(Genesis 1:31, emphasis mine).

Truth is, on the seventh day God ceased His creative work. He
declared it holy as a way to endorse and celebrate His masterful
accomplishment. He called it His day of rest or you could say, His
day of satisfaction of accomplishment. That means every seventh
day is a reminder to worship the God who is so very proud of you and
all of creation that He has given you.

---

*My Prayer: Thank You for giving me a special day each week to
celebrate and worship You and all Your accomplishments. I'm glad
You created me, and I want You always to be proud of me. Help me
say or do something today that will make us both proud. Amen.*

Here and Everywhere

My Bible Reading:
"Am I a God who is only close at hand?" says the LORD.
"No, I am far away at the same time. Can anyone hide
from me in a secret place? Am I not everywhere in all the
heavens and earth?" says the LORD. (Jeremiah 23:23–24)

You're at your school's championship game. Your team is leading by a slim margin with only minutes left in the game. Suddenly you feel the vibration of your phone. It's a text from your friend who is headed to the hospital due to a car accident. You don't want to leave the game, but you want to be with your injured friend too.

The problem is that you are limited by time and space. You can't humanly be in more than one physical place at a time. That's not the case with God. He can be everywhere at the same time.

Truth is, your God is so awesome that He can be with you at your game and with your friend at the hospital at the same time. Because God is here with you, and yet everywhere, you can know He is available all the time for all who call upon Him.

My Prayer: You are an awesome God who is ever-present to be there for all who call upon You for help. Thank You for always being there for me. And while I do not have the power to be ever-present, help me be there for a friend today who is in need. Amen.

January 15

Know Me

My Bible Reading:
Jesus prayed to his Father, "This is the way to have eternal life—
to know you, the only true God, and Jesus Christ,
the one you sent to earth." (John 17:3)

What does it take to have a close relationship with another person? One teenager wrote that being close to someone "is to be real with another person. . .no facade, no barriers." That's pretty good. A close relationship is about really knowing another person and letting that person really know you.

That's what God wants. Jesus said the way to eternal life was to know Him and His Father God. He told the children of Israel He wanted them to know and love Him. God said, "I want you to show love, not offer sacrifices. I want you to know me more than I want burnt offerings" (Hosea 6:6).

Truth is, if God had a sign hung around His neck it would read: PLEASE KNOW ME. Because He made you in His relational likeness and image, you have that same sign hung around your neck. God wants you to learn to know Him, and He wants you to open up to let Him know everything that is going on in your life too.

My Prayer: God, even though You sometimes seem far away, I want to learn to know You better. And I want to learn to be open to You by sharing what's happening to me. Help me do that, even today. Amen.

His Greatest Joy

My Bible Reading:
Jesus said, "I have told you this so that my joy may be
in you and that your joy may be complete." (John 15:11 NIV)

Can you imagine God laughing? How about a God who smiles? A lot of people see a stern, authoritarian God with no sense of humor. You may have run across some people that are that way. But that's not what God is like.

God told his children that "the joy of the LORD is your strength" (Nehemiah 8:10). The fruit or expressions of God the Holy Spirit in your life should be "joy" (Galatians 5:22). The Bible says you are to live a life of "joy in the Holy Spirit" (Romans 14:17). And Jesus said that when His followers enter into heaven each of them will hear His Father say, " 'Enter into the joy of your Master' " (Matthew 25:23 NASB).

Truth is, God is the originator of joy. And since you were made in His relational image, He wants you to experience joy too. God's greatest joy is to have a close relationship with you so your joy can be made complete. Isn't it great that your Creator is the source of joy and that He wants you to be happy and full of His joy?

My Prayer*: Thank You that You're the God of joy and that You want me to experience the deep sense of joy and happiness that You experience. I want to sense Your smile today. And help me express the "joy of the Lord" to someone before this day is over. Amen.*

A Good Anger

My Bible Reading:

Sing to the LORD, all you godly ones! Praise his holy name. For his anger lasts only a moment, but his favor lasts a lifetime! (Psalm 30:4–5)

Have you ever been ticked—really angry? Your anger may have been a result of someone hurting you, doing something against you, or maybe you didn't get your way on something and you really got ticked. Many times anger is self-centered and vindictive. But God's anger isn't like that.

God's anger is holy, with a pure purpose. God gets angry when the innocent suffer. That probably angers you too. His anger is at times measured out to protect the innocent and bring the guilty to justice. The Bible says, "He will judge the world with justice, and the nations with his truth" (Psalm 96:13). In anger God will discipline and cause pain on people for a short time so they will turn back to Him. He did this a lot to the children of Israel.

Truth is, God is "slow to get angry and filled with unfailing love" (Psalm 103:8). God's anger is always holy and comes out of a motivation of love. All of God's actions toward you are always in your best interest, because He loves you.

My Prayer: I'm glad, God, that You are angry at all the evil in the world and that You are at work to see justice prevail. Help me love the good and hate what evil does to this world just like You do. Amen.

When Anger Isn't Good

My Bible Reading:
Don't sin by letting anger control you.
Think about it overnight and remain silent. (Psalm 4:4)

God's holy anger is always good. That isn't the case for a lot of people. Has your anger ever caused you to do some crazy things, even wrong things? That may be, but sheer anger isn't really the problem. Anger becomes a problem when it overpowers and controls you.

Truth is, it's not always easy to control anger. Yet scripture gives you clear direction on what to do with anger. It says to sleep on it and don't talk. When you control your anger you win all the way around. You keep from hurting yourself and others. Wise Solomon said, "Sensible people control their temper; they earn respect by overlooking wrongs" (Proverbs 19:11). Try it the next time you get steamed. Seal your lips and sleep on it. Keeping your anger under control really pays off.

My Prayer: Thank You for the wisdom of Your Word. Give me the strength to be sensible. When I begin to get angry help me keep my lips zipped until I can respond in a way that honors You. Give me the strength to control my anger today. Amen.

A Footprint

My Bible Reading:
"The heavens proclaim the glory of God. . . . Day after day
they continue to speak; night after night they make him
known. They speak without a sound or word; their voice
is never heard. Yet their message has gone throughout
the earth, and their words to all the world." (Psalm 19:1–4)

Some say the universe and everything in it had a naturalistic cause. They claim there was no Creator God who spoke the world into existence; rather this planet and life as we know it is a product of a natural billion-year evolutionary process. Given enough time and matter, they say, anything can be formed by mere chance. But that doesn't mean God is not the Creator of the universe.

Look at your watch. Glance at your smartphone. Take note of what you are holding—a book with printed words in it. Did your watch, smartphone, or even this book get assembled by chance with no outside help? Your reason probably tells you there was someone— an intelligent being—who put them together. There is a footprint of intelligent design behind this book, your watch, and phone.

Truth is, this planet and all its vastly complex life-forms point to a masterful Intelligent Designer too. The Bible contends that people really do "know the truth about God because he has made it obvious to them. For ever since the world was created, people have seen the earth and sky. Through everything God made, they can clearly see his invisible qualities [his footprint]—his eternal power and divine nature. So they have no excuse for not knowing God" (Romans 1:19–20). God as the Intelligent Designer has left His footprint so we can conclude with confidence He is the great Creator.

My Prayer: *Thank You for creating me and all that exists. Help me be more thankful for Your creativity each time I gaze up at the stars at night or see a newborn child. You are an awesome God! Amen.*

Sadder than Sad

My Bible Reading:

The LORD observed the extent of human wickedness on the earth, and he saw that everything they thought or imagined was consistently and totally evil. So the LORD was sorry he had ever made them and put them on the earth. It broke his heart. (Genesis 6:5–6)

Have you ever had a broken heart? It's that overwhelming sadness or emotional pain from the loss of someone or something. God felt it repeatedly as humans rejected Him and refused a relationship with Him. Feeling heartache isn't a weakness. You inherited the capacity to painfully feel rejection and loss from a God who created you in His relational image.

Jesus, God's Son, was about to take the weight of the world's sins to the cross, and He pulled three of His disciples aside. The Bible says Jesus "became anguished and distressed. He told them, 'My soul [heart] is crushed with grief to the point of death. Stay here and keep watch with me' " (Matthew 26:37–38).

Truth is, your God is the One who can relate to any heartache you may ever feel and He is there to help. "The LORD is close to the broken-hearted; he rescues those whose spirits are crushed" (Psalm 34:18).

My Prayer*: Thank You that You are a God who knows how I feel when I'm brokenhearted. And thank You that You are especially close to me then. Help me take my cares and burdens to You and openly share them with You rather than keeping them to myself. You are an awesome, caring God. Amen.*

Seeing Is Not Always Believing

My Bible Reading:
It was by faith that Moses left the land of Egypt,
not fearing the king's anger. He kept right on going because
he kept his eyes on the one who is invisible. (Hebrews 11:27)

Moses had numerous encounters with God but never really saw Him. One time when he was talking to God, he asked Him to become visible to him. But God said, " 'I will make all my goodness pass before you. . . . But you may not look directly at my face, for no one may see me and live' " (Exodus 33:19–20).

Truth is, Moses never really did see God directly, yet he believed in Him. He "kept his eyes on the one who is invisible." It didn't take seeing God directly for Moses to allow God to direct him through life. You don't have to see Him visibly either to believe He is there guiding you every day. God's goodness is evident all around you in creation (Romans 1:19–21), in your moral conscience (Romans 2:14–15), in His Word (2 Timothy 3:16–17), in history (1 Samuel 17:46–47). Visibly seeing is not always believing. But there is plenty of evidence to give you good reason to keep your eyes on the invisible One to guide you every day.

My Prayer: You are the invisible God full of goodness and love. And even though I haven't seen You with my physical eyes, I have seen You with my spiritual eyes. Thank You for being there for me. Help me be a visible reflection of You to my friends today. Amen.

Wonderfully Complex

My Bible Reading:
You made all the delicate, inner parts of my body and
knit me together in my mother's womb. Thank you for
making me so wonderfully complex! (Psalm 139:13–14)

The more scientists learn how the body functions, the more mind-blowing their discoveries. Advanced imaging technology is able to magnify a human cell a billion times. And it reveals nano-engineering so sophisticated that they liken the cell to a technologically advanced automated city.

Your body contains about one hundred trillion cells with molecular robotic systems that do thousands of precise and accurate operations per second. These operations are controlled by a computerlike system that stores terabytes of data in compressed molecules. When you cut your finger, for example, millions of microscopic nanotech-like robots go into action to rebuild and heal your wounded finger at the molecular level.

The emerging response system notifies your cells by a central control system and reprograms them to divert molecules to your wound. Within seconds the mechanical activities of your cells begin to clot your blood, clear away debris, and destroy harmful bacteria. Soon the development of new cells begins rebuilding tissue.

Truth is, the human cell is a technological wonder with perhaps more sophistication and complexity than anything on earth. God made you wonderfully complex! He is an awesome God!

My Prayer: Thank You, God, that You created me with such wonderful complexity to enjoy life and the world You have given me. Help me always be grateful for all You have given me. Amen.

The Origin of Morals
Proves Something

My Bible Reading:
For the truth about God is known to them instinctively
[those people who push God away]. God has put this
knowledge in their hearts. (Romans 1:19 NLT)

There is no argument that some things are just wrong. Instinctively you and everyone else know, for example, that abusing innocent children is wrong. No one has to pass a law protecting children to tell you it's wrong—you just know it is.

You and everyone else accept the objective moral value that harming the innocent is not right. But where did that value come from? Scripture says God, the great Value Giver, planted His knowledge of morality inside you. And that in itself is another piece of evidence that God exists.

The reasoning goes like this:

- If objective morals exist, a Value Giver (God) must exist.
- Objective morals do exist.
- Therefore, a Value Giver (God) must exist.

Truth is, you possess a "morality center" that wasn't put there by your parents, school, or society. God the Value Giver hardwired you to know instinctively that certain things are flat-out wrong.

My Prayer: You, O God, exist above me and beyond me as the great Value Giver. Thank You that You are the very origin of morality— of what is right and wrong. And thank You for planting a sense of morality within me. Help me detect right from wrong today and follow the right and avoid the wrong. Amen.

How Big Is Big?

My Bible Reading:
"I am the one who made the earth and created people
to live on it. With my hands I stretched out the heavens.
All the stars are at my command." (Isaiah 45:12)

You are on planet Earth, which is suspended in a vastness of space. That space stretches on and on and on sprinkled with stars that seem endless. The size of the known universe is really impossible to comprehend, but let's take a stab at it.

The universe is so immense that it is measured using light-years. That's the distance light travels in 365 days. Traveling at 186,282 miles per second, light will go almost 6 trillion miles in a year!

You live in the Milky Way galaxy, which is more than 100,000 light-years in diameter. Your nearest sister galaxy is the Andromeda galaxy. It's about 2.5 million light-years away. And how many galaxies are there in the universe, with how many stars? Scientists say there are probably more than 100 billion other galaxies spread over a space of at least 93 billion light-years that contain over a septillion stars! That's a one followed by twenty-four zeros.

Truth is, that's a big universe with a lot of stars. And God commands them all!

My Prayer: *You are a big God who created a big universe. I can't comprehend how truly big You are and all that You created. But I thank You that even though You are Almighty God that oversees a big universe, You take thought of small me. Thank You for that. Amen.*

January 25

Before God?

My Bible Reading:
The LORD, your Redeemer and Creator, says: "I am the LORD, who made all things. I alone stretched out the heavens. By myself I made the earth and everything in it." (Isaiah 44:24 NLT)

If God was the Master Creator and caused everything to come into being, then who or what caused God? The short answer is, since God is eternal and has always existed, He doesn't need a cause. Ancient philosopher Thomas Aquinas made an argument that anything in motion, like the universe, could not have been brought into motion by itself. Rather, he said, things in motion must be caused to move. That may be a little hard to follow, but the conclusion is that there had to be an Unmoved Mover, and that Mover's name is God.

Some say the creation of the universe, which began to exist at some point, didn't need a cause. But that doesn't make sense because everything that begins to exist must logically have a cause.

Truth is, God is the Mover outside the universe that caused everything to begin. "Have you never heard? Have you never understood? The LORD is the everlasting God" (Isaiah 40:28). Since He has always existed He didn't need to begin in order to be caused.

My Prayer: While my mind, O God, cannot fathom how You have always existed, it doesn't mean it is illogical to believe that You are eternal. You are the everlasting God, the Creator of all that exists. I praise You for being who You are and that You are my hope for an eternal life with You. Amen.

How Do You Know?

My Bible Reading:

"I don't know whether he [Jesus] is a sinner," the man replied. "But I know this: I was blind, and now I can see!" "But what did he do?" they asked. "How did he heal you?" (John 9:25–26)

Jesus had healed the man who was born blind. The skeptics of that day didn't want to acknowledge Jesus as the Messiah and give him credit for the healing. They didn't want the man to acknowledge Jesus had that kind of power either. So they asked him, "How did He (Jesus) do it?"

Truth is, the man couldn't explain how Jesus could perform such a powerful miracle. He just knew it was so because he had experienced it. You may not be able to explain to people how God created the universe, or how He has always existed, or how He is a real God that people can know personally. But if you have personally experienced His forgiveness and He has made you His child, you know He is real. Like the blind man who experienced Jesus' eye-opening power, you can say, "I know God is real because I too have experienced Him!"

My Prayer: God, I may not have all the answers to the questions people ask me about how You created the universe. But I know You are real by the fact that You have changed my life from a lost child in sin to a forgiven child who knows You as Savior and Friend. Thank You for being a personal God. Help me let people see a little of You in my life today. Amen.

The Origin of Love

My Bible Reading:
God is love, and all who live in love live in God,
and God lives in them. And as we live in God,
our love grows more perfect. (1 John 4:16–17)

It feels good to have someone love you. It feels pretty good to love someone in return too. And it really feels good not to be judged, criticized, rejected, or disrespected in any way. That all feels good because real love is accepting, caring, patient, and kind. That's what love does and doesn't do, but that doesn't tell us what love really is.

Love is more than an emotion or feeling. Love, original love, is actually a person—the person of God. He defines everything that love is and ever will be. Jesus said the motivating factor behind a real love is to " 'do to others whatever you would like them to do to you' " (Matthew 7:12). In other words, Godlike love is always other-focused. It looks out for the interests of others and isn't selfish.

Truth is, it's not always easy to give out that kind of unselfish love. But as you accept God loving you in that way, your ability to love others "grows more perfect."

My Prayer: Thank You that You are the very definition of unselfish love. You love me unconditionally and I want to love others that same way. Help me say or do things to those around me with an other-focused love. Amen.

When Intolerance Is a Beautiful Thing

My Bible Reading:
Your eyes are too pure to look on evil;
you cannot tolerate wrongdoing. (Habakkuk 1:13 NIV)

Generally you think of being intolerant as a bad thing and being tolerant of people as the loving thing to do. Well God has certainly shown tolerance to a world of wrongdoers with His expression of love, acceptance, and mercy. That's a beautiful thing. But think of this. What is more beautiful than God's intolerance expressed in His moral outrage toward the tragedies of child abuse, poverty, racism, slavery, AIDS, bigotry, and other such evils?

I was so struck by the beautiful nature of intolerance that I created a T-shirt that read on the front "Intolerance Is a Beautiful Idea." On the back it read:

> *Mother Teresa was intolerant of poverty.*
> *Bono was intolerant of AIDS.*
> *Nelson Mandela was intolerant of apartheid.*
> *Martin Luther King was intolerant of racism.*
> *Jesus was intolerant of bigotry.*

Truth is, God's hatred toward sin that so hurts His children reflects God's holy intolerance—that's a beautiful thing.

My Prayer: Thank You that Your holy character gives tolerance and intolerance their proper definition and understanding. I want to more clearly see how wrong hurts others and be intolerant of it by helping to alleviate the heartache and pain from people's lives. Help me do some of that today. Amen.

The Infinite Source of Light

My Bible Reading:
Jesus said, "I am the light of the world. If you follow me,
you won't have to walk in darkness, because you will
have the light that leads to life." (John 8:12)

Jesus, God's Son, is the light of the world and He has always been in existence. Some believe when God created the universe He let His light penetrate the known world. But the light you are able to see is just a small part of the entire spectrum of what is called electromagnetic radiation (EMR).

The visible light range or wavelength of the EMR is from about 380 nanometers to about 740 nanometers. But the EMR spectrum is much, much broader than that. It actually extends from thousands of miles down to a fraction of the size of an atom. This includes low frequencies like radio waves to high frequencies like gamma rays, none of which can be seen by the naked eye. Scientists say that in principle the EMR spectrum is infinite and continuous. While time, space, and mass can all change, the speed of EMR is always constant in all frames of reference.

Truth is, Jesus is the light of the world and He is constant, infinite, and continuous too. And Jesus is the One who brings His pure light, seen or unseen, to every dimension of the universe, from the distant stars to a fraction of the diameter of a proton. His spiritual light dispels the darkness and "leads to life!"

---

*My Prayer: Your light is eternal and extends everywhere.
I am so glad that You have shed Your light on me and
given me eternal life. Help me reflect Your light today
so my friends can also know about You. Amen.*

Crowned With

My Bible Reading:

What are mere mortals that you should think about them, human beings that you should care for them? You made them only a little lower than God and crowned them with glory and honor. (Psalm 8:4–5)

God created you in His image, and even though you and everyone else, past and present, has tarnished that image, He wants you to regain your crown of glory and honor. If you have trusted in Christ as your Savior, scripture says a lot about the honorable position you now hold with God. Here are six of them:

- You are God's masterpiece (Ephesians 2:10).
- You are His child (John 1:12).
- You are where His Spirit lives (1 Corinthians 3:16).
- You are His ambassador or representative (2 Corinthians 5:20).
- You are His chosen people, a royal priest, and His very own possession (1 Peter 2:9-10).
- You are an heir that will inherit His kingdom (Romans 8:17).

Truth is, because you have a relationship with God through Christ, you are crowned with a meaningful life now and a marvelous future that will last forever!

My Prayer: Even though I don't deserve a crown of glory and honor, because of Your sacrifice and love I have one. Thank You for that and for the reality that I can live with You for all eternity. Help me show my gratefulness by being a good representative of You—maybe by befriending someone who needs some encouragement today. Amen.

What's in a Name?

My Bible Reading:
Those who know your name trust in you, for you, O Lᴏʀᴅ,
do not abandon those who search for you. (Psalm 9:10)

Those who know God's name—what He is really like—trust in Him. This month you have learned more about who God is and that you can know He really exists. And when you know Him (His name) you can really trust Him. Here are a few names or titles of God:

- "In the beginning God [*élohim*] created" (Genesis 1:1). God's name means the all-powerful supreme one who has no equal.
- "I AM WHO I AM [*Yahweh*]" (Exodus 3:14–15). He is the self-existent one with no beginning and no end.
- "Blessed be Abram by God Most High [*El-Elyon* or *El-Shaddai*]" (Genesis 14:19). God's name here means the Almighty one who is sovereign or controller over all things.
- "Abraham named the place *Yahweh-Yireh* (which means 'the Lᴏʀᴅ will provide')" (Genesis 22:14).
- "The Lᴏʀᴅ is my shepherd [*Jehovah-Rohi*]; I have all that I need" (Psalm 23:1). As shepherd, He is my perfect guide in life.
- "The virgin will conceive a child! She will give birth to a son and will call him Immanuel (which means 'God is with us')" (Isaiah 7:14).
- "And he [Jesus] will be called: Wonderful Counselor, Mighty God, Everlasting Father, Prince of Peace (Isaiah 9:6).

Truth is, you can trust a God whose name is all-powerful, self-existent, sovereign—a God who is in control, a provider, shepherd and guide—who is always with you as a Wonderful Counselor, Mighty God, Everlasting Father, and a Prince of Peace.

My Prayer: *I am so thankful that Your name tells me You are worthy of my trust. You will never abandon me because You are faithful and true. I seek after You. Thank You for allowing me to find You. Amen.*

FEBRUARY

Totally Inspired

God Spoke

My Bible Reading:

"Now search all of history, from the time God created people on the earth until now, and search from one end of the heavens to the other. Has anything as great as this ever been seen or heard before? Has any nation ever heard the voice of God speaking from fire—as you did—and survived? . . . He showed you these things so you would know that the LORD is God and there is no other. He let you hear his voice from heaven so he could instruct you." (Deuteronomy 4:32–33, 35–36)

Moses had a one-on-one meeting with God on Mount Sinai. God told Moses to have the children of Israel gather at the foot of the mountain so they could hear God speak. Flames shot up from the top of the mountain and God spoke out of the flames.

Nothing had ever happened like that before, or since. He spoke words to His human creation because He wanted to instruct them on how to find redemption and gain eternal life. So Moses carefully wrote down everything God said, because, after all, this was God speaking.

Truth is, those words have been accurately preserved all these years and have been published as the most widely circulated book in all of history. Some have called those writings the Bible. Others simply refer to them as God's Word. Understand the meaning of those words and you will understand the real meaning of life itself!

My Prayer: Thank You God for speaking Your Words of Life so many years ago. And thank You for preserving those words over the centuries in Your holy scriptures so I too could hear from You. Teach me to understand Your Word. Amen.

It's Alive?

My Bible Reading:

For the word of God is alive and powerful. It is sharper than the sharpest two-edged sword, cutting between soul and spirit. . . . It exposes our innermost thoughts and desires. (Hebrews 4:12)

The words your friends speak to you today will be words that are alive because your friends are alive—they are living beings. But how can an ancient book written by people who have long died contain living words? Simple. An eternal living God breathed those words thousands of years ago, and He is still here today as the Holy Spirit to keep those words alive.

The Bible says that "all Scripture is inspired by God" (2 Timothy 3:16). The New Testament was originally written in the Greek language. The Greek word (the original language the New Testament was written in) for "inspired" is *theopneustos*. It literally means "God-breathed." The apostle Paul, who penned much of the New Testament, said he and the other apostles wrote down "words given to us by the Spirit, using the Spirit's words to explain spiritual truths" (1 Corinthians 2:13). The Holy Spirit brings life to God's Word.

Truth is, when you read God's Word today it is just as alive and powerful as it was when God spoke His words from Mount Sinai over three thousand years ago. When the prophets wrote words in the Old Testament and the apostles of Jesus wrote the words in the New Testament, they were living words breathed out by an ever-living God.

My Prayer: *Thank You that through Your Holy Spirit Your words of scripture are alive and real for me today. Help me be more motivated to know what Your words mean to me. Today and every day give me more of a hunger to read Your Words of Life. Amen.*

No Killjoy

My Bible Reading:
Joyful are people of integrity, who follow the
instructions of the LORD. Joyful are those who obey his
laws and search for him with all their hearts. (Psalm 119:1–2)

Have you ever had the impression that the Bible with all its dos and don'ts is meant to be a killjoy? "Stop that"; "Don't do this"; "Avoid that attitude"; "Follow this way"—on the surface it all seems so negative and restrictive. But King David didn't see it that way at all. He went on to pray to God: "Make me walk along the path of your commands, for that is where my happiness is found" (Psalm 119:35). He knew that God's instructions and commands were never meant to simply restrict him or keep him from being happy. It's quite the opposite.

Truth is, God and His ways are designed to lead you to live in right relationship with Him so you can enjoy life as it was meant to be lived. God's way of living is the happiest way of life and He wants you to experience it. Even God's negative commands are positive, because they are meant to protect you from harm and provide for your happiness.

My Prayer*: Thank You for giving me all Your instructions
and commands so I can live a life of joy and happiness. Help me
remember that when I start to think that following Your commands is
a restriction to my happiness. Thanks that You love me and want me
to be happy. Help me share that truth with someone today. Amen.*

From a Heart of Love

My Bible Reading:

"So remember this and keep it firmly in mind: The LORD is God both in heaven and on earth, and there is no other. If you obey all the decrees and commands I am giving you today, all will be well with you and your children." (Deuteronomy 4:39–40)

Every instruction, story, admonition, parable, and guideline from God's Word comes out of the loving heart of God to provide for you and protect you. Did your parents ever keep you away from a hot stove or tell you to look both ways before crossing the street? The reason was to protect you. It is in your best interest to avoid getting burned or being run over by a car. God's Word is for your benefit. God spoke through Moses to say: "'You must always obey the LORD's commands and decrees that I am giving you today for your own good'" (Deuteronomy 10:13).

Truth is, God gave you His words because He loves you. Think of it. When you love God back by doing what He asks you to do, you reap the reward of your own happiness. That's what a good relationship is all about—pleasing one another and bringing each other joy.

My Prayer: You are a loving God who wants to see me happy. I am so grateful that Your words of scripture are meant to guide me onto a path of happiness. Help me share this very truth with my friends today. Amen.

True Person, True Words

My Bible Reading:
For the word of the LORD holds true, and we can trust everything
he does. He loves whatever is just and good; the unfailing
love of the LORD fills the earth. (Psalm 33:4-5)

Have you ever had a friend you could completely trust? Like, whatever he or she told you was actually true and you could count on it. That works when a person's character is honest and true. Because true words will naturally come out of a true person.

The Bible says, "God's way is perfect. All the LORD's promises prove true. He is a shield for all who look to him for protection" (Psalm 18:30). The instructions God gives on how to act flows out of who He is (perfect goodness) and how He himself acts (perfectly good). His ways are true and good because His very nature is true and good.

Truth is, you can always know that every one of God's commands and instructions is in your best interest because they come out of a perfectly true and good God. "Whatever is good and perfect is a gift coming down to us from God our Father" (James 1:17).

My Prayer: Thank You that behind every one of Your words in scripture stands a perfect and true God that I can trust. Your Word is true because You are true. You are so worthy of my life and my trust. Help me share something about Your truth and goodness with someone today. Amen.

Revived

My Bible Reading:
The instructions of the LORD are perfect,
reviving the soul. (Psalm 19:7)

God is perfect and His instructing Word has the power to revive you. Before you had a relationship with God you were spiritually dead. Everyone born on this earth was born spiritually dead and in need of being revived to new life.

The perfect Word of God is alive, and when you trusted in Christ for salvation the Holy Spirit of life revived your soul and gave you eternal life. That is what the amazing and powerful Word of God can do. But there's more. God wants His Word to keep reviving you when you are feeling a little low, like discouraged or disheartened. There are a lot of things in life that can make you feel like that.

Truth is, God's Word is alive and powerful and is there to lift your spirits and encourage your heart. The Holy Spirit is real and offers His encouraging and comforting words to you. His words revive the soul and turn discouragement into encouragement. "God is our merciful Father and the source of all comfort. He comforts us in all our troubles so that we can comfort others" (2 Corinthians 1:3-4).

My Prayer: Thank You that Your perfect instructions can revive my soul. Help me go to Your Word and find You as my comfort when I am in need of encouragement. Allow Your words of comfort to flow through me to comfort and encourage others. Allow me to be an encouragement to someone, even today. Amen.

Made Wise

My Bible Reading:
The decrees of the LORD are trustworthy,
making wise the simple. (Psalm 19:7)

Have you ever met someone who was truly wise? Sure there are a lot of people who are smart—they have a great deal of head knowledge—but there are few who are truly wise. A wise person is someone who sees the bigger picture, one who has sound judgment and can make right decisions.

You can trust in God's Word because God Himself is trustworthy. And when you rely on God's Word and follow it, you become wise. Solomon, known as the wisest of all men, said, "The LORD grants wisdom! From his mouth come knowledge and understanding. . . . Then you will understand what is right, just, and fair, and you will know how to find the right course of action every time. For wisdom will enter your heart" (Proverbs 2:6, 9–10 NLT).

Truth is, real wisdom is seeing life as God sees it, and when you trust in His Word He grants you the ability to make right choices every time.

My Prayer: *Thank You that Your trustworthy Word grants me wisdom. Help me trust more and more in what You have to say and less and less in what I think is best. You see the big picture of life and the right path. Let me see life from Your perspective and guide me down the path of wisdom today. Amen.*

The Right Path = Joy

My Bible Reading:
The commandments of the LORD are right,
bringing joy to the heart. (Psalm 19:8)

Let's face it, doing the right thing isn't always the fun thing. Doing what you feel like, eating what you're hungry for, or going wherever you please whenever you want, can be much more fun—at least in the short term. But God's Word teaches that over the long haul, walking down the right path according to God will bring lasting joy. Fun can be short-lived, but a deep-seated joy can last forever.

Truth is, following God's path, which is always right, brings joy to the heart. "Trouble chases sinners, while blessings reward the righteous" (Proverbs 13:21). "The LORD will withhold no good thing from those who do what is right. . . . What joy for those who trust in you" (Psalm 84:11–12). "There is joy for those who deal justly with others and always do what is right" (Psalm 106:3). In the long run, the right path will always equal joy.

My Prayer: Thank You that You are a God of joy and Your way is always the right way. Help me remember that. Guide me this day to follow Your commands, for I know that in the long run Your way is a way of joy. My friends also need to know this, so help me be a living example of it to them. Amen.

Clear Insight

My Bible Reading:
The commands of the LORD are clear,
giving insight for living. (Psalm 19:8)

Have you ever experienced someone trying to pull one over on you, but you saw right through it? Have you been in a situation that made you feel uncomfortable because you sensed something wasn't quite right? If so, you had good discernment, which is another way to say you had clear insight into the person or situation.

Would you like to have more clarity, discernment, and insights to live a more fulfilled life? Following the instructions of God's Word provides just that. They teach you to peer clearly into people and situations so you can avoid wrong and do right.

Truth is, you need discernment to even understand and apply God's truth to your life. That's why the psalmist prayed, "Give discernment to me your servant; then I will understand your laws" (Psalm 119:125). Wise Solomon said that the instructions from God "will give insight to the simple, knowledge and discernment to the young" (Proverbs 1:4).

My Prayer: *Thank You for giving me a road map to life through Your Word, the Bible. Your Word gives such clear insights on doing the right things and avoiding the wrong things. Your clear words help me get where You want me to be. Even today, continue to teach me Your ways so that I can discern the right paths You want me to follow. Amen.*

True Blue

My Bible Reading:
The laws of the LORD are true; each one is fair. (Psalm 19:9)

Someone whom you can count on to be loyal and always stick by you is sometimes called a "true blue" friend. Have you ever heard that phrase? It is said that in the late Middle Ages the English town of Coventry gained a unique reputation. The town's dyers could produce material that didn't fade with washing. In other words, the colors in the fabric remained "fast" or "true" and were known as being "true blue." So the town gained the reputation for being "true blue."

God's Word is "true blue" because God is true. "He is not human," the Bible says, "so he does not change his mind" (Numbers 23:19). And "God will continue to be true even when every person is false" (Romans 3:4 NCV). You can count on God's instructions to be "true blue" for everyone and therefore fair. "Everything [God] does is just and fair" (Deuteronomy 32:4). How can it get any better than that?

Truth is, you can always count on the instructions from God being fair to everyone because He is so right and true. It is in God's nature to be true, so He can't be anything but fair and just to everyone. God's Word can be trusted because God can be trusted.

My Prayer: *Thank You that Your Word can be counted on.
All of Your commands come from You who are perfectly
just and true and fair. Life isn't fair, but You are.
Thank You for giving me such a just and true Word. Amen.*

The Bottom Line

My Bible Reading:
"You must worship no other gods, but only
the LORD, for he is a God who is passionate about
his relationship with you." (Exodus 34:14 NLT)

The bottom line? The real reason God wants you to worship Him, know His ways (His Word), and follow them—is because He is passionate about a relationship with you. He told the prophet Hosea, "'I want you to know me'" (Hosea 6:6). And when you study His Word you get to know God and deepen your relationship with Him. That's the bottom line—God loves you so much and wants you to return that love by getting to know Him and experiencing joy by living according to His ways.

Truth is, God's Word reflects the heart of a God who wants to be your best friend. The Bible may at first be difficult to understand and may seem like a lot of rules to obey, but it's not. It's really a book about God and His Son, Jesus, who wants to have a deep love relationship with you. Moses understood this and begged God, "'If you are pleased with me, teach me your ways so *I may know you*'" (Exodus 33:13 NIV, emphasis mine).

My Prayer: *Thank You that You want a love relationship with me,
like being best friends. And thank You for giving me Your Word,
the Bible, as my guide to unlocking that deep friendship.
Help me share the truth today that You are passionate about
Your relationship with me and everyone. Amen.*

School's Not Out

My Bible Reading:
All Scripture is inspired by God [God-breathed] and
is useful to teach us what is true. (2 Timothy 3:16)

You may love school and all the teachers that have ever taught you. Maybe you wish you could be in school for the rest of your life. If that's not true, it's really okay. But in a real sense, learning is a lifelong journey, because God and His Word are there to be your teacher for life. And count on it; He is the absolute best teacher.

The God-breathed words of scripture and the Holy Spirit are there to teach you what is right and true. Jesus said, "'Come to me, all of you who are weary and carry heavy burdens, and I will give you rest. Take my yoke upon you. Let me teach you, because I am humble and gentle at heart, and you will find rest for your souls'" (Matthew 11:28–29).

Truth is, Jesus wants to personally be your teacher, and, believe me, He's the best teacher in the world. Even though He knows everything there is to know, He's not arrogant and He doesn't get impatient. He is humble and gentle and His course of life is designed just for you.

My Prayer*: Thank You that You want to teach me with Your words that are true and relevant for me. I want to learn from You. So I pray today: "Teach me, O LORD, to follow every one of your principles. Give me understanding and I will obey your law; I will put it into practice with all my heart" (Psalm 119:33–34 NLT). Amen.*

A Time Out?

My Bible Reading:
All Scripture is inspired by God and is useful to teach us what
is true and to make us realize what is wrong in our lives.
It corrects us when we are wrong. (2 Timothy 3:16)

Have you ever had someone put you in a "time out" when you were young? A lot of parents use the "time out" thing to try and help a person realize he or she is misbehaving. The hope is that it will act as a corrective. Well, another purpose of God's Word is to give you a "time out"—to make you realize what actually is wrong and bring about a correction in what you think and how you act.

For example, a lot of people say it's okay to give some pushback to those who dislike you and disrespect you. Because the only way some people get it is when you give them some negative pushback, right? But God's Word says differently. Jesus said, "'Love your enemies! Pray for those who persecute you! In that way, you will be acting as true children of your Father in heaven'" (Matthew 5:44-45). So Jesus gives a corrective to the "get even" thinking with a "love your enemy" thinking.

Truth is, God's Word gives you the right standard for thinking and doing. It is there to let you know what attitudes and actions are right and to correct you when you need it.

My Prayer: Lord, I'm not perfect. So I'm glad that Your loving Word is there to show me the right way and to correct me when I'm wrong. Help me be more sensitive to Your Word. I pray the prayer that King David wrote: "Search me, O God, and know my heart; test me and know my anxious thoughts. Point out anything in me that offends you, and lead me along the path of everlasting life" (Psalm 139:23-24). Amen.

A True Valentine

My Bible Reading:
"For God so loved the world that he gave his
only Son, so that everyone who believes in him
will not perish but have eternal life." (John 3:16 NLT)

Valentine's Day. Where did that come from? One legend has it that a priest named Valentine served during the third century in Rome. The Emperor of Rome outlawed marriage because he decided that single men made better soldiers than those that had wives and families. Valentine believed in love and continued to perform marriages in secret for young lovers. When Valentine's actions were discovered, he was put to death. From that time on people began celebrating a day for lovers in honor of Valentine. There are similar legends of how Valentine's Day got started, most with the idea that a person named Valentine sacrificed himself in the name of love.

Truth is, the greatest "Valentine" story is a historically true one. God, who is the very definition of love, longed to be reconnected to each human being ever born. All were separated from Him because of sin. So God sacrificed His only Son to offer a reunited life with Him forever. Jesus' death on the cross was like God calling out to you, "Be My Valentine."

My Prayer: Your sacrifice demonstrates how much You love me and the whole world. Thank You that Your love got to me and I finally accepted Your Son's sacrifice as Your way to give me eternal life. I am so grateful! Help me show a little of Your love to someone today. Amen.

Life Training

My Bible Reading:
All Scripture is God-breathed and is useful
for [teaching. . .correction and]. . .training in
righteousness [right living]. (2 Timothy 3:16 NIV)

Can a book do all that—teach me, correct me, and train me to live right? How can a set of words in a book do all that? Actually, mere words can't.

When the Bible says that the God-breathed words are useful for training, it uses a special word in the Greek translation—*paideia*. It means to "bring up," as in to "raise" or "parent." That's sort of a strange thought, because when you think of parenting you think of a person, not a set of words, right?

Exactly! Parenting isn't a correspondence course; it's a person-to-person function. And that is exactly what Jesus said, "'I will ask the Father, and he will give you another Advocate [a Counselor], who will never leave you. He is the Holy Spirit, who leads into all truth'" (John 14:16–17).

Truth is, God sent His Holy Spirit to "parent" you. God has given you a one-on-one personal trainer to guide you through life as you study and read His training manual—the Bible!

My Prayer: Thank You that Your words are true and that You are my personal trainer. I believe Your words that "the LORD is good and does what is right; he shows the proper path to those who go astray. He leads the humble in doing right, teaching them his way. The LORD leads with unfailing love and faithfulness" (Psalm 25:8–10). Help me be humble today and please keep training me in right living through Your Spirit and Your Word. Amen.

Passed Down Accurately

My Bible Reading:
Jesus said, "I tell you the truth, until heaven and
earth disappear, not even the smallest detail of God's law
will disappear until its purpose is achieved." (Matthew 5:18)

Have you ever misread a text—someone meant one thing but you interpreted it wrong? Before there were texts or even the printing press, any writings that were to be preserved had to be copied by hand. And that opened up the possibility for mistakes by the copiers, who were called scribes. And since the scriptures were all written before the printing press, who is to say the scribes literally copied every word accurately? It's a big problem if scribes didn't copy the scriptures as they were originally penned.

The good news is that Jesus said that not even the smallest detail of God's Word would disappear until it achieves its purpose. And God accomplished that through a very disciplined set of Old Testament scribes. These copiers, known as Talmudic and Masoretic scribes, were so disciplined that before a copy of scripture could be certified as accurate, other scribes would count every word and letter. Why? They had to know that the newly copied scripture contained precisely the same number of letters and words as the one they were copying from. Every line even had to begin and end with the same word and letter as the source, so that the new copy was reproduced as an exact duplicate of the old one.

Truth is, when you read God's Word you can be confident you are reading the God-breathed words He wanted you to read.

My Prayer: Thank You that You have seen to it that I have an accurate transmission of Your words. That demonstrates that You really want me to know what You have to say. And I really want to hear what You have to say to me, even this very day. Amen.

February 17

How Many?

My Bible Reading:
Jesus said, "Heaven and earth will disappear,
but my words will never disappear." (Matthew 24:35)

Have you ever heard of the old movie *Gladiator* that won the
Academy Award for Best Picture the year it was released?
It was based on Caesar's *Gallic Wars* written between 58–44 BC.
Everything you learn in school about Caesar's wars is found in just
over 250 historical writings, called manuscripts. The earliest known
manuscript dates back to AD 900. The first copies made from the
original were probably finished twenty years after the historian
began penning them. But the only copies that exist today are dated
some 950 years after the original was written.

One way you evaluate the reliability of an ancient manuscript is to
determine how many manuscript copies have survived and the time
that elapsed between the original writings and the earliest existing
copy. The more copies you have and the nearest in time those copies
are to the original, the better.

Jesus' words were written down and then copied over the centuries. There are no originals of them just like there are no originals of
the *Gallic Wars*, Homer's *Iliad*, Plato's writings, or of the writings before
Christ or during His time on earth. There are just over 1,800 manuscripts
of Homer's *Iliad* with a 400-year time gap between the original and the
first copy. That's better than the *Gallic Wars* and better than any other
ancient first-century writing—except for the New Testament.

Truth is, Jesus said His words would never disappear. So how have
the New Testament manuscripts written in the first century survived?
There are over 24,000 manuscripts in existence today dating back to
within fifty years of the very first originals!

My Prayer*: Thank You that You have allowed so many manuscripts
of Your words to survive. And thank You that they were copied so
carefully. That gives me such confidence that I am reading the
accurate words written in the New Testament. Amen.*

Eye Witnesses

My Bible Reading:
Jesus' disciple John wrote, "We are telling you about what we ourselves have actually seen and heard." (1 John 1:3 NLT)

Have you ever been at an event and told some friends about it who weren't there so they could experience it themselves? What if those friends told others about what you saw? Then what if those people told others, and that process was repeated a hundred times? By the time the hundredth person heard about what you experienced, it is likely some important information was either left out or badly twisted. It is unlikely your original story was accurately related on that hundredth telling.

That isn't the way the words of Jesus and His apostles were passed on. The people who wrote down the words of Jesus actually lived during the time of Jesus. They heard Him teach, they saw Him perform miracles, they witnessed His crucifixion, and they saw Him after He rose from the dead. The words of Jesus and the experiences of His time on earth were recorded by those who were eyewitnesses of those events.

Truth is, you can count on the words of Jesus and the whole New Testament to have been accurately recorded. Jesus' words were reported by people who knew what they were talking about because they were there to see and hear Jesus.

My Prayer: Thank You that Your words to me are true. Thank You that the people You spoke to on earth are the ones You had to report it. It gives me confidence that what I read is coming directly from You. Help me pass on Your reliable truths to others today. Amen.

It's How I See It

My Bible Reading:
Be a good worker, one who does not need to be ashamed
and who correctly explains the word of truth. (2 Timothy 2:15)

Have you ever had someone ask you to explain what a particular scripture verse means to you? The Bible deals with a lot of issues and it's not always easy to understand their meaning. And some people take a stab at it and explain what scripture personally means to them.

But explaining the meaning of scripture isn't a matter of personal interpretation. Peter, a disciple of Jesus, wrote, "Know this first of all, that no prophecy of Scripture is a matter of one's own interpretation" (2 Peter 1:20 NASB). It really isn't a matter of how you see it or how anyone else sees it; it is really a matter of how God sees it.

Truth is, God has an intended meaning for every verse and book in the Bible. Your task is to understand what God intended for you to know when He spoke through His writers "using the Spirit's words to explain spiritual truths" (1 Corinthians 2:13). He wants you to read His words and understand their proper meaning as He intended.

My Prayer: Thank You that You are the author of the Bible and that You want me to understand the meaning that You intended. Help me understand Your words and apply them to my life. The truth for today is that You are a personal God who loves me enough to want me to get to know You intimately. Help me absorb that truth throughout the day. Amen.

Clear Mind, Open Heart

My Bible Reading:

No one can know a person's thoughts except that person's own spirit, and no one can know God's thoughts except God's own Spirit. And we have received God's Spirit (not the world's spirit), so we can know the wonderful things God has freely given us. (1 Corinthians 2:11–12)

Have you ever talked to someone who got so emotional that you couldn't get him or her to understand what you meant? Maybe you've experienced someone who was so dogmatic about an issue that he or she wouldn't listen to reason. Some people simply aren't very open-minded. As a result, they shut out other people's views and opinions.

God has expressed His views and opinions in His Word. And unless you keep a clear mind and an open heart, it will be very difficult to absorb what He wants you to understand. One of the biggest mistakes people make in interpreting the meaning of the Bible is by injecting their own views or emotions into scripture.

Truth is, God has given you His Spirit to guide you into understanding how His truth is to apply to your life. Jesus told His disciples that His Father would send His Spirit for this very reason. "'He is the Holy Spirit, who leads into all truth'" (John 14:17).

My Prayer: I want to know Your thoughts. Help me keep a clear mind and open heart so Your Spirit can reveal You and Your thoughts to me in Your words of scripture as You meant them to be understood. Thank You that You have given me Your Spirit of Truth. Amen.

Okay, I'm Wrong!

My Bible Reading:
If you ignore criticism, you will end in poverty and disgrace;
if you accept correction, you will be honored. (Proverbs 13:18)

How hard is it for you to admit you're wrong? It may be easier for some than others. Yet, it seems no one really likes saying, "I'm wrong." But the reality is no one is perfect, so everyone needs to accept healthy criticism. Healthy growth, both relationally and spiritually, depends upon accepting criticism and correction.

Criticism never feels good, but it's part of the process of growing up spiritually. That is how we become spiritually mature. In fact, success in practically everything in life depends on owning up to your mistakes and correcting them. Wise Solomon said, "A man who refuses to admit his mistakes can never be successful. But if he confesses and forsakes them, he gets another chance" (Proverbs 28:13 TLB).

Truth is, accepting criticism and discipline from God is always good because it teaches you how to be more like Christ. The Bible says, "God's discipline is always good for us, so that we might share in his holiness" (Hebrews 12:10). Sharing in Jesus' holiness is actually becoming more like Him.

My Prayer: *It's not easy to accept criticism, but help me accept it anyway. I know You love me and want to see me grow to be more like You every day. Help me express some of Your likeness to those around me today. Amen.*

It's Who You Know

My Bible Reading:
As we know Jesus better, his divine power gives us
everything we need for living a godly life. (2 Peter 1:3 NLT)

Sometimes the Bible may seem like a book of dos and don'ts. There are a lot of commands that say to avoid this or admonitions to be more like that. While the Bible does give clear guidelines, it's not so much about telling you what to do as it is revealing to you the person you need to know.

Sure, God wants you to live a godly life, but for good reason. Because when you live like Him you live a maximum life of joy and peace. He designed you that way. That's why a growing relationship of knowing Jesus more and more is so important. The more you know what the God of the Bible is like, the more you are given the power to live like Him.

Truth is, God gave you His Word because He wants you to know Him and enjoy an ongoing intimate personal relationship with Him that will last forever. That's the main reason to read His Word—to know Jesus better in order to be and live more like Him.

My Prayer*: Thank You for revealing Yourself in Your Word. Help me know You more and more as I discover the true meaning of Your truth in my life. Help me share some of Your loving characteristics with others, even today. Amen.*

Spiritual IQ

My Bible Reading:
I pray for you constantly, asking God...to give you
spiritual wisdom and insight so that you might grow
in your knowledge of God. (Ephesians 1:16–17)

To become an attorney you'll need insights into the law and the legal system. To become a medical doctor you'll need insights into the human body and medicine. To become an accountant you'll need insights into mathematics and bookkeeping. But to become knowledgeable of God you'll need different kinds of insights—spiritual insights.

Growing in your knowledge of God isn't like studying law or medicine or mathematics. Those require certain mental insights. Knowing God requires a spiritual insight that is only possible if you have been made God's child by His Spirit. The apostle Paul wrote that "people who aren't spiritual can't receive these truths from God's Spirit. It all sounds foolish to them and they can't understand it, for only those who are spiritual [made alive through a relationship with Christ] can understand what the Spirit means" (1 Corinthians 2:14).

Truth is, only those who have been made alive to God and have His Spirit can listen and understand the spiritual insights of scripture. Jesus said, " 'Anyone who belongs to God listens gladly to the words of God' " (John 8:47). To grow in your knowledge of God you need to be in tune with His Spirit.

My Prayer*: Thank You for making me alive to You by Your Holy Spirit. Help me keep in tune with Your Spirit by relying on You for wisdom and insights from Your Word. I want to keep growing in my knowledge of You. Amen.*

Got It from God

My Bible Reading:
I want you to understand that the gospel message I preach is not based on mere human reasoning. I received my message from no human source, and no one taught me. Instead, I received it by direct revelation from Jesus Christ. (Galatians 1:11–12)

There are thirty-nine books in the Old Testament and twenty-seven books in the New Testament. Over three thousand years ago God began speaking through Moses to write down His words. He would eventually inspire more than forty different prophets and apostles to pen all the scriptures. He carefully communicated "the words of the Lord" through His human spokesmen. That word choice "the words of the Lord" is used more than three thousand times in scripture to tell us that the words of the Bible are from God.

Truth is, when you read from the Bible you are reading God's words as if He were writing them for you. These were men chosen by God and they "were moved by the Holy Spirit, and they spoke from God" (2 Peter 1:21). Some will say the Bible is merely religious writings made up by religious men. But scripture is a supernatural book that has come from God Himself.

My Prayer: Thank You that You spoke through Your chosen writers to pen Your words for me and everyone who will listen. Help me always remember the words of scripture are Your words of truth. Let them be alive in my life today as I share some of Your truth with others. Amen.

Never Out of Stock

My Bible Reading:
"The grass withers and the flowers fade, but the
word of our God stands forever." (Isaiah 40:8)

Have you ever been online to buy something and the notice comes up "out of stock"? Sometimes items are just not popular enough and they're listed "no longer available." The prophet Isaiah was saying that some things, like the grass, wither to nothing and flowers fade away. But not God's Word. That stands forever.

Scripture has been hand-copied over the centuries until the mid-1400s when printing presses began printing Bibles. Since then the Bible has been printed and published more than any other book in the world. Today the Bible, or portions of the Bible, has been translated into some 2,650 languages with distribution totaling billions of copies.

Truth is, God's Word will never be out of stock or out of print. Remember what Jesus said? " 'Heaven and earth will disappear, but my words will never disappear' " (Luke 21:33). The Bible stands out as one-of-a-kind. No other book is God-breathed with a collection of writings that are the very thoughts and concepts of God. And because of that it will last forever!

*****My Prayer:** You, O God, are forever and Your words of
truth will last forever. Thank You that I can count on Your
Word to be right and true today, tomorrow, and forever.
Help me share that truth with someone today. Amen.*

Can't Believe Everyone

My Bible Reading:
Do not believe everyone who claims to speak by the Spirit.
You must test them to see if the spirit they have comes from God.
For there are many false prophets in the world. (1 John 4:1)

One group claims their truth is right, while another claims they're the true way. You can find 101 different churches and religions—all of which say their views are the correct ones. Scripture cautions you not to believe just anyone.

The disciple John went on to explain one way to tell whether someone has wrong teaching or not. He said that if someone "does not acknowledge the truth about Jesus, that person is not from God" (1 John 4:3). Jesus is the test. If what a person says doesn't agree with Jesus, you can be confident that person isn't presenting the truth.

Truth is, Jesus proved He was God's Son by being born of a virgin, performing incredible miracles including the big one—rising from the dead. He is the one who stated, " 'I am the way, the truth, and the life. No one can come to the Father except through me' " (John 14:6).

My Prayer: You, Jesus, are the Son of the one true God. Your truth is the final word on all truth. Thank You that You made it so clear that You are the "Chosen One" of God. And thank You for giving me Your true words of scripture. Help me always compare other people's teaching to Your true words. Amen.

A Special Place in Your Heart

My Bible Reading:
I have hidden your word in my heart,
that I might not sin against you. (Psalm 119:11)

Have you ever had anyone dislike you? Maybe that person was envious of you or didn't like it that you had more friends than he or she had, and maybe they were even glad when things didn't go your way. Was it rather easy to ignore and reject that person?

Now think of your current best friend. It's that friend you enjoy hanging out with, that special friend who would do almost anything for you, and the one you know will stick by you when you need him or her most. You don't think about rejecting that kind of friend or doing something that would hurt him or her, do you? Why not?

You don't want to hurt people you are connected with and close to because you have come to care for them. In a real sense you have a special place in your heart for them. That's what the writer of this psalm meant. By having a special place in his heart for God and His Word, it kept him from wanting to hurt or do something against God, his closest friend.

Truth is, the more you make room in your heart for Christ and His Word, the more you are going to avoid doing anything that will hurt and displease Him. The closer you draw to Jesus, the more you want to please Him.

My Prayer: *Help me keep hiding Your Word in my heart.*
I want to learn to know You more. I want to please You.
Thank You for being such a relational God. Amen.

Pointing

My Bible Reading:
Jesus said: "I tell you the truth, those who listen to my message and believe in God who sent me have eternal life. They will never be condemned for their sins, but they have already passed from death into life.... You search the Scriptures because you think they give you eternal life. But the Scriptures point to me." (John 5:24, 39)

You're sitting around with your friends after a sporting event. You see three students walking by that you don't know. They all look your way and one points directly at you. What goes through your mind? How does it make you feel?

Pointing is rude, right? It singles you out and probably not for a good reason. But in Jesus' case, it was for a very good reason. All of scripture is pointing a finger at Jesus and in effect saying, "All the laws and regulations, all of its hopes and promises, and all of its protection and provisions begin and end with You—the Chosen One of God, the one who brings meaning to all of God's Word."

Truth is, Jesus is the centerpiece of all scripture because He and He alone accomplishes its purpose. When Jesus said, "Scripture points to me," He was acknowledging He was the Word and the reason it existed. Jesus went on to say, "'Don't misunderstand why I have come. I did not come to abolish the law of Moses or the writings of the prophets. No, I came to accomplish their purpose'" (Matthew 5:17).

My Prayer: Thank You that all of scripture points to You, because following laws and obeying rules cannot give me life. Only You can give me eternal life. Thank You for being You, the eternal, life-giving God who loves me. Help me share Your love with someone today. Amen.

Thirsty

My Bible Reading:
As the deer longs for streams of water, so I long for you,
O God. I thirst for God, the living God. (Psalm 42:1–2)

When was the last time you had a cold, refreshing drink? Was it an hour, five hours, a day, or three days ago? Your last drink was no doubt only hours ago, not days. Why? Because your body requires liquid on a constant basis—it longs to be hydrated. That is the way you were designed physically.

Spiritually you were designed to be thirsty for God, to long after Him. Without Him there is no true life, happiness, joy, or satisfaction in this existence. Scripture says that God " 'gives life and breath to everything, and he satisfies every need. . . . His purpose was for the nations to seek after God and perhaps feel their way toward him and find him—though he is not far from any one of us. For in him we live and move and exist' " (Acts 17:25, 27–28).

Truth is, God wants you to long after Him, because as you do you become closer to Him and that pleases Him. God gets great joy out of your loving Him. And what do you get? You get a life of meaning, fulfillment, and joy!

My Prayer: It's hard to imagine that a mighty and all-powerful God who is self-sustaining really loves me. Knowing this gives me a longing to know You more. Please keep me thirsty for You. You are an amazing God who gives me meaning and purpose in life. Amen.

MARCH

You Choose

Trust Me

My Bible Reading:

The LORD God warned him [Adam], "You may freely eat the fruit of every tree in the garden—except the tree of the knowledge of good and evil. If you eat its fruit, you are sure to die." (Genesis 2:16–17)

Did you ever try to have a relationship with someone you didn't fully trust and he or she didn't fully trust you? It's a guarantee for a disastrous relationship. The hallmark of a close and lasting love relationship is trust.

God wanted Adam to trust in Him. God told him that he had total freedom to eat from all the trees, except one. He wanted Adam to freely and voluntarily make a love choice. He had to answer the question: "Is God keeping something good from me?" God longed for Adam to trust that He truly loved him and had his best interest at heart. A choice to obey God was a choice to trust in God.

Truth is, that's what God wants from you too—He wants you to trust in Him. God wants you to believe that He always has your best interest at heart when He asks you to obey Him.

My Prayer: Lord, You are a good God who always has my best interest at heart when You ask for my obedience to Your ways. I want to keep trusting You, believing that You love me and always want what is best for me. And help me love You by obeying Your Word. Help me demonstrate that today by living out Your command to love others as You love me. Amen.

Choices Have Consequences

My Bible Reading:

When Adam sinned, sin entered the world. Adam's sin brought death, so death spread to everyone, for everyone sinned. (Romans 5:12)

Life is full of consequences. Turn the electricity off in your house and you'll have a dark house. Unplug your TV and it won't show a picture. Remove the battery from your smartphone and you won't be able to text. In each case a separation from the power source brings a death to lights, TVs, and smartphones. Actually that's what death is—a separation from the power source of life.

When Adam sinned he experienced a separation from God, his true power source of life. He was immediately separated from God relationally (died spiritually) and years later his life separated from his body (died physically). As a result all humans have inherited this condition of being separated from God. "All have sinned," the Bible says, "and fall short of the glory [or standard] of God" (Romans 3:23 NIV).

Truth is, that's what sin has done. It has separated all humans from God because as scripture states, "The wages of sin is death" (Romans 6:23). And while God has provided a plan to forgive sin and reverse the death sentence of humans, it's important to acknowledge that choices have consequences.

My Prayer: As I am reminded that choices have consequences, O Lord, help me make choices today that please You. You are my source of life and I am so glad You are merciful and patient with me. I echo these words of scripture, "I have chosen to be faithful; I have determined to live by your regulations" (Psalm 119:30). Amen.

Who Knows Best?

My Bible Reading:
She [Eve] saw that the tree was beautiful and its fruit looked
delicious, and she wanted the wisdom it would give her.
So she took some of the fruit and ate it. (Genesis 3:6)

What was the "wisdom" Eve wanted? She wanted to be wise enough to decide for herself what fruit was good for eating and what wasn't. She wanted to be the one to determine what was right and what was wrong. Rather than looking to God as the true definer and standard of what was right, she decided she would be her own standard.

That was a big mistake! But humans are still making that mistake today. It seems a lot of people want to be the one who decides what is right for them and wrong for them. They want to be the one who "knows best" what choices to make for themselves. What they consider right for them at any given time becomes their own definition of morality.

Truth is, God and God alone is the perfect standard for right and wrong; He defines morality. "He is the Rock," scripture says, "his deeds are perfect. Everything he does is just and fair. He is a faithful God who does no wrong; how just and upright he is!" (Deuteronomy 32:4). When you look to God and His Word to define right and wrong, you honor Him and are in effect saying, "I love You, will obey You, and trust that You know what is best for me."

My Prayer: *You are the all-knowing holy God who does no wrong. I want to always look to You and Your Word to determine what is right and what is wrong. Thank You for being my moral compass. Amen.*

The Devil Made Me Do It!

My Bible Reading:
Jesus said, "From the heart come evil thoughts, murder, adultery, all sexual immorality, theft, lying, and slander." (Matthew 15:19)

It's not easy to own up to your faults. When you really blow it you may temporarily feel better if you blame someone else, like "The devil made me do it." Of course, in the end it's always better to own up to whatever was done and admit it was no one else's fault but your own.

There may be outside forces that influence your choices, but Jesus made it clear that wrong attitudes and actions really come from within the heart. The apostle Paul said that because of Adam's sin everyone is born with a sinful nature. He explained the problem wasn't with God's laws that point to the right way to live. "The trouble is with me," he said, "for I am all too human, a slave to sin. . . . And I know that nothing good lives in me, that is, in my sinful nature" (Romans 7:14, 18). Paul asked and answered the real question: "Who will free me from this life that is dominated by sin and death? Thank God! The answer is in Jesus Christ our Lord" (Romans 7:24–25).

Truth is, you can't accept Jesus as the answer unless you admit you have a sinful heart in the first place. King David knew he was a sinner from the start when he said, "I was born a sinner" (Psalm 51:5). The good news is there is blessing for people who know they have the problem of sin. Jesus said, " 'God blesses those who realize their need for him, for the Kingdom of Heaven is given to them' " (Matthew 5:3 NLT).

My Prayer*: I'm so glad that You have the power to change hearts that want to do wrong to new hearts that want to do right. Thank You for changing my heart and help me continue to realize my need for You every day. Amen.*

March 5

Separated but Not Abandoned

My Bible Reading:
The LORD God banished them [Adam and Eve] from the Garden of Eden, and he sent Adam out to cultivate the ground from which he had been made. (Genesis 3:23)

Some people think God is intolerant of people who disagree with Him. They say He should be less demanding and even overlook human weaknesses and failures. They assert He isn't a very understanding God. Those who say that don't really understand what God is like.

There is a reason God separates Himself from sin as He did in the case with Adam and Eve. The Bible says, "You [God] are holy" (Psalm 22:3). He is so holy and pure He "cannot allow sin in any form" (Habakkuk 1:13 NLT). "Your eyes are too pure to look on evil; you cannot tolerate wrongdoing" (Habakkuk 1:13 NIV). To tolerate or accept sin would violate God's nature.

Truth is, God is a merciful God. You "delight to show mercy" (Micah 7:18 NIV). He is the God who said, " 'I will never fail you. I will never abandon you' " (Hebrews 13:5). Even though God simply can't overlook sin, He steps up in mercy to make a full payment for your sins. A payment that cost Him the death of His only Son.

My Prayer: Thank You that You are a holy God. Your holiness and purity make You intolerant of sin. It is understandable that You had to separate from humans that were sinful. But thank You for Your loving mercy that paid an enormous price to forgive even me of my sins. Help me share that truth with someone today. Amen.

Authentic Love Is Risky

My Bible Reading:
Joshua said to the people: "If serving the LORD seems undesirable to you, then choose for yourselves this day whom you will serve.... But as for me and my household, we will serve the LORD." (Joshua 24:15 NIV)

God never forces anyone to love and serve Him. He gave the children of Israel a choice, he gave the first couple (Adam and Eve) a choice, and He gives you a choice. That's what love is—a choice. But in giving humans a choice God took a big risk.

The risk was that humans might not choose to love and serve God. That means God would feel the rejection of His creation. Of course He could have programmed humans to automatically love Him. But that alternative wouldn't be fulfilling either. Would you want to be loved by a robot-type person programmed to love or by someone who was forced to love you? That's not fulfilling.

Truth is, if love isn't a choice it is not an authentic love. Real love can't be programmed, forced, or manipulated. God wants you to be free to love Him because you choose to. And that opens up the possibility of you choosing not to love Him. Of course He'll do everything in His power to form a love relationship with you. But He will leave it up to you to choose to love Him back. Doesn't that just blow your mind that God loves you so much that He gives you the freedom to choose?

My Prayer: Thank You that You gave me a choice to love You. And it humbles me to think You have gone to such lengths so I can love You back even though I was born a sinner separated from You. You are such a merciful and awesome God. Amen.

Amazing Patience

My Bible Reading:
The Lord isn't really being slow about his promise, as some people think. No, he is being patient for your sake. He does not want anyone to be destroyed, but wants everyone to repent.... And remember, our Lord's patience gives people time to be saved. (2 Peter 3:9, 15)

How patient are you? Say you had a friend who rejected you once for no good reason, maybe even rejected you twice. Would you be patient with him or her? What if that kind of disloyalty was repeated over and over and over again? That would take a lot of patience, wouldn't it?

When humans rejected God the Bible says, "It broke his heart" (Genesis 6:6). Yet He has been patient even though the human family has rejected Him again and again. That's an amazing amount of patience. God really does care about you and all the world and wants everyone to be saved.

Truth is, God's patience is a motivator. "Don't you see how wonderfully kind, tolerant, and patient God is with you?" the Bible says. "Can't you see that his kindness is intended to turn you from your sin?" (Romans 2:4). God's kindness and patience act as a motivator to turn away from sin.

My Prayer: *Your kindness and patience with me do motivate me to turn away from wrong. It makes me want to be better and do better. I mess up, but You remain patient with me. Thank You for that. I never want to take advantage of Your never-ending patience. I always want to please You. You are an amazing God and I love You. Amen.*

A Judge Who Is Always Right

My Bible Reading:
Righteousness and justice are the foundation of your throne.
Unfailing love and truth walk before you as attendants. (Psalm 89:14)

Have you ever been judged unfairly? Maybe you were accused of something you really didn't do. Maybe you took the fall when it was someone else's fault. It's not fair to be blamed for something that wasn't your fault. But you never need to worry about getting unfair judgments from God. Because His judgments are always right.

"O LORD of Heaven's Armies, you make righteous judgments, and you examine the deepest thoughts and secrets" (Jeremiah 11:20). "The LORD reigns forever, executing judgment from his throne. He will judge the world with justice and rule the nations with fairness" (Psalm 9:7-8). Because God is righteous by nature, He judges perfectly right every time.

Truth is, you can rely on God not only to be fair in His judgments, but to point you in the right direction when you blow it. "The LORD is good and does what is right; he shows the proper path to those who go astray" (Psalm 25:8). God is a Judge who is always right and always wants what is right and good for you.

My Prayer: Thank You that You are a righteous and fair Judge who loves me enough to not just point out my wrongs, but also show me the right way. It is Your rightness—Your holy and perfect nature—that I love and want to reflect in my own life. Help me reflect fairness to those I come in contact with today. Amen.

Consequences—A Purpose for Pain

My Bible Reading:
My child, don't reject the LORD's discipline, and don't be upset
when he corrects you. For the LORD corrects those he loves, just as
a father corrects a child in whom he delights. (Proverbs 3:11-12)

Have you ever burned your finger? It didn't feel good, did it?
But let's say your hand never felt the consequences of a burn.
What would happen? Without the pain of a burn you would most
likely experience severe damage to the point of losing the use of your
fingers or hand. Pain is what tells you to pull away from those things
that will burn you.

The consequences of wrong behavior are oftentimes God's way
of telling you to "pull away from those things that will burn you." The
discipline from God is a good thing. It is designed to help you avoid
those things that can really cause you severe damage spiritually,
emotionally, or relationally.

Truth is, you should be happy for discipline. The fact that God allows
you to experience the consequences of bad behavior is a good thing.
Consequences are there to bring you back to the right path—a path of
joy and happiness. Job said to " 'consider the joy of those corrected
by God! Do not despise the discipline of the Almighty when you sin' "
(Job 5:17). There is a purpose for the pain of your wrongdoing; it is
meant to bring you back to God's arms.

*My Prayer: Help me thank You for the consequences of my
misbehavior. You are allowing me to feel the consequences of my
wrongs so I can learn to avoid wrong and follow right. You always
want what is best for me and You are happy when I am living a life of
joy. Thank You that You are that kind of a loving Father to me. Amen.*

Seriously Jealous

My Bible Reading:
"You must worship no other gods, for the LORD,
whose very name is Jealous, is a God who is jealous
about his relationship with you." (Exodus 34:14)

Here's a question: If it's wrong for me to be jealous, why is God jealous? Here's a good answer: God's jealousy isn't wrong because He isn't being selfish about it. He is other-focused. He wants you to love Him exclusively and be in relationship with Him because that is what will bring you joy and completeness.

God has no wrong in Him. He doesn't get jealous if you don't return His love because His pride is hurt or He can't stand rejection. He is passionate about His relationship with you and He becomes jealous if you turn away from Him because He knows that broken fellowship with Him will cause you pain. And that would break His heart.

Truth is, God's jealousy reveals His caring heart for you. He wants nothing but the best for you. Your happiness is His joy. Jesus said, " 'I have told you this so that my joy may be in you and that your joy may be complete' " (John 15:11 NIV). He knows His joy can't be in you to its fullest unless you are continually loving Him.

My Prayer: To be honest, it's hard to believe You are seriously jealous for me. I feel so unworthy of that kind of love from You. But I will thank You for Your love and be grateful that You love me so. I want to love You back with the kind of love You have for me. Help me do that every day. Amen.

The Living Dead

My Bible Reading:
Put to death the sinful, earthly things lurking within you. . . .
Put on your new nature, and be renewed as you learn to know
your Creator and become like him. (Colossians 3:5, 10)

In the real world, people are either alive or dead. The idea of the living dead, the undead, or zombies walking around is the stuff of TV or movie fiction. But that is not the case spiritually. To be spiritually alive and healthy, you must die to your selfish nature.

Jesus said, " 'If you try to keep your life for yourself, you will lose it. But if you give up your life for me, you will find true life' " (Luke 9:24 NLT). What Jesus and scripture mean by "put to death" or "give up your life" is to resist your selfish nature and not be controlled by it. Everyone is plagued by selfishness. Yet the more you resist (put to death) your selfish nature, the more alive you are spiritually.

Truth is, you are spiritually healthy when you are the "living dead"— dying daily to your selfish nature and filling your heart and mind with the living Christ and His Word. The Bible says to "consider yourselves to be dead to the power of sin and alive to God through Christ Jesus. Do not let sin control the way you live; do not give in to sinful desires" (Romans 6:11-12).

My Prayer: I realize there are sinful desires in my life. Help me resist those desires and put my selfishness to death by refusing to allow them to control me. To do that, I need the strength of Your Word and Your Holy Spirit. I look to You, for "God is [my] refuge and strength, always ready to help in times of trouble" (Psalm 46:1). Amen.

Owning Up Is Hard to Do

My Bible Reading:
God is faithful and reliable. If we confess our sins, he forgives
them and cleanses us from everything we've done wrong.
If we say, 'We have never sinned,' we turn God into a liar
and his Word is not in us. (1 John 1:9–10 GWT)

What are the three hardest words in the world to say? For most people it's "I am wrong." Confessing that you're wrong is tough. Owning up to a failure or admitting that you've really blown it is hard to do. There's a reason it's hard. It feels like others will look down on you or even reject you when you've done wrong. And who wants that?

Truth is, God is loving and faithful and doesn't reject people who confess their sin. In fact, you can count on it; He is definitely a forgiving God. Rather than looking down on you for confessing you have blown it, He is overjoyed that you are owning up to your sin. King David, who committed some real serious sins, said, "You will not reject a broken and repentant heart, O God" (Psalm 51:17). He is pleased with those who own up to their sin. That is what it means to have a repentant heart.

My Prayer: Thank You that You are such a forgiving God. Help me readily confess my sins when I do wrong. Thank You that You are my friend and Savior, a God who "is compassionate and merciful, slow to get angry and filled with unfailing love" (Psalm 103:8). Amen.

A Chain Reaction

My Bible Reading:
Knowing God leads to self-control. Self-control leads to patient
endurance, and patient endurance leads to godliness. Godliness
leads to love for other Christians, and finally you will grow
to have genuine love for everyone. (2 Peter 1:6–7 NLT)

You've got them all lined up just right. The dominoes snake down the table in perfect position. You carefully tap the first domino against the next and the chain reaction begins. Within seconds all the dominoes fall as predicted. You may have caused a physical chain reaction like this with dominoes or seen someone else do it.

Simply speaking, a physical chain reaction happens when a series of events precipitates the next. One event leads to the next, to the next, and so on. While it's possible to cause physical chain reactions, it is also possible to cause a good spiritual chain reaction in your life. Peter says that knowing God sets off an incredible chain reaction that leads to all kinds of good things, like self-control leading to patient endurance to godliness to loving other Christians to eventually genuine love for everyone.

Truth is, knowing God is what the Christian life is all about and where it all begins. When Jesus was praying to His Father He said, " 'This is the way to have eternal life—to know you, the only true God' " (John 17:3). That is what sets up this fantastic spiritual chain reaction. Knowing God for who He is and how He relates to you leads to becoming more like Him—patient, godly, loving other Christians, and loving everyone.

My Prayer: *Let the chain reaction from knowing You more and more take place in my life every day. As I know how patient, kind, and loving You are, let a chain reaction of Your patience, kindness, and love shine through my life. Amen.*

In the End

My Bible Reading:
I have seen wicked and ruthless people flourishing
like a tree in its native soil. But when I looked again,
they were gone! (Psalm 37:35–36)

L et's face it, sometimes good things happen to bad people and bad things happen to good people. So how can it be said that following God and His ways brings protection and provision? There are plenty of bad people who don't get caught and live seemingly happy lives. And there are a lot of good and innocent people who suffer pain and heartache.

Living out God's ways doesn't mean that in the short term people will always avoid difficulty. And those who violate God's ways will not always suffer for it in the short term. Positive rewards and negative consequences may not be measured out fully until this life is over.

Truth is, in the end the righteous will reap their reward even though they may suffer in this life for a while. And the wicked may flourish for a while, but like King David indicated, in the end they will get their just reward.

My Prayer: *Thank You for being a just God who rewards Your children who follow You and Your ways. And thank You that You give those that reject You what they deserve. You are a righteous and fair judge. "He is coming to judge the earth. He will judge the world with justice, and the nations with his truth" (Psalm 96:13). Thank You for that. Amen.*

Choices

My Bible Reading:
A wise person chooses the right road;
a fool takes the wrong one. (Ecclesiastes 10:2)

You will make literally hundreds of choices today. Most of them are almost automatic. You chose what time you got up this morning, what to wear, what to eat, what time to leave for school, and made many other decisions throughout your day. You take little time or effort to consider those kinds of choices.

However, there are other types of choices that are more important—moral choices. Those are the choices that you should pause and consider. Moral choices are like being at a crossroad. You must decide which is the right road and which is the wrong road. You must decide between the path according to God and His Word or the path according to your selfish desires.

Truth is, when you look to God and His ways, you gain wisdom and understanding to make the right choices. Wise Solomon said, "Trust in the LORD with all your heart; do not depend on your own understanding. Seek his will in all you do, and he will show you which path to take" (Proverbs 3:5–6).

My Prayer: *Help me pause and consider my options when it comes to the moral choices I face. I know that Your way is the right way. Give me wisdom and strength to choose Your way even though it may mean that those around me might reject me or ridicule me. "Make me walk along the path of your commands, for that is where my happiness is found" (Psalm 119:35). Amen.*

Precept—Principle—Person

My Bible Reading:

Before this faith came, we were all held prisoners by the law. We had no freedom until God showed us the way of faith that was coming. In other words, the law was our guardian leading us to Christ so that we could be made right with God through faith. (Galatians 3:23-24 NCV)

You may not remember it, but your parents probably taught you to stop at a crosswalk and look both ways to be sure no cars were coming before you went across. The rule or *precept* was "Stop, and look both ways before crossing the street." But that precept was based on or pointed to a *principle* of safety. And that principle was based on or pointed to a *person* as your physical protector. Your parents gave you a specific precept based on a principle of safety because they were people who wanted to physically protect you.

Truth is, every precept from scripture is based on a principle that points to the person of God who always has your best interest at heart.

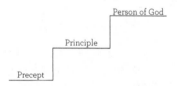

The precepts give you the commands—what to do or not to do. These point to the principles, which give you the "why" behind the commands. But all that simply points or leads you to the person of God. When you see rules or precepts from that perspective, you understand they are given out of the heart of God who always wants to provide for your good and protect you from harm.

My Prayer: *Thank You that You stand behind every law and instruction from scripture with the loving motivation to provide for me and protect me. I can easily lose sight of that when I focus only on the restriction of rules. Help me always remember that Your precepts and principles for me come from Your loving heart. You are an awesome God! Amen.*

The Great Definer

My Bible Reading:
Whatever is good and perfect comes to us from God above,
who created all heaven's lights. Unlike them, he never
changes or casts shifting shadows. (James 1:17 NLT)

You may have never heard of Noah Webster, but you've probably heard of his dictionary. In 1828, Noah, at the age of seventy, published his *American Dictionary of the English Language.* Today the *Merriam-Webster's Collegiate Dictionary* includes more than 200,000 definitions. But before Webster defined words, before words were ever printed on a page, God defined moral truth.

Everything that is "good and perfect comes down to us from God." He is the "God of truth and without iniquity, just and right is he" (Deuteronomy 32:4 KJV). Moral truth isn't something He decides or makes up definitions for off the top of His head—truth is something He *is.* It is His very nature that defines moral truth and all that is good.

Truth is, the reason honesty is right and deceit is wrong is because God is true. The reason love is a virtue and hatred is a vice is because God is love. The reason fidelity in marriage is honorable and cheating on a spouse is immoral is because God is faithful and pure. Everything that is moral, right, good, and beautiful is defined by and measured up against the Great Definer, God Himself.

My Prayer*: I am so glad that knowing moral truth is knowing
You and who You are. That means Your truth isn't a set of cold rules
to follow, but a person with whom I can have a close relationship.
Thank You that You are a relational God who defines moral
truth so I can tell right from wrong. You are my Great Definer.
Help me share this truth with someone today. Amen.*

An Umbrella of Protection & Provision

My Bible Reading:

He [God] is a shield to those who walk with integrity.
He guards the paths of the just and protects those
who are faithful to him. (Proverbs 2:7–8)

It was a beautiful day. You had a great time hanging out with your friends. You say good-bye and begin walking home. The wind kicks up a bit and the sky grows dark. There are a few sprinkles at first, but soon the rain is pouring down. You remember that you put an umbrella in your backpack for just this kind of situation. You pull it out, pop it open, and enjoy the rest of your walk home under the protection of your umbrella.

That's what umbrellas do—they provide a shelter and protect you from a soaking rain. That is what obedience to God and His Word does too—it acts as an umbrella of protection and provision. Scripture states, "God's way is perfect. All the LORD's promises prove true. He is a shield for all who look to him for protection" (Psalm 18:30). "They [God's commands] are a warning to those who hear them; there is great reward for those who obey them" (Psalm 19:11 NLT).

Truth is, you can count on God's protection and provision as you live in faithfulness to Him and His Word. "The LORD protects all those who love him" (Psalm 145:20).

My Prayer: Thank You that You are my provider and protector. Help me stay under Your umbrella by remaining faithful to You and the instructions from Your Word. You are an awesome God. Amen.

March 19

What Makes Dishonesty Wrong

My Bible Reading:

"Do not steal. Do not deceive or cheat one another. Do not bring shame on the name of your God by using it to swear falsely. I am the LORD. Do not defraud or rob your neighbor." (Leviticus 19:11–13)

Have you ever heard someone who's done something wrong say something like "Hey, I didn't hurt anyone by what I did"? The concept is based on the belief that if an action or attitude doesn't directly hurt another person, then it's not wrong for that person. The fact is, every sin is an affront to at least one person and that person is God.

Cheating on a test seems like a victimless act, right? Who is it hurting exactly? First and foremost it hurts God. It "brings shame on the name of your God," scripture states. King David understood that point all too well. He had lied and defrauded another man's wife. The King took a wife away from a soldier. He had no right to do that. Yet he said, "Against you [God], and you alone, have I sinned. . . . You will be proved right in what you say, and your judgment against me is just" (Psalm 51:4).

Truth is, sins like dishonesty do hurt other people, even the person who is sinning. But more importantly it hurts God and brings shame on His true character. Why? Because everything about God—His very nature—is true and right. That is why scripture says, "It is impossible for God to lie" (Hebrews 6:18). And since you were created in God's image (an image of truthfulness), if you act dishonestly it dishonors Him and goes against who He is. And that hurts God.

My Prayer: You are so perfectly right and true. Thank You for creating me to be honest. You are my loving God and I don't want to hurt You by being deceitful in any way. You are so honest with me. I want to reflect honorably upon You this day by being honest in all my dealings with others. Help me do that. Amen.

The Rewards of Honesty

My Bible Reading:
Choose a good reputation over great riches; being held
in high esteem is better than silver or gold. (Proverbs 22:1)

You just completed a job application. You were asked to list three people for recommendations. You named your English teacher, your coach, and principal. The company called you back to say the summer job is yours. You ask why they chose you over all the other applicants. The response: "Your teacher, coach, and principal all said you were a good student, but most of all they said you had a reputation of being an honest person. Our company is looking for people of integrity."

That's one of the rewards of being honest. It provides you with a good reputation. Honesty also protects you from feeling guilt. "Their heart is deceitful," the prophet said, "and now they must bear their guilt" (Hosea 10:2 NIV). Another thing, being honest with people provides for a trusting relationship and it protects from possible ruined relationships.

Truth is, when you live an honest life and avoid lying, cheating, and being deceitful you are protected from guilt, a cycle of deceit, and possible ruined relationships. You're also provided with a clear conscience and a reputation of integrity.

My Prayer: Thank You that I can count on Your provision and protection as I live a life of integrity before You and others. Help me always see Your commands and instructions as Your way of protecting and providing for me. Thank You for loving me that way. Amen.

March 21

What Makes Sexual Purity Right

My Bible Reading:
God's will is for you to be holy, so stay away from
all sexual sin. . . . God has called us to live holy lives,
not impure lives. (1 Thessalonians 4:3, 7)

Do you know why a goldfish can't enjoy life outside the fish bowl? Because fish were created to enjoy life within the pure boundaries of water. God created you to enjoy sex within the pure boundaries of marriage. Go outside that pure boundary and you will suffer negative consequences. For your benefit God wants you to live a sexually pure life.

In biblical terms, sexual immorality is all sexual relations that occur outside of a marriage between one man and one woman (extramarital and premarital sex). God's design is that sexual relations be experienced within an unbroken and pure union between two people entering into the exclusive relationship of marriage. That pure union can be broken even *before* marriage if a person doesn't wait to enjoy sex within the boundary of marriage.

Truth is, sexual purity (experiencing sexual relations within the pure boundaries of marriage) is right because a pure God created you in His image to live sexually pure. "All who have this eager expectation [of being like Christ when He returns] will keep themselves pure, just as he is pure" (1 John 3:3). God by nature is pure and when you live sexually pure, before or after marriage, you are living rightly.

My Prayer: Thank You that You are so holy and pure and that You created me to enjoy sexual relations within the pure boundaries of marriage. Help me resist the temptation to cross outside Your boundaries of purity. You have given me these boundaries so I can enjoy sex as it was meant to be enjoyed. Thank You for that. Amen.

The Rewards of Sexual Purity

My Bible Reading:
You can't say that our bodies were made for sexual immorality. They were made for the Lord, and the Lord cares about our bodies. (1 Corinthians 6:13)

Waiting to enjoy sexual relations until marriage isn't easy. Tell me about it—I waited and didn't get married until I was almost thirty-two! No, it wasn't easy, but it was worth it. Because God cares about you and your body, He tells you to be sexually pure.

"Run from sexual sin!" the Bible says, "No other sin so clearly affects the body as this one does. For sexual immorality is a sin against your own body" (1 Corinthians 6:18). Remain sexually pure and you'll never have to worry about having a sexually transmitted disease, an unplanned pregnancy, or struggle with the stress of guilt.

Truth is, there are great rewards that come with being sexually pure. Not only are you protected from those things mentioned above, but you are also provided with peace of mind, a guilt-free conscience before God, and the opportunity to gift yourself to your future husband or wife as someone who saved yourself for him or her. Remaining sexually pure from this day forward is a loyalty pledge to God, yourself, and your future spouse. Honoring that pledge gives you great rewards.

My Prayer: Thank You that I can count on Your protection and provision as I live a life of sexual purity. You care about my sex life because You care about me. You want me to experience sexual relationships in a way that will promote lasting happiness and joy in my life. Thank You for that. Amen.

What Makes Showing Mercy Right

My Bible Reading:

"This is what the LORD Almighty says: Judge fairly and honestly, and show mercy and kindness to one another." (Zechariah 7:9 NLT)

Friends aren't perfect. Even with the best of intentions your friends can sometimes be insensitive or inconsiderate and end up hurting you. What do you do? You show mercy and forgive them, because that's the right thing to do, right?

But what if someone isn't your friend? What if he or she hurts you intentionally? Do you show that person mercy? Mercy is showing kindness to those who need it and even your enemies need it. Jesus said, "Love your enemies! Do good to those who hate you. Bless those who curse you. Pray for those who hurt you" (Luke 6:27-28). According to Jesus and His Word you are to show mercy on the deserving (your friends) and the undeserving (your enemies).

Showing mercy is right because it comes from the very nature of God. King David said that "his [God's] mercy endures forever" (Psalm 107:1 NKJV). Paul stated that "God is so rich in mercy" (Ephesians 2:4). Mercy isn't something that God just shows; it is something He is.

Truth is, God created you in His image to reflect His nature of mercy in your own life. When you show mercy to those who need it (deserving or not) you are living out the image of God, who is forever merciful. And that is the right thing to do.

My Prayer: Thank You that You are a God of mercy and You created me to show mercy too. It's not easy for me to extend mercy to those who are not my friends. Help me be merciful to the deserving and undeserving today just as You are merciful to me. Amen.

The Rewards of Showing Mercy

My Bible Reading:
"God blesses those who are merciful,
for they will be shown mercy." (Matthew 5:7)

Some say it is satisfying to get revenge on those who try and hurt them. There may be something to that. It can feel good to see bad people get punished, especially if they have been bad to you. But there is no lasting reward in revenge, because what you give out will eventually come back to bite you.

When you resist revenge and show mercy, you receive mercy in return. Jesus promised, " 'If you give, you will receive. . . . Whatever measure you use in giving—large or small—it will be used to measure what is given back to you' " (Luke 6:38 NLT). If you show mercy, you will reap the reward of being shown mercy. Forgive people, even those whom you feel are undeserving, and you will reap the reward of being forgiven. Jesus said, " 'If you forgive those who sin against you, your heavenly Father will forgive you' " (Matthew 6:14).

Truth is, there is great reward in showing mercy to others. You can be protected from the retribution and revenge of those you don't show mercy to and you avoid facing the unforgiveness of those you don't forgive. Being merciful can provide you with the blessing, leniency, and forgiveness of others.

My Prayer: Thank You that I can count on Your protection and provision as I show mercy to others. Help me remember how merciful You are to me so that I can allow Your mercy to flow through me to others. Help me be merciful to someone today. Amen.

What Makes Disrespect Wrong?

My Bible Reading:
For the Lord's sake, submit to all human authority—
whether the king as head of state, or the officials he has
appointed. . . . Respect everyone. (1 Peter 2:13–14, 17)

God's big on respect. His Word says to respect and honor all those in authority: God (Psalm 29:1–2); the government (Romans 13:1); parents (Ephesians 6:2–3); the elderly (Leviticus 19:32). He wants everyone to respect each other: husbands, wives, children, parents, brothers, sisters, friends, and neighbors. Why? What is so important about respect?

When God created humans He created them in His likeness and image "and crowned them with glory and honor" (Psalm 8:5). God is the most respected and honorable of all and He "crowned" or placed on each of His human creation some of His glory and honor. It was His own breath that He breathed into the first human to elevate him to a living soul (Genesis 2:7).

Truth is, respecting others is right and disrespecting people is wrong because respect and honor are part of who God is. He is the one who sets the standard of respect and if you disrespect those in authority, you disrespect God (Romans 13:2). When you honor and respect others you show honor and respect to God Himself. For, " 'You are worthy, O Lord our God, to receive glory and honor and power. For you created all things, and they exist because you created what you pleased' " (Revelation 4:11).

My Prayer: God, I always want to respect You. And when I show respect to my parents, teachers, law enforcement officers, family, and friends, help me remember that I am showing respect and honor to You too. Today, help me especially show respect to my parents by letting them know I want to follow their instructions and make them proud. Amen.

The Rewards of Showing Respect

My Bible Reading:

Would you like to live without fear of the authorities? Do what is right, and they will honor you. The authorities are God's servants, sent for your good. But if you are doing wrong, of course you should be afraid, for they have the power to punish you. (Romans 13:3-4)

Have you heard of the law of reciprocity? The idea is when you do something nice (like show respect) to someone, he or she feels obliged to show you respect. It's like if you do positive things, you get positive in return—do negative things, you get negative in return.

When you obey traffic laws, you enjoy the privilege of driving. Break traffic laws repeatedly and you're apt to lose your driving privileges. Respect your teachers by being mannerly and doing your homework and you'll not only be more apt to pass the class, but your teacher will be more apt to be mannerly toward you.

Truth is, showing others respect and treating them with decency can provide you with healthier relationships, praise from others, and a more attractive personality—someone who is considered a pleasure to be around. Showing respect also protects you from damaging relationships, feeling the punishment of the law, and actually feeling disrespected by others.

My Prayer: Thank You that I can count on Your protection and provision as I show others honor and respect. You have established authorities over me and created me in Your image. Help me honor you by honoring the laws of our land and respecting the dignity of every person I meet today. Amen.

What Makes Self-Control Right?

My Bible Reading:

We all make many mistakes, but those who control their tongues can also control themselves in every other way. (James 3:2)

Have you said things to people that later you wish you hadn't? Everyone has at some time or another. Holding back your anger or restraining yourself from saying something that could hurt someone requires self-control.

Controlling your tongue takes discipline and a measure of maturity. It means thinking ahead and asking yourself what the words you're about to say might cause. Solomon said, "Wise people think before they act; fools don't—and even brag about their foolishness" (Proverbs 13:16). "Spouting off before listening to the facts is both shameful and foolish" (Proverbs 18:13).

Truth is, exercising self-control is right because God, the very standard of right, is a God of self-control. God had every right to be angry at rebellious humans and let them suffer the consequences of their sins. But over and over God has demonstrated His mercy and self-control. God said, " 'I am slow to anger and filled with unfailing love and faithfulness' " (Exodus 34:6). When you show self-control you demonstrate a quality of God—in whose image you were created.

My Prayer: Thank You that You created me in Your image of self-control. Help me control my tongue and hold back when I get frustrated with people. Help me show Your patience and love to them. Thank You that You show me so much patience and love, even when I don't deserve it. Amen.

The Rewards of Self-Control

My Bible Reading:
The children of Israel's "hearts were not loyal to [God]. They did
not keep his covenant. Yet he was merciful and forgave their
sins and did not destroy them all. Many times he held back his
anger and did not unleash his fury!" (Psalm 78:37–38)

Who would you rather hang with, a person who spouts off un-
controllably and trashes everyone and everything, or a person
who is restrained and measured in what he or she feels and says?
That's not a hard choice. People enjoy being around a person who
exercises self-control.

Exercising self-control in your life can help you avoid getting
caught up in the addiction of nicotine, alcohol, and drugs. Healthy
eating even requires self-control. Addictions and excess are a path
to pain and heartache. In contrast, there are great benefits to living
a life of self-control relationally, emotionally, and physically. That's
why James tells us to "be quick to listen, slow to speak, and slow to
get angry" (James 1:19).

Truth is, a life of self-control provides you with a greater sense of
self-respect, admiration from others, and a deeper joy in life. You
are equally protected from physical addictions, lower self-esteem,
and disrupted relationships. God is your standard and model of self-
restraint. And He offers His Holy Spirit to help you maintain your
self-control. Scripture says, "Don't drink too much wine, for many
evils lie along that path; be filled instead with the Holy Spirit and
controlled by him" (Ephesians 5:18 TLB).

My Prayer: *God, I can count on Your protection and provision as I
exercise self-control in my life. Help me honor You, my own body,
and those around me today as I exhibit self-control through the
power of Your Holy Spirit. You are an awesome God. I love you. Amen.*

What Makes Injustice Wrong?

My Bible Reading:
"Those who wish to boast should boast in this alone: that they truly know me and understand that I am the LORD who demonstrates unfailing love and who brings justice and righteousness to the earth, and that I delight in these things." (Jeremiah 9:24)

Starving nations, abused children, enslaved people, heartless criminals who get away with murder, merciless warlords who prey on the innocent—these are some of the great injustices in the world. But how do you know these things are actually unjust? What is it that makes injustice wrong? To have a true sense of what is just and unjust you must have a true right and wrong. Without true rightness there can be no true definition of justice.

Many times when scripture speaks of God's justice it also speaks of His righteousness. "Righteousness and justice are the foundation of your throne" (Psalm 89:14). "The LORD gives righteousness and justice to all who are treated unfairly" (Psalm 103:6). God shows His people "righteousness and justice, unfailing love and compassion" (Hosea 2:19). It is God's universal rightness that defines what is just and unjust.

Truth is, you cannot know that any injustice is wrong without knowing the righteousness of God. It is the nature of His rightness that cries out against starvation, abuse, enslavement, crimes, hurting of the innocent, and every other injustice in the world. You can know any injustice is wrong by comparing the action to a just and right God.

My Prayer: Thank You that You are a righteous God who defines all that is right and holy. And thank You that You hate injustice and love mercy. Help me reflect Your justice in my life as I take a stand for right and help those who are being treated unjustly in the world. Amen.

The Rewards of Promoting Justice

My Bible Reading:
Jesus said, "Do to others whatever you would like them
to do to you. This is the essence of all that is taught
in the law and the prophets." (Matthew 7:12)

Think for a moment how you want to be treated. You no doubt want people to treat you with respect, be courteous and kind to you, acknowledge it when you do well, be fair with you and give you the opportunity and freedom to be all you can be. If you want to be treated that way, Jesus said to treat others in that same way. If you want to be treated justly, then act and promote the idea of others being treated justly.

Truth is, there are rewards in promoting justice for all. Every day some student somewhere is being unfairly teased and picked on. When you see it happening and take a stand for that person, you become a promoter of justice. Your reward is one of honor, a clear conscience, and the satisfaction of being a protector of the innocent. On a larger scale, there is perhaps no better feeling than being part of a humanitarian effort to feed the hungry, clothe the naked, give homes to the homeless, and care for those less fortunate. "[God] gives justice to the oppressed and food to the hungry.... He cares for the orphans and widows, but he frustrates the plans of the wicked" (Psalm 146:7–9). God too loves it when you bring a sense of justice to the lives of others.

---

*My Prayer: You are the God of justice, a defender of the weak.
Help me show fairness and kindness to someone today who
may be feeling unfairly treated. Allow me to be a source of
comfort and encouragement to that person. Amen.*

Thought Life & Choices

My Bible Reading:
Fix your thoughts on what is true, and honorable, and right,
and pure, and lovely, and admirable. Think about things
that are excellent and worthy of praise. (Philippians 4:8)

Have you ever heard the old saying, "We are what we eat"? The idea is that you become a by-product of what you put in your body. There may be a certain truth to that physically, but it is certainly true spiritually.

If people focus their thoughts and minds on hateful gossip, revenge, trash talk, dirty jokes, porn, violence, and selfish pleasures, what kind of choices do you think they'll make? The things people fill their minds and hearts with will determine the kind of choices they make. What people feed on is what they become.

Truth is, focus on what is true and honorable and your choices will be true and honorable. Keep your thought life focused on what is right and pure and your choices will reflect what is right and pure. Think on those things that are lovely, admirable, excellent, and worthy of praise and your life will be an example of the same. The principle works: spiritually feed on the goodness of God and you will choose godly things. "Let all that I am praise the LORD. . . . May all my thoughts be pleasing to him" (Psalm 104:1, 34).

My Prayer: Help me keep my thoughts and heart focused on You and Your Word. Let me keep my mind filled with what is pure and honorable today so my choices will be right and true. Amen.

APRIL

He Entered My World

No April Fools

My Bible Reading:
Though he [Jesus] was God. . .he gave up his divine
privileges; he took the humble position of a slave and
was born as a human being. (Philippians 2:6–7)

Your "friend" comes running up to you in the hallway and says, "I just saw the list—you're on it for homecoming queen!" Or, your "buddy" pulls you aside and says, "I just overheard Renee (the most popular girl in school) say she hoped you'd ask her out!" After a moment of perhaps feeling shocked and flattered your "friend" says, "April fools!"

A lot of jokes are pulled off on unsuspecting people on April 1st. Something happened some two thousand years ago that might seem like a joke because of how amazing it was—but it was no joke. The Almighty God of the universe was actually born into the human family!

Truth is, God gave up His supernatural privilege as Master Creator of everything and took on the form of a human being for *you*. It is called the miraculous incarnation—God becoming human. It was His masterful plan to reverse your death sentence of sin and give you eternal life with Him.

My Prayer: You cared enough about me to come to earth as a human to allow me to escape eternal death and enjoy life with You forever. While I don't feel worthy of Your love and mercy, I will not be so foolish as to reject Your offer of eternal life. Thank You for coming to earth to rescue and redeem me. I love you. Amen.

A God-Man

My Bible Reading:

Christ is the visible image of the invisible God. He existed before anything was created and is supreme over all creation, for through him God created everything. (Colossians 1:15–16)

Practically everyone and every religion of the world recognizes Jesus as a great teacher and role model. He taught people to be kind and considerate and to do to others what you want them to do to you. But Jesus wasn't just a prophet of God and a great human teacher. He *was* God.

God didn't create Jesus. He eternally "existed before anything was created" and in fact, He was the one who created everything in the first place. As a human you enjoy the same essence of humanness as your human parents. And Jesus enjoys the same essence of character and nature by being God's Son. Scripture says, "The Son radiates God's own glory and expresses the very character of God" (Hebrews 1:3).

Truth is, Jesus is as human-like as you are and as God-like as His Father God. He is both fully God and fully human at the same time. And that gives Him a unique ability. As infinite God of the universe He has the ability to communicate with finite humans. You may never be able to know God exhaustively in His infinite existence as Almighty God, but you can know Him truly as the God-man Jesus. Now that's amazing!

My Prayer: Because You are uniquely God and man You can allow me to know You. Thank You that You want me to know You and that You made it possible for me to have a relationship with You. Help me get to know You better. Amen.

Just like You

My Bible Reading:
And while they [Mary and Joseph] were there, the time came for her baby to be born. She gave birth to her firstborn son. She wrapped him snugly in strips of cloth and laid him in a manger. (Luke 2:6–7)

Your birthday was a very important day, but you don't remember anything about it. Nothing made sense to you in those first few hours and days. You left a warm dark "room" where you were enveloped by your mother to enter a brightly lit room where your arms and legs flailed wildly. Eventually you opened your eyes, felt the warm touch of your mom, and began the journey of living independently from your mother.

It's hard to imagine that God went through that same human process of being born a baby, but He did. Mary rocked Jesus to sleep, fed Him, changed His diapers, etc. He encountered the human experience from birth to adulthood just like you.

Truth is, Jesus as a human is as real as you are right now. As God, Jesus was the one who formed the human body, yet like you, He had to learn to walk. He spoke the universe into existence, yet like you, He had to learn to speak. Just like you, He was helpless as a baby and grew to become a teenager and eventually into a grown-up.

My Prayer: *Knowing that You were once as helpless and in need of constant care as I was helps me realize You can relate to me. It helps me know that You truly understand what I go through. Thank You that You are a relatable God. I love you. Amen.*

Just like God

My Bible Reading:
Everything was created through him [Jesus] and for him.
He existed before anything else, and he holds
all creation together. (Colossians 1:16–17)

Sure, God was born as a human baby and grew from childhood. But Jesus' humanness doesn't make Him any less mighty and God-like. He literally "holds all creation together." As God "he sustains everything by the mighty power of his command" (Hebrews 1:3). He is still the all-powerful One whom we live in awe of and worship.

Truth is, God's humanness as Jesus doesn't make Him weak and Jesus' all-powerful nature as God doesn't make Him any less approachable. He is the baby Jesus who knows what it is like to be human and He is the all-powerful God who holds your life in His hand. Yet He wants you to "come boldly to the throne of [your] gracious God. There [you] will receive his mercy, and [you] will find grace to help [you] when [you] need it most" (Hebrews 4:16).

My Prayer: *I am able to relate to You, Jesus, because You became human. And I am in awe of You as my Almighty God of the universe. Help me learn to come boldly to You for what I need without ever taking You for granted. Help me share this wonderful truth with someone today. Amen.*

He Brought a Light to My World

My Bible Reading:
Jesus said, "I am the light of the world. If you follow me,
you won't have to walk in darkness, because you will
have the light that leads to life." (John 8:12)

Were you ever afraid of the dark? There is something about darkness that's scary. You can't see where you're going when it's dark. Someone or something might be out there to do you harm. Darkness is just creepy.

When sin entered the human race the God of light had to separate Himself from it because a holy God "cannot allow sin in any form" (Habakkuk 1:13 NLT). It was like the whole world went dark and every person who came into existence after that was born into the darkness of sin. No humanly created light could ever dispel the darkness of sin.

Truth is, Jesus is the true and holy light that can dispel the darkness of sin. "His life brought light to everyone. The light shines in the darkness, and the darkness can never extinguish it" (John 1:4–5). No matter how much sinful darkness you have experienced, Jesus' light can destroy and eliminate every bit of it. Scripture says, "For once you were full of darkness, but now you have light from the Lord. So live as people of light! For this light within you produces only what is good and right and true" (Ephesians 5:8–9).

My Prayer: Thank You that You came into this world as my shining light to expel my darkness. Help me live today as a person of light who produces what is good and right and true. Amen.

He Brought Eternal Life to My World

My Bible Reading:
"For God loved the world so much that he gave his
only Son so that anyone who believes in him
shall not perish but have eternal life." (John 3:16 TLB)

When Jesus entered this world He found humanity in the darkness of sin and as dead as dead could be. "When Adam sinned, sin entered the world. Adam's sin brought death, so death spread to everyone" (Romans 5:12). The reality is that when God entered your world as a human, He did it to bring you life eternal. "Yes, Adam's one sin brings condemnation for everyone, but Christ's one act of righteousness brings a right relationship with God and new life for everyone" (Romans 5:18).

Truth is, it required God stepping into human existence and taking on human form in order to offer you a resurrected life with Him. You were dead in your sin, and Jesus offered life through belief in Him. " 'I am the resurrection and the life,' " Jesus said. " 'Anyone who believes in me will live, even after dying. Everyone who lives in me and believes in me will never ever die' " (John 11:25–26).

*My Prayer: I "know that the Son of God has come, and he has
given [me] understanding so that [I] can know the true God. . . .
He [Jesus] is the only true God, and he is eternal life" (1 John 5:20).
Thank You that You loved me enough to personally show up in
human form to offer me eternal life. In my new life in You, help me
today to share Your life-giving message with others. Amen.*

April 7

He Brought Freedom to My World

My Bible Reading:
Jesus said, "The Spirit of the LORD is upon me, for he has
anointed me to bring Good News to the poor. He has sent
me to proclaim that captives will be released, that the blind
will see, that the oppressed will be set free." (Luke 4:18–19)

One day Jesus was in a synagogue on the Sabbath and He quoted
the words from Isaiah 61 that appear above. It was a prophecy
about Himself coming to earth to set people free. Scripture says that
"once you were slaves of sin" (Romans 6:17). You needed someone
with the power to set you free and Jesus is that One!

Truth is, "it is for freedom that Christ has set [you] free" (Galatians
5:1 NIV). Jesus came to break the chains of sin and give you spiritual
freedom. Scripture says, "When the right time came, God sent his Son,
born of a woman, subject to the law. God sent him to buy freedom for
us who were slaves to the law" (Galatians 4:4–5). God never intended
for you to live as a slave to sin and the law. You were not meant to be
a slave.

_____

My Prayer: *"[I] have been called to live in freedom" (Galatians 5:13).
The need to live free was implanted within me by You, and I
thank You that You have freed me. Help me always be thankful
for a life of freedom in You. Help me share Your message of
freedom with those who are still slaves to sin. Amen.*

He Broke the Power of Death in My World

My Bible Reading:
Because God's children are human beings—made of flesh
and blood—the Son also became flesh and blood. For only as a
human being could he die, and only by dying could he break
the power of the devil, who had the power of death. Only in
this way could he set free all who have lived their lives
as slaves to the fear of dying. (Hebrews 2:14-15)

Have you ever had someone take something of yours they had no
right to take? It probably ticked you off because that person had
what belonged to you. Well the devil—God's archrival—has a power
that doesn't belong to him. It's the power of death. Another reason
Jesus came to earth is to take that power away from him.

Truth is, it was by Jesus' death on the cross and His mighty resurrection that He broke the power of death that was to be your eternal
destiny. God "sent his own Son in a body like the bodies we sinners
have. And in that body God declared an end to sin's control over us
by giving his Son as a sacrifice for our sins" (Romans 8:3).

My Prayer: *Thank You for entering my world as a human and dying
for me to break the power of my death sentence. I now can live
without the fear of eternal death. You are so merciful and so loving.
Help me share Your mercy and love with someone today. Amen.*

The Cornerstone

My Bible Reading:

"For Jesus is the one referred to in the Scriptures, where it says, 'The stone that you builders rejected has now become the cornerstone.' There is salvation in no one else! God has given no other name under heaven by which we must be saved." (Acts 4:11–12)

Have you ever played the Jenga game? It's where players take turns removing one block at a time from a tower constructed of fifty-four wooden blocks. The winner is the last person to successfully remove and place a block on the tower without it falling. What every successful player knows is that you can't remove the bottom foundational blocks or the tower will fall. The foundation to the tower is its cornerstone.

In Acts 4, Peter and John told the people that scripture called Jesus "the cornerstone." In other words, He is the foundation upon which your salvation is based; "there is salvation in no one else!" (Acts 4:12).

Truth is, Jesus made it clear that as God in human form He was your only hope of eternal life. " 'Unless you believe that I Am who I claim to be,' " He said, " 'you will die in your sins' " (John 8:24). Jesus, the God-man, is your cornerstone and you can count on Him to break the power of death and give you eternal life.

My Prayer: Thank You that You are the Cornerstone of my salvation—the One who grants me eternal life in relationship with You. I am so glad You made it clear that You and You alone are my only hope of salvation. My trust is in You. Amen.

The Chosen One

My Bible Reading:
John [the Baptist] saw Jesus coming toward him and said, " 'Look!
The Lamb of God who takes away the sin of the world! He is the
one I was talking about when I said, " 'A man is coming after me
who is far greater than I am, for he existed long before me.'...
I testify that he is the Chosen One of God." (John 1:29-30, 34)

Israel at the time of Jesus was looking for the Messiah—the Chosen
One from God to deliver them from the oppression of the Romans.
Moses and the prophets prophesied that this Chosen One would
come, and John the Baptist identified him.

John said, "When God sent me to baptize with water, he told
me, 'The one on whom you see the Spirit descend and rest is the one
who will baptize with the Holy Spirit.' I saw this happen to Jesus, so
I testify that he is the Chosen One of God" (John 1:33-34). The word
began to spread. A man named "Philip went to look for Nathaniel and
told him, 'We have found the very person Moses and the prophets
wrote about! His name is Jesus, the son of Joseph from Nazareth' "
(John 1:45). Soon hundreds began accepting Jesus as the Messiah.

Truth is, throughout Jesus' life He fulfilled the prophecies about the
Messiah. He did miracles that only God could do. God didn't want you
to be without clear evidence that Jesus was in fact who He claimed
to be—God's Son. Luke, an astute historian, drew on eyewitness
accounts to further reinforce that Jesus was God. Luke wrote, "Many
people have set out to write accounts about the events that have been
fulfilled among us. They used the eyewitness reports circulating
among us from the early disciples. Having carefully investigated
everything from the beginning. . .you can be certain of the truth of
everything you were taught" (Luke 1:1-4).

My Prayer: *Thank You Jesus that You don't want me to believe in You
blindly. I am glad You have offered evidence that You were the true
Son of God. You are the Chosen One, and You have given me clear
reason to believe in You. Thank You for that. Amen.*

April 11

He Made the Claim

My Bible Reading:
The high priest asked him, "Are you the Messiah, the Son of the Blessed One?" Jesus said, "I Aᴍ. And you will see the Son of Man seated in the place of power at God's right hand and coming on the clouds of heaven." (Mark 14:61–62)

Some people say that it was Jesus' followers who made Him into a god to be worshipped and that Jesus Himself never did. They say, instead, He always referred to Himself as the "Son of Man." But His reference to Himself as the Son of Man was in fact a claim to be God's Son.

Jesus' use of the words "Son of Man" can be traced back to the book of Daniel. He prophesied that he saw "a son of man coming with the clouds of heaven...[with] authority, honor, and sovereignty over all the nations of the world.... His rule is eternal—it will never end. His kingdom will never be destroyed" (Daniel 7:13-14). Daniel's use of the words "son of man" is a clear reference to the divinity of the sovereign Lord.

Truth is, Jesus even referred to Himself with the words "Son of God" in John 5:25, and the religious leaders who opposed Jesus knew He was claiming to be God's Son. When Jesus asked why they wanted to kill Him, they said, " 'For blasphemy! You, a mere man, claim to be God' " (John 10:33).

My Prayer: *Jesus, You made it clear that You are the Son of the one true God. You have not simply become a religion that humans concocted. You entered my world and proved You were God in the flesh on a mission to rescue me and everyone who would believe in You from eternal death. Help me share that great news with others. Amen.*

Two Alternatives

My Bible Reading:
Jesus said, "I tell you the truth, before
Abraham was even born, I AM!" (John 8:58)

Jesus claimed to be the eternal God when He used the words "I AM." God had told Moses that His name was "I AM" in Exodus 3:14. And when Jesus used that name He was stating He was the one true God who offers humans eternal life.

This exclusive claim by Jesus gives us only two alternatives. If Jesus is not God in human form, then His offer of salvation is either a sham or a lie. There are no other options. Jesus' claim to be God is either a false claim or a true one.

Now some say that it really doesn't matter if Jesus was God in the flesh or not. They claim Jesus was just a great moral teacher. But that doesn't make sense. Because if Jesus wasn't the Son of God He either knew it and was a liar, or He didn't know it and was a lunatic. Either alternative rules Him out as being a great moral teacher.

Truth is, Jesus really is the true Son of God. People have one of two choices: accept Him as Lord of the universe or reject Him. Aren't you glad you have found His claims credible and have accepted Him?

My Prayer: *Thank You for showing me through scripture that You are neither a foolish liar nor a deluded lunatic. You have demonstrated that You are God in flesh who came to offer me eternal life. Thank You for being You. Help me share this amazing truth with someone today. Amen.*

Born of a Virgin

My Bible Reading:
This is how Jesus the Messiah [the Chosen One] was born. His mother, Mary, was engaged to be married to Joseph. But before the marriage took place, while she was still a virgin, she became pregnant through the power of the Holy Spirit. (Matthew 1:18)

You know a little about the "birds and the bees," right? Virgins don't get pregnant and stay virgins! Yet that is precisely what the prophet Isaiah wrote would happen seven hundred years before Jesus was born. "The virgin will conceive a child! She will give birth to a son and will call him Immanuel (which means 'God is with us')" (Isaiah 7:14).

Scripture states that Jesus was virgin-born, and there is evidence that backs that assertion. Joseph was an honorable Jewish man, and no honorable man would marry a Jewish woman who'd had sex with another man before marriage. But he had a dream from God that convinced him that "'the child within [Mary] was conceived by the Holy Spirit.... And you are to name him Jesus'" (Matthew 1:20–21). Joseph simply wouldn't have gone through with his marriage to Mary unless he had been convinced she had been made pregnant by the Holy Spirit.

Also, Jesus' hometown people all knew that Joseph was not Jesus' birth father. While many didn't accept He was God's Son, they at least recognized He wasn't conceived through Joseph.

Truth is, those closest to Mary and Joseph knew Jesus was miraculously conceived by God. The prophecy foretold it and the accurate historical accounts of scripture record it. Jesus was born of a human mother but conceived through God the Holy Spirit!

My Prayer: You, Jesus, are truly the God-man. You are human, yet You are God. You are able to relate to me in Your humanity, yet You offer me eternal life because You are God. Thank You for Your wonderful plan of salvation. Amen.

He Understands

My Bible Reading:
Since he [Jesus] himself has gone through suffering and testing, he is able to help us when we are being tested. . . . [He] understands our weaknesses, for he faced all of the same testings we do, yet he did not sin. (Hebrews 2:18; 4:15)

L ife happens and it isn't always pretty. You have undoubtedly suffered disappointments, rejection by others, unjust criticism, and at times feel like no one really understands. There may be times you thought there was no way God could identify with your suffering. Yet because God entered your world as a human being, He knows experientially what you go through.

Truth is, there is nothing you have experienced that God in Jesus does not understand. He wants you to know that He is there for you, accepting you no matter what. He truly understands. Scripture says, "He [Jesus] was despised and rejected—a man of sorrows, acquainted with deepest grief" (Isaiah 53:3).

My Prayer: Things get hard sometimes. It is great to know that You can understand what I go through and are there for me. You are such an understanding and accepting God that I can relate to and rely upon. Help me go to You and Your Word more often when I feel I need someone to understand. Thank You that You are an understanding God. Amen.

His "Weird" Acceptance

My Bible Reading:
God showed his great love for us by sending Christ
to die for us while we were still sinners. (Romans 5:8)

Why do your family and friends accept you? Why do you accept them? Well, when you have good friends, you accept them, right? And with family, they're just family and what else can you do—you're related to them.

Acceptance is usually based on mutual friendship or blood relationship. To accept people who reject you or dislike you is a little weird. But that is exactly what God demonstrated when He sent His Son to this earth. You were not His friend at all. Because you were born a sinner the Bible says you were God's enemy. You "were once far away from God. You were his enemies, separated from him by your evil thoughts and actions" (Colossians 1:21).

Truth is, God loved you so much that He accepted you without any conditions. In spite of your sin, He accepted you and in fact died for you. That may be a weird kind of acceptance, but it sure feels good. It feels good to know that you are wanted and loved based on the person you are regardless of what you have or haven't done. That's God's kind of acceptance.

My Prayer: Thank You that before I could even respond to Your love, You accepted me for who I am—a sinner. And it blows my mind that this was Your plan from the beginning. Your Word says this about You: "God decided in advance to adopt us into his own family by bringing us to himself through Jesus Christ. This is what he wanted to do, and it gave him great pleasure" (Ephesians 1:5). Thank You, thank You, thank You! Amen.

The Uncondemning Jesus

My Bible Reading:

Jesus said, "For God did not send his Son into the world to condemn the world, but to save the world through him." (John 3:17 NIV)

Have you ever known someone who has been fined for a traffic violation? If so, that person was pronounced guilty or condemned for breaking the law by a judge and sentenced to pay a fine. It doesn't feel good to be condemned.

The book of John tells the story of the religious leaders who brought to Jesus a woman who had been caught in the act of adultery. The Jewish law condemned her to death and they wanted to know if Jesus thought she should be stoned. He answered them by saying, " 'Let the one who has never sinned throw the first stone' " (John 8:7). One by one all those who had condemned the woman walked away.

Truth is, Jesus, who had never sinned, could have rightfully condemned the woman. But He asked her, " 'Where are your accusers? Didn't even one of them condemn you?' 'No, Lord,' she said. And Jesus said, 'Neither do I. Go and sin no more' " (John 8:10–11). You have an uncondemning Jesus. He didn't come into this world to condemn you; He came to forgive you.

My Prayer: *I know my sins condemn me. But I am so thankful that You are a forgiving God. You came to earth to sacrifice Yourself so that my sins can be forgiven and not held against me. Thank You for being a redeeming and not a condemning Jesus. I love You for that. Help me demonstrate my love by telling others about Your forgiving heart. Amen.*

Why Jesus Associated with Scum

My Bible Reading:

Matthew invited Jesus and his disciples to his home as dinner
guests, along with many tax collectors and other disreputable
sinners. But when the Pharisees saw this, they asked his disciples,
"Why does your teacher eat with such scum?" (Matthew 9:10–11)

D o you know some people who might be considered scum? They
may be the weirdos and outcasts at your school. They are often
the ones some students put down, make fun of, and may even bully.
Well, there were some of those in Jesus' day. And He accepted their
invitation to hang out and eat with them.

The religious leaders wanted to know why Jesus would associate
with "the scum." Jesus' answer was simple: " 'Healthy people don't
need a doctor—sick people do. . . . I have come to call not those who
think they are righteous, but those who know they are sinners' "
(Matthew 9:12–13).

Truth is, Jesus' merciful and compassionate heart causes Him
to accept people for who they are. It's in His nature to reach out to
the hurting, outcasts (scum), and those who need forgiveness. The
expression used most often in the New Testament to describe Jesus'
heart of love and acceptance is that He was "moved with compassion"
to meet every person at the point of their need.

---

*My Prayer: I am so thankful for Your compassionate heart that
looked beyond my faults, failures, and even sins to see my needs.
Thank You that You came as such a loving and accepting God.
Help me be accepting today of those who need a friend. Amen.*

Accepting Others

My Bible Reading:
Accept each other just as Christ has accepted
you so that God will be given glory. (Romans 15:7)

Your friend comes to you and says, "Hey, I really need a hundred bucks right now. I can't wait; can you give it to me?" You reach into your wallet or purse but you don't have more than twenty dollars. You shrug and say, "I'm sorry I don't have a hundred bucks on me. And so I can't give you what I don't have."

There is a principle here: you can only give to others what you have received. Jesus said, " 'Give as freely as you have received' " (Matthew 10:8). Since God has accepted you in spite of your failures, you can accept others in spite of their failures. God didn't put any condition on you before He accepted you. So you can accept others without putting any conditions on them.

Truth is, accepting others like God accepts you means you accept people for who they are, no matter what. And when you do, God is "given glory." That means God gets recognized, praised, and honored when you pass on a Godlike acceptance to others. And there's a bonus: you get blessed when you act Christlike. God's Word says, " 'All who follow my ways are joyful' " (Proverbs 8:32).

My Prayer: Thank You that You accept me for who I am, no matter what. Help me accept others in that same way, even today. I want to express an accepting heart to someone who especially needs it. I know when I follow Your ways, it honors You and brings me joy. Amen.

How Does He Do It?

My Bible Reading:
He has removed our sins as far from us as the east is from
the west. The LORD is like a father to his children, tender and
compassionate to those who fear him. (Psalm 103:12–13)

Your "friend" lies about you and you get in trouble. Do you accept
him or her anyway? Or do you just say, "Oh, that's okay. A little
lie here or there is no big deal anyway, right?" That's not easy to do,
but more importantly, you shouldn't pass off lying as "no big deal."
God certainly doesn't. Yet God accepts people in spite of their wrong
behavior. How does He do that?

Because God is absolutely holy He cannot embrace your sin in
any form. So to accept you in spite of your sin He does something
very unique. He makes a distinction between your "essence" created
in His image and your "nature" infected because of sin. He sees a
difference between you as His lost child and what you do. Because
what you do is *not* the same as who you are. Otherwise, God could not
remove sins "as far from us as the east is from the west."

Truth is, God is in effect saying, *"I am the tender Father you long for
and you are My lost child. That is who you are. While I hate what sin
has done to you—it has separated you from Me—I can still accept you
for who you are. And because I want a Father-and-child relationship
with you, I have sent My Son to die for you so that I can forgive you
completely for all your sins."*

*My Prayer: Thank You that You accept me for who I am and
do not reject me as a person because of what I've done wrong.
And thank You that You died to offer me a way to be forgiven.
Help me accept others today as You accept me. Amen.*

He Enters Your World

My Bible Reading:
So the Word [God] became human and made his home among us.
He was full of unfailing love and faithfulness. And we have seen
his glory, the glory of the Father's one and only Son. (John 1:14)

L et's say you really like someone and that person claims to really like you. You see this person in the hall, in a few classes, and across the lunchroom. But all he or she ever does is smile a little at you and wave. That would not be a very fulfilling relationship, would it?

What tells your mind and emotions that a person really cares about you begins when he or she truly enters your everyday world. That is what tells you a person is interested in who you are, what you do, what you like, what you really care about—your dreams and aspirations. By entering your world that person lets you know you are loved and accepted for who you are.

Truth is, that is what God did. When He took on human skin, He left His royal, perfect existence and entered your world. Today through the power of the Holy Spirit, He enters your world to say He cares about you and everything concerning you. He doesn't ask you to come up to His level of perfect existence; He meets you exactly where you are.

---

*My Prayer: You are an available God who comes to me because
You care about me. Your unfailing love and faithfulness to me
motivate me to be faithful to You and love You even more.
Help me demonstrate that love to You by showing someone
today that I care about him or her. Amen.*

April 21

He Prays for You

My Bible Reading:
"Simon, Simon, Satan has asked to sift each of you
like wheat. But I have pleaded in prayer for you,
Simon, that your faith should not fail." (Luke 22:31–32)

Simon Peter was an outspoken disciple of Jesus. He had his good traits, but he had some bad ones too. He was rather impulsive, impatient, and a little overconfident. He told Jesus, " 'I'm ready to die for you' " (John 13:37), yet he denied even knowing Jesus after the Lord was arrested.

But just before Jesus predicts that Peter is going to deny his Lord, He says, " 'I have pleaded in prayer for you.' " Then Jesus says, " 'So when you have repented and turned to me again, strengthen your brothers' " (Luke 22:32). That means Jesus really believed in Peter. He wasn't about to give up on him, so He prayed for him.

Truth is, Jesus won't give up on you either, even though you may fail Him from time to time. When you're about to be tested or tempted, guess who is praying for you? Yes, Jesus is praying specifically for you. It says in 1 John: "There is someone to plead for you before the Father. He is Jesus Christ, the one who pleases God completely" (1 John 2:1 NLT). And the Holy Spirit even prays so intensely for you that His groaning "cannot be expressed in words" (Romans 8:26).

My Prayer: It blows my mind to think that You care for me so much that You actually pray for me. I admit I need Your prayers and I need to know that You believe in me. Thank You for that. Help me find strength in You, and may Your prayers keep me close to You today. Amen.

He Weeps with You

My Bible Reading:

"When Jesus saw her [Mary] weeping. . .[He asked] 'Where have you put him [Lazarus]?'. . . . They told him, 'Lord, come and see.' Then Jesus wept. The people who were standing nearby said, 'See how much he loved him!' " (John 11:33–36)

Mary, Martha, and Lazarus (two sisters and a brother) were very good friends of Jesus. So when Lazarus got sick, the sisters sent word to Jesus to come with the hope that He would heal their brother. But by the time Jesus got there, Lazarus had died. When He met up with Mary, she was crying.

Then something extraordinary happened. Jesus wept. But why? He knew that in a few short minutes He would perform the miracle of raising Lazarus from the dead. So what was He crying for—*who* was He crying for?

Jesus was weeping for His dear friend Mary. At that moment in time she was heartbroken, and Jesus wanted to identify with her pain and cry with her. Sure He was going to raise Lazarus, but right then Mary needed the comforting tears of Jesus, and He was there for her.

Truth is, when your heart cries out in pain or discouragement, Jesus is there crying with you too. He was there for Mary and He is there for you whenever you need Him. He is "the same yesterday, today, and forever" (Hebrews 13:8). You can count on Him.

My Prayer: Thank You that You care enough about me and my problems that You even weep with me. Thank You for being such a dear friend and Savior like that to me. Help me be that kind of close friend to someone today. Amen.

Help When You Need It

My Bible Reading:

[Jesus] understands our weaknesses, for he faced all of the same testings we do, yet he did not sin. So let us come boldly to the throne of our gracious God. There we will receive his mercy, and we will find grace to help us when we need it most. (Hebrews 4:15–16)

Life has its ups and downs. It's great when things are going well, people are getting along, and there are no major problems erupting. But when friends turn on you or people say mean things about you that aren't true, it can really hurt. What do you need most when you are feeling misrepresented and misunderstood by others?

It's always good to try to clarify things with people and correct misconceptions. But at the moment of being misunderstood, you need a friend who understands what it's like and can identify with your pain. That's Jesus.

Truth is, Jesus felt misunderstood. He spent years telling His followers who He was and why He came to earth. "But they didn't understand any of this. . .and they failed to grasp what he was talking about" (Luke 18:34). Because Jesus faced misunderstanding He is able to identify with your hurt and give you the help you need when you need it.

My Prayer: *Thank You that You are there for me when I'm being misunderstood by others. Help me in those times to remember to "come boldly" to You for help. You want me to rely on You as my gracious God and friend. Help me do that. You are such an awesome God! Amen.*

Resist Getting Even

My Bible Reading:

"Don't repay evil for evil. Don't retaliate with insults when people insult you. Instead, pay them back with a blessing. That is what God has called you to do, and he will grant you his blessing." (1 Peter 3:9)

The religious teachers of Jesus' time were big on getting a satisfying revenge. If someone wronged you, then you could wrong them back to the same degree. But Jesus taught something else. He said, in effect, if someone wrongs you, don't give in to the idea of getting even. Instead, He taught to " 'love your enemies! Pray for those who persecute you!' " (Matthew 5:44).

Paying back an insult with a blessing, like a kind word, a gift, or a prayer for your enemy, is not easy. Yet look what Jesus did. He was betrayed, denied, falsely accused, slapped, spit on, beaten, and then crucified. And instead of retaliating, He endured it all and prayed, " 'Father, forgive them, for they don't know what they are doing' " (Luke 23:34).

Truth is, Jesus understands what it's like to be insulted and put down, even to the point of death. He can relate to how you feel when someone wrongs you. Instead of getting even, He wants you to love those who would try to hurt you and in return receive a blessing. His Word says, "If you want to enjoy life and see many happy days, keep your tongue from speaking evil and your lips from telling lies. . . . Search for peace, and work to maintain it' " (1 Peter 3:10–11).

My Prayer: I want to live out Your kind of love and acceptance so I can respond to those who would hurt me with a blessing. You are such an accepting Jesus. Help me be accepting today, even to those who would like to harm me. Amen.

April 25

When Facing Rejection

My Bible Reading:
He came into the very world he created, but the
world didn't recognize him. He came to his own people,
and even they rejected him. (John 1:10–11)

Rejection hurts. The emotional pain from feeling rejected can hurt as much as a physical injury. It is virtually impossible to escape some form of personal and emotional rejection in your life. God knows that and is there for you.

The all-powerful God of the universe, who never did wrong, even faced rejection. When Jesus went to His hometown of Nazareth, "They scoffed, 'He's just the carpenter's son....' And they were deeply offended and refused to believe in him" (Matthew 13:55, 57). These were the people He grew up with. His childhood "friends" and their families rejected Him. Not only that, all four of His brothers initially rejected Him. Scripture says, "For even his brothers didn't believe in him" (John 7:5).

Truth is, when you feel rejection you have a friend in Jesus who can identify with you and be there for you. Your God who cannot lie says, " 'Never will I leave you; never will I forsake you.' So we say with confidence, 'The Lord is my helper; I will not be afraid. What can mere mortals do to me?' " (Hebrews 13:5–6 NIV).

---

*My Prayer: Thank You that You are my constant helper—
my dearest friend who is there for me when others turn away
and reject me. You are the one who knows me best, yet loves me
most. "God is [my] refuge and strength, always ready to help
in times of trouble" (Psalm 46:1). Thank You for that. Amen.*

Enduring Insults

My Bible Reading:
Be happy if you are insulted for being a Christian, for then
the glorious Spirit of God will come upon you.... It is no shame
to suffer for being a Christian. Praise God for the privilege of
being called by his wonderful name! (1 Peter 4:14, 16 NLT)

It is a great privilege for you to be called by God Himself to be His
child. That is the greatest honor of all! And if you are criticized
and insulted for being His follower, "Be happy" the scripture says.
Because it is at that point God "will come upon you"—which means
He is really closest to you.

Jesus also experienced insults, was made fun of and ridiculed
even by his own family and people. But Jesus knew who He was—
God's Son—and that His Father would give Him everything He
needed to endure. His Father would never fail Him.

Truth is, you too can endure insults because God will always be with
you. "So if you are suffering in a manner that pleases God, keep on
doing what is right, and trust your lives to the God who created you,
for he will never fail you" (1 Peter 4:19). You can count on it. Jesus will
always be with you no matter what you go through.

*My Prayer: Jesus, when I endure insults and even if I'm persecuted
for being Your child, help me always remember Your Word: "If God
is for us, who can ever be against us? Since he did not spare even his
own Son but gave him up for us all, won't he also give us everything
else?... Can anything ever separate us from Christ's love? Does it
mean he no longer loves us if we have trouble or calamity, or are
persecuted?... No, despite all these things, overwhelming victory is
ours through Christ, who loved us" (Romans 8:31-32, 35, 37). Amen.*

It's Not Fair

My Bible Reading:
For God is pleased when, conscious of his will, you patiently
endure unjust treatment.... For God called you to do good, even if
it means suffering, just as Christ suffered for you. (1 Peter 2:19, 21)

Have you ever said something like, "That's not fair," and someone
replied, "Well, life isn't always fair!"? It's true. Many things in
life aren't fair. But God is pleased when you endure the unfairness by
not lashing back in an unkind spirit. He wants you to patiently take it.
But does that mean it's right for people to get away with treating you
unfairly? Not at all!

Truth is, God is the righteous judge and people will eventually get
what they deserve. The important thing is to leave it all in God's
hands. He says, " 'I will take revenge; I will pay them back. In due time
their feet will slip. Their day of disaster will arrive, and their destiny
will overtake them' " (Deuteronomy 32:35).

Jesus, the perfect One who was sinless, endured the most unfair
treatment of all. And what did He do when He was tortured and
crucified? He did not retaliate "nor threaten revenge when he suffered. He left his case in the hands of God, who always judges fairly"
(1 Peter 2:23).

My Prayer: *Thank You that You are my example to follow.
Even You trusted in Your Father to handle unfairness. Help me
put my trust in You when I'm treated unfairly. I know that will
please You, and I long to please You. You are so great! Amen.*

He Became a Servant

My Bible Reading:

Jesus said, "Those who are the greatest among you should take the lowest rank, and the leader should be like a servant. Who is more important, the one who sits at the table or the one who serves? The one who sits at the table, of course. But not here! For I am among you as one who serves." (Luke 22:26–27)

Jesus is the Creator of the universe. His title is the "King of all kings and Lord of all lords" (Revelation 19:16). No one can know more, do more, or be more than He is, and rightfully so. He is God. Yet when He entered the world He didn't demand His place as King, but rather lowered Himself as a servant. He was, in part, teaching you an attitude of the heart and how to treat others.

Truth is, Jesus had a servant's heart and was a humble leader. And He wants you to follow His example. Scripture says, "All of you, serve each other in humility, for 'God sets himself against the proud, but he shows favor to the humble' " (1 Peter 5:5). Jesus said good things happen to those who have a servant's heart of humility. "God blesses those who are humble, for they will inherit the whole earth" (Matthew 5:5).

My Prayer: Thank You for humbling Yourself, taking on human skin and dying so that I could live. Your life and example motivates me to serve others. Help me today to serve someone with a humble heart like Yours. Amen.

Only God

****

My Bible Reading:

"Seeing [the people's] faith, Jesus said to the paralyzed man, 'My child, your sins are forgiven.' But some of the teachers of religious law who were sitting there thought to themselves, 'What is he saying? This is blasphemy! Only God can forgive sins!'" (Mark 2:5-7)

What's the biggest problem in the world? War? Starvation? Disease? Global warming? Death? You might cite a lot of big problems in the world, but if you go back to the root problem of everything mentioned above you are left with a singular issue—sin.

When sin entered the world, it brought every problem imaginable. So if the sin issue of the world could somehow be addressed, then every problem would eventually be solved.

Truth is, Jesus came to earth with the mission in mind to solve the problem of sin. His purpose was to restore the relationship between sinful humanity and a perfect and sinless God. No one, except God, has the power to forgive the sins of humanity. And Jesus, as the sinless Son of God, is the perfect and only candidate to do just that. "For the sin of this one man, Adam, brought death to many. But even greater is God's wonderful grace and his gift of forgiveness to many through this other man, Jesus Christ" (Romans 5:15).

My Prayer: I am so thankful that You came to earth as the God-man to enable me to be forgiven of my sins. Only You can forgive my sins, and thank You that in Your mercy and love You did. Help me share with someone today how grateful I am for Your forgiveness. You are a gracious and forgiving Savior. Amen.

Centered on Christ

My Bible Reading:

Even before he made the world, God loved us and chose us in Christ to be holy and without fault in his eyes.... God's secret plan has now been revealed to us; it is a plan centered on Christ, designed long ago according to his good pleasure. (Ephesians 1:4, 9 NLT)

Before God spoke the universe into being, before He shaped this planet into a beautiful paradise, before He breathed into humans the breath of life...He had a plan to deal with sin and death. He knew sin would enter your world and you would be separated from Him. His plan was miraculous and merciful. It was centered on Christ with the mission to restore your relationship with Him.

Truth is, without Jesus coming to earth to die, you and all who have lived before you or will live after you are doomed. There is no hope of forgiveness by God unless Jesus showed up in human form and offered Himself as a sacrifice for sin. He was, and is, your only hope of forgiveness. "For he has rescued us from the kingdom of darkness [death] and transferred us into the Kingdom of his dear Son, who purchased our freedom and forgave our sins" (Colossians 1:13–14). God's entire plan of salvation was, and is, centered on the amazing Incarnation (God in Christ becoming human) and purchasing your freedom from death.

My Prayer: Thank You for Your plan of salvation. "You saw me before I was born. Every day of my life was recorded in your book. Every moment was laid out before a single day had passed" (Psalm 139:16). And You reached out to me through Your Son Jesus to have an eternal relationship with You. Words cannot express how deeply grateful I am for Your love and mercy. Thank You for Your wonderful plan of salvation. Amen.

MAY

The Price of Forgiveness

A Life for a Life

My Bible Reading:

God told Moses: "When you present an animal as an offering to the LORD...it must be a male with no defects.... Lay your hand on the animal's head, and the LORD will accept its death in your place to purify you, making you right with him." (Leviticus 1:2–4)

L ife is a wonderful thing. You can experience the close connection with a friend, feel the excitement of an adventure, enjoy the relaxation of a quiet moment, or take a break with a peaceful walk. Death, on the other hand, is a terrible thing. You enjoy absolutely nothing in death. The real problem is that you were born spiritually dead.

That's where the God of life comes in. Before He even created this world He devised a plan to bring you back to life in a relationship with Him. But for that plan to work meant there had to be a "life-for-a-life" exchange.

Truth is, when people of Old Testament times sacrificed an animal to God, He accepted its death in their place. The death of an animal without defects substituted for the death of the sinner. But sacrificing animals wasn't God's permanent solution. That was only a symbol of what was to come. In order for the consequences of sin and death to be reversed, a more powerful and perfect sacrifice or ransom had to be paid. And Jesus paid that price. "God chose him [Jesus] as your ransom long before the world began" (1 Peter 1:20).

My Prayer: Thank You that You had a plan to save me from eternal death, even before You created humans. You were willing to accept Jesus' death for my life. I am so thankful for Your mercy. Help me live every day with a heart of gratitude for Your wonderful plan of salvation. And encourage me to share Your plan with others. Amen.

Can't Just Let It Slide

My Bible Reading:
O Lord my God, my Holy One, you who are eternal... You are pure and cannot stand the sight of evil. (Habakkuk 1:12–13)

Your friend gets mad, says some nasty things to you, and goes home because you beat him or her in an electronic game. Later your friend apologizes for saying mean things. You may let it slide and say, "Sure, that's okay; everything's cool." But God can't overlook meanness and sin like that.

God has many characteristics. He is all-powerful, all-knowing, loving, just, merciful, gracious, and so on. But above all, the very essence and being of God is something that defines all of His characteristics. By nature God is *holy*! That means His love is holy, His justice is holy, His anger is holy, His mercy is holy, etc. And in all His holiness and purity He cannot tolerate that which is unholy or sinful.

Truth is, God's merciful and masterful plan of a life-for-a-life exchange is to make those who are unholy, holy. "Even before he made the world, God loved [you] and chose [you] in Christ to be holy and without fault in his eyes" (Ephesians 1:4). That's God's solution. A holy God who can't overlook your sin makes you holy through Christ so that you and He can have a personal relationship. "God chose you to be the holy people he loves" (Colossians 3:12).

My Prayer: You are a holy God and there is no wrong in You. Thank You for Your merciful plan to make me holy in and through Christ. Without Jesus I could never have a relationship with You. Thank You for Your love and mercy to me. Help me share Your love with someone today. Amen.

The Holy Sacrifice

My Bible Reading:
For God made Christ, who never sinned, to be the
offering for our sin, so that we could be made right
with God through Christ. (2 Corinthians 5:21)

Have you ever met a perfectionist? It's the type of person who wants things just right. Maybe you're a perfectionist. But the ultimate perfectionist is God. The offering and sacrifice for your sin had to be a perfect and sinless offering. The sacrifices of lambs and goats in the Old Testament were only temporary—a more perfect sacrifice was needed.

Truth is, there was only one sacrifice that was the perfectly holy sacrifice that a holy God could accept—and that was Jesus. Not only was Jesus the holy sacrifice who never sinned, He became our holy priest as well. "He [Jesus] is the kind of high priest we need because he is holy and blameless, unstained by sin" (Hebrews 7:26).

God's holiness is satisfied because of a holy Jesus. His sacrificial death atones or satisfies the payment for sin so you can be redeemed and saved from eternal death. It was "redemption that came by Christ Jesus. God presented Christ as a sacrifice of atonement, through the shedding of his blood—to be received by faith" (Romans 3:24–25 NIV).

My Prayer: I am so thankful for what You, Jesus, have done for me. You became the holy sacrifice God needed to forgive me of my sins. I will always be grateful for Your mercy and love for me. Help me share Your love and mercy with someone today. Amen.

The Price of Freedom

My Bible Reading:
For you know that God paid a ransom to save you from the empty life you inherited from your ancestors. And it was not paid with mere gold or silver, which lose their value. It was the precious blood of Christ, the sinless, spotless Lamb of God. (1 Peter 1:18–19)

Have you ever visited a prisoner who is serving a sentence? Normally the way a prisoner is set free from confinement is to serve the sentence he or she has been given. The jail sentence is the "wages" of the crime committed.

The sentence for your "crime" of sin is death. That's a pretty stiff sentence that you don't want to serve, right? As a slave to sin and death, you have no hope, except for one merciful act by the only person able to get your sentence overturned.

Truth is, Jesus, the "sinless, spotless Lamb of God," paid for your sentence so you could be set free. You are rescued from the eternal wages of death. "Christ has rescued [you] from the curse pronounced by the law. When he was hung on the cross, he took upon himself the curse for [your] wrongdoing" (Galatians 3:13). God's holy justice was fully satisfied because of Jesus' holy sacrifice for you.

My Prayer: Jesus, what can I say to express my heart of gratitude for rescuing me from a sentence of eternal death? Thank You! I will join in with the millions of angels, living creatures, and elders who sing in a mighty chorus: " 'Worthy is the Lamb who was slaughtered—to receive power and riches and wisdom and strength and honor and glory and blessing' " (Revelation 5:12). You are an awesome and merciful God. Amen.

A Forever Promise

My Bible Reading:

Jesus gave a cup of wine to His disciples at the Passover meal and said, "Each of you drink from it, for this is my blood, which confirms the covenant between God and his people. It is poured out as a sacrifice to forgive the sins of many." (Matthew 26:27–28)

Has anyone ever made a promise to you? Did he or she keep it? Well, God made a forever promise—it is called "the blood of the covenant." When Jesus met with His disciples that night for the Passover meal, He reminded them of the blood covenant God made with the children of Israel. And when Jesus sacrificed Himself on the cross, that covenant was sealed as a forever promise.

Truth is, your forgiveness of sins was assured when you trusted in Christ as your Savior. "Christ offered himself to God as a perfect sacrifice for our sins. That is why he is the one who mediates a new covenant between God and people, so that all who are called can receive the eternal inheritance God has promised them" (Hebrews 9:14–15). And you can be sure God keeps His promises. In fact, God "bound himself with an oath, so that those who received the promise could be perfectly sure that he would never change his mind. . . because it is impossible for God to lie" (Hebrews 6:17–18).

My Prayer: *I have trusted in Your Son, Jesus, as my Savior and I receive Your promise of eternal life. Thank You for Your "blood of the covenant." You are a merciful and loving God to me. I love You. Help me share Your promise of eternal life with others today. Amen.*

Bought and Paid For

My Bible Reading:
Don't you realize that your body is the temple of the Holy Spirit,
who lives in you and was given to you by God? You do not belong
to yourself, for God bought you with a high price. So you must
honor God with your body. (1 Corinthians 6:19–20)

Have you ever heard someone say something like, "Hey it's my
life, and I can do what I want with it"? A lot of people think that
way, but as a follower of Jesus you have been bought and paid for by
the death and resurrection of Jesus. You no longer belong to yourself.

What were you before God saved you? You were the "walking
dead." You were spiritually dead and a slave to sin. But Jesus "purchased [your] freedom and forgave [your] sins" (Colossians 1:14). You
are no longer a slave to sin; rather you serve God out of a heart of love
and gratefulness.

Truth is, you belong to God like lovers do when they give themselves
to one another in marriage. In love you want to honor the one who
did so much for you. "We don't live for ourselves or die for ourselves.
If we live, it's to honor the Lord. And if we die, it's to honor the Lord.
So whether we live or die, we belong to the Lord. Christ died and rose
again for this very purpose" (Romans 14:7–9).

*My Prayer: When I think of how much You loved me
and died to purchase my salvation, I could do no less than
be Yours and honor You with how I live. Help me to think
and say and act in every way so as to bring honor to You.
And one of the best ways to honor You is to love others as You
have loved me. Let me show Your love to someone today. Amen.*

A Guarantee

My Bible Reading:

When you believed in Christ, he identified you as his own by giving you the Holy Spirit. . . . The Spirit is God's guarantee that he will give us the inheritance he promised and that he has purchased us to be his own people. (Ephesians 1:13–14)

Have you ever purchased something that came with a warranty? A warranty is a guarantee that if the product malfunctions or breaks, the company will fix it. But warranties expire, usually about the time your product breaks or fails. God's guarantee is different.

Truth is, when you believed in Christ you became a child of God. And He gave you His Holy Spirit to guarantee you that He has purchased your salvation and that you have eternal life. "For his Holy Spirit speaks to us deep in our hearts and tells us that we are God's children" (Romans 8:16 NLT).

My Prayer: *I praise You for giving me Your Holy Spirit that assures me of my salvation. May I never doubt that I am Your child. You are so worthy of my praise. And let me glorify You today by sharing the assurance of my salvation with others. Amen.*

Back to the Future

My Bible Reading:
The sacrifices under that [Old Testament] system were
repeated again and again, year after year, but they were
never able to provide perfect cleansing for those who
came to worship. . . . For it is not possible for the blood of
bulls and goats to take away sins. (Hebrews 10:1, 4)

Have you ever known someone who has received a bad check?
He or she went to the bank to cash the check and the teller said,
"I'm sorry, but there are insufficient funds in this account. I can't
cash this check." A check written today will be worthless tomorrow,
unless someone makes sure enough funds have been deposited in
the account to cover the check.

Prior to Jesus dying as a sacrifice for sin, it was like there weren't
enough "funds" in God's account to forgive people of their sins.
Animal sacrifices amounted to "insufficient funds." Jesus' sacrifice
is the only one that really counts. The Bible says, " 'There is salvation
in no one else!' " (Acts 4:12). But God took care of this "insufficient
funds" problem in a unique way.

Truth is, Jesus' sacrifice reached back in time to allow God to forgive
those who relied on the old system and save them. God "held back
and did not punish those who sinned in times past, for he was looking
ahead and including them in what he would do in this present time"
(Romans 3:25-26). Jesus' offering of Himself is so powerful that it is
able to save the first person created in ages past to the last person to
ever be born in the distant future.

---

*My Prayer: Your death on the cross was a powerful sacrifice. It
reminds me just how powerful Your love is for me and every person
who has or ever will be born. Thank You that I can experience Your
amazing love. Help me share Your love with someone today. Amen.*

No Place like Home

My Bible Reading:
Christ suffered for our sins once for all time. He never sinned, but he died for sinners to bring you safely home to God. (1 Peter 3:18)

No one has a perfect home, mainly because no human being is perfect. But if you had a perfect home, what would it be like? You might say the perfect home is a safe place where you can be who you are and always feel accepted. It would probably be a place where you can truly love and be loved, share your hopes and dreams, feel close and connected and know that no matter what, people are there for you, wanting you, and caring for you so you would never feel alone.

Truth is, Jesus went to extraordinary lengths to "bring you safely home to God"—to a perfect place where you are loved beyond belief. God wanted you so much that Jesus suffered a torturous death so you could enjoy the perfect home experience with Him. But that home isn't just in this life—it exists for all eternity with Him and all your loved ones who are His children. God promised that "'all who are victorious will inherit all these blessings [a perfect home], and I will be their God, and they will be my children'" (Revelation 21:7).

My Prayer: Thank You that You wanted me as Your child, to be part of Your home. Thank You that You are the perfect Father who cares for me and will always be there for me so I will never, ever be alone. Help me be more of a grateful and loving child who honors You. I love You. Amen.

He Broke the Power

My Bible Reading:
When he [Jesus] died, he died once to break the power of sin. . . .
So you also should consider yourselves to be dead to the power
of sin and alive to God through Christ Jesus. (Romans 6:10–11)

Have you ever gotten caught by someone for doing something wrong, but instead of telling on you, the person used it as leverage? It's like the person had power over you to do what he or she wanted—otherwise you'd be "found out." That's not comfortable. Who wants to be under the control of someone like that?

The problem is that someone has had leverage over you since birth. You were born a sinner because of Adam's sin and consequently you became a slave to sin (Romans 6:17). The devil had the upper hand. The power of sin had leveled a charge against you that you couldn't deny because you had sinned.

Truth is, you had no hope of breaking free from the power of sin. . . except for Jesus. He died for you to break the power of sin. "You were dead because of your sins. . . . Then God made you alive with Christ, for he forgave all [your] sins. He canceled the record of the charges against [you] and took it away by nailing it to the cross" (Colossians 2:13–14).

My Prayer: *I had a record of sin charged against me and had no way to cancel it. Thank You that You died and rose again "to remove the power of sin forever by [Your] sacrificial death for [me]" (Hebrews 9:26 NLT). I will live this day praising You for loving me enough to die for me. Thank You that the power of Your love and sacrifice broke the power of sin over my life. Help me share that truth with someone today. Amen.*

In Need of a High Priest

My Bible Reading:

So Christ has now become the High Priest.... With his own blood—
not the blood of goats and calves—he entered the Most Holy Place once
for all time and secured our redemption forever. (Hebrews 9:11–12)

Jesus, a high priest? Where did the idea of priests come from in the first place?

From the very beginning God's plan was to have a direct and personal relationship with humans. But because humans commit sin, a holy God couldn't have direct interaction with them. So He instructed Moses to build a Tabernacle as a temporary means so the children of Israel could enjoy God's presence. And in that Tabernacle God accepted animal sacrifices for the forgiveness of sin. But only a certain group of individuals was allowed to offer the sacrifices before God on behalf of the people. Those individuals were called priests, and the most important one was called the high priest.

Truth is, the high priest of the Old Testament offered sacrifices for the forgiveness of sins on a continuing basis. But his responsibility ended when the Great High Priest "[Jesus] Christ offered himself to God as a perfect sacrifice for our sins" (Hebrews 9:14). Now Jesus gives you direct access to His Father God.

My Prayer: Thank You that You are my High Priest. You have heard my prayers, and God has forgiven me of my sins because of Your sacrificial death. In Your mercy, You have secured my redemption—saved me from eternal death—and have granted me eternal life with You. I love You, Jesus. Amen.

Once and Forever

My Bible Reading:
Because Jesus lives forever, his priesthood lasts forever.
Therefore he is able, once and forever, to save those
who come to God through him. (Hebrews 7:24–25)

Have you ever glued a model plane, car, or ship together? The model is a replica or copy of the real thing. When God told Moses to build the Tabernacle and the things in it, they too were a replica of what God had in heaven. God never intended for Jesus to remain on earth to be a high priest in some Tabernacle or church made by human hands.

God's plan was for Jesus to enter the Most Holy Place in heaven (God's Tabernacle), offer Himself as a sacrifice, and live forever as your High Priest, your Savior and King. No other offering is needed for sins of the past, sins in the present, or for any sins that are committed in the future.

Truth is, a sacrifice doesn't need to be made continually for people's sins. Scripture says, "If that had been necessary, Christ would have had to die again and again, ever since the world began. But now, once for all time, he has appeared at the end of the age to remove sin by his own death as a sacrifice" (Hebrews 9:26). So, "when sins have been forgiven, there is no need to offer any more sacrifices" (Hebrews 10:18). Jesus' sacrifice was the once and forever sacrifice offered to God in heaven for you.

My Prayer: Because You were sinless and eternal, You were the one and only sacrifice Your Father needed. Thank You that You are all I need to have eternal life. Jesus, Your plan to save me and all those who trust in You was merciful and ingenious! Help me share that plan with someone today. Amen.

Really Confident

My Bible Reading:
Philip went to look for Nathanael and told him, "We have
found the very person Moses and the prophets wrote about!
His name is Jesus, the son of Joseph from Nazareth." (John 1:45)

One thing is clear: if Jesus was not truly God's Son, then His death
on the cross meant nothing. You can believe all you want that
His sacrifice allowed God to forgive you, but if He was not God in
human form, God's Chosen One, then the power of sin isn't broken,
your freedom isn't purchased, and His offer of eternal life isn't real. If
Jesus wasn't the "person Moses and the prophets wrote about," you
have no confidence you are a child of God.

Truth is, God wants you to be really confident that Jesus is the true
Son of God—" 'the Lamb of God who takes away the sin of the world' "
(John 1:29). That's one of the reasons He had the prophets foretell
or prophesy about who the Chosen One would be and how to tell if
Jesus was truly God's Son.

Philip had obviously done his homework. He probably found the
many prophecies that were fulfilled in Jesus, like the prophecy that
Jesus would be from the family line of David (Jeremiah 23:5), be born
in Bethlehem (Micah 5:2), be preceded by a messenger (John the
Baptist) (Isaiah 40:3), and begin His ministry in Galilee (Isaiah 9:1).
And that's just four out of sixty major Old Testament prophecies
that were fulfilled in Jesus, all of which were written more than four
hundred years before Jesus was born. God wants you to be really
confident that Jesus is His perfect sacrificial Lamb that takes away
your sins. And these many prophecies give you that confidence.

---

*My Prayer: You have given me so much evidence from
the Old Testament prophets that Jesus is Your Son and
He is my Savior. You don't want me to just believe blindly,
but believe with confidence. Thank You for that. Amen.*

What Are the Chances?

My Bible Reading:
So the Word [God] became human and made his home among us.
He was full of unfailing love and faithfulness. And we have seen
his glory, the glory of the Father's one and only Son. (John 1:14)

Jesus entered the world and many people soon became convinced He was in fact the Son of God. One reason is because Jesus fulfilled the Old Testament prophecies about the Messiah, the Chosen One of God. In fact, there are sixty major prophecies that were fulfilled in Him. But isn't it possible that those prophecies just *happened* to coincide with His life? Possibly, but what are the chances?

To answer that question, you need only to turn to the science of statistics and probabilities. A verified analysis was conducted by the American Scientific Affiliation that concluded that the probability of just *eight* prophecies being fulfilled in one person is 1 in 10^{17} (that's 100,000,000,000,000,000).

To get an idea of that probability, assume you had that many Oreo cookies and you spread them across the state of Texas. That many cookies would not only cover the state, but you would be surrounded by Oreos two feet deep. Now, take a bite out of one cookie and toss it into the pile and stir all the cookies up thoroughly. Then blindfold yourself and start walking the full breadth of the state of Texas, stooping just once along the way to pick up a single cookie. What are the chances you'd pick up the cookie from which you took a bite?

Truth is, it is the same chance that one person could have fulfilled just eight prophecies about the Chosen One in a single lifetime!

My Prayer: *It is unbelievable to imagine that eight Old Testament prophecies about Jesus could have come true by chance—let alone sixty prophecies! Thank You, God, for making it so very clear that Your Son was Jesus of Nazareth and that He died so I could be forgiven and granted eternal life. Help me share this truth with someone today. Amen.*

Wrong Proof

My Bible Reading:
The crowd watched as Jesus was hanging on the cross and the leaders scoffed. "He saved others," they said, "let him save himself if he is really God's Messiah, the Chosen One." (Luke 23:35)

Jesus had been beaten to within an inch of His life. A cruel crown of thorns was jammed onto His head. Then He was nailed to a cross. What if He had done what His accusers suggested? Say He popped the nails out of His hands and feet and jumped off the cross, ripped off His crown of thorns and said, "See, I really am the Chosen One. So believe in Me now!"

If Jesus had accepted their challenge to save Himself from a cruel death, He would have provided the wrong proof. His very purpose was to come to earth, suffer and die, and then rise again for your salvation. In one day, the very day Jesus was crucified, He fulfilled twenty-nine specific prophecies about what would take place in those short, dreadful hours.

Truth is, the proof the scoffers were looking for was being fulfilled right before their eyes. Even their statement, "He saved others, let him save himself" was prophesied in Psalm 22:8 hundreds of years before Jesus was born. The Savior had to stay on the cross until He died and then rise from the dead to become the Savior of the world!

My Prayer: Jesus, as horrible as it was to die like that, I am so thankful You did. Rather than coming off the cross to save Yourself, You died that I might be saved. Thank You for doing that for even me. Help me share Your loving mercy of salvation to those around me. Amen.

Wanting to Be Remembered

My Bible Reading:
The criminal hanging beside Jesus on the cross said, "Jesus, remember me when you come into your Kingdom." And Jesus replied, "I assure you, today you will be with me in paradise." (Luke 23:42–43)

Got the picture? Jesus is being crucified—along with two criminals who are guilty as charged. And one of the criminals who deserved to die for his crimes asks Jesus for mercy—that is what the man meant when he said, " 'Jesus, remember me. . . .' " It's clear that in his dying hours he believed that Jesus was the Chosen One who could give him life after death.

Truth is, the criminal hanging there beside Jesus was as good as dead. So are you. Like that dying criminal, you are guilty of sin as charged. Your sin stands between you and a holy God without hope of forgiveness. You are dead to Him with no ability in yourself to change your death status. That is, unless Christ remembers you as He did the criminal crucified beside Him. And He does!

Jesus remembers you, forgives you, and in love gives you eternal life in Him. That is the amazing love of God! "You are a God of forgiveness, gracious and merciful, slow to become angry, and rich in unfailing love" (Nehemiah 9:17).

My Prayer*: Thank You that You remembered me. Even though it was my sins that helped nail You to the cross, You remembered me and forgave me. One day I will live forever in Your paradise. Help me share Your amazing love with someone today. Amen.*

Promise to Forgive

My Bible Reading:
If we confess our sins, He is faithful and righteous to forgive us our sins and to cleanse us from all unrighteousness. (1 John 1:9 NASB)

People make promises. There are money promises, work promises, friendship promises, love promises, all kinds of promises. And people who keep their promises are considered to be faithful people.

When you confess your sins, God is faithful to forgive you because He made a promise to do so. And that promise can be kept all because of Jesus' sacrificial death on your behalf. Amazingly, His plan to forgive you was made even before He created the world. You can have confidence of forgiveness because you "have eternal life, which God—who does not lie—promised [you] before the world began" (Titus 1:2).

Truth is, "our evil consciences have been sprinkled with Christ's blood to make us clean. . . . [So] let us hold tightly to the hope we say we have, for God can be trusted to keep his promise" (Hebrews 10:22–23 NLT). You can count on it; if you confess your sins to God, He will forgive. "He [God] keeps every promise forever" (Psalm 146:6).

My Prayer: Thank You that You are a promise-keeping God. You are faithful to forgive me because of what Jesus has done for me. I am so thankful for Your mercy and love. My relationship with You means everything. Amen.

Forgave Them All

My Bible Reading:
Though we are overwhelmed by our sins,
you forgive them all. (Psalm 65:3)

How many sins have you committed in your life? You no doubt haven't counted them, but God surely knows how many times you have sinned. So how many times do you think He'll hear your confessions and forgive your sins before He runs out of love and mercy? One hundred times? Two hundred times? Five hundred times?

Truth is, God has an unlimited amount of compassion and mercy to all who repent (those who are sorry and turn their back on wrong). "Give thanks to the LORD because he is good, because his mercy endures forever" (Psalm 106:1 GWT).

God will never turn away from those who are sorry for their sin no matter how many sins have been committed. The heart of God is actually moved by your brokenness over wrongdoing. King David prayed to God, "The sacrifice you desire is a broken spirit. You will not reject a broken and repentant heart, O God" (Psalm 51:17). "The LORD is close to the brokenhearted; he rescues those whose spirits are crushed" (Psalm 34:18).

My Prayer: Lord, while I don't want to do wrong, I am so thankful that You are merciful to forgive me when I do. And thank You that You have forgiven every one of my past sins. You are a merciful and loving God. Help me share Your mercy and love with someone today by sharing how forgiving You are of the sins that are committed. You are an awesome God! Amen.

To Infinity and Beyond

My Bible Reading:
For his unfailing love toward those who fear him is as great
as the height of the heavens above the earth. He has removed
our sins as far from us as the east is from the west. (Psalm 103:11–12)

Start hiking due north. What would be your final destination?
Obviously, the North Pole. Head due south and you'll arrive where?
Naturally, the South Pole. But what would be your final destination if
you hiked due east or west? Where would be your stopping point?

If you hike east or travel west, you will simply keep going around
and around the globe for eternity. King David purposely used the
phrase "as far from us as the east is from the west." It is the Hebrew
expression for infinity.

Truth is, your sins are forgiven, to quote Buzz Lightyear, "to infinity
and beyond." Those sins are nowhere to be found. When God forgives,
He infinitely forgives.

-----

*My Prayer: Thank You that Your forgiveness is final and my sins are
forever gone. Help me remember that if my sins come to my memory
to haunt me, You have mercifully removed them from me. Let me rest
in that amazing truth and share it with someone today. Amen.*

Truly Forgivable

My Bible Reading:

"Come now, let's settle this," says the LORD. "Though your sins are like scarlet, I will make them as white as snow. Though they are red like crimson, I will make them as white as wool." (Isaiah 1:18)

What's the worst sin you ever committed? What do you think is the worst sin in the world? Are some sins so bad that God can't forgive a sinner who confesses them in true repentance and remorse?

King David knew about hideous and terrible sins. He committed some awful sins in his life. Yet God forgave the worst of his sins. He said, "Finally, I confessed all my sins to you and stopped trying to hide my guilt. I said to myself, 'I will confess my rebellion to the LORD.' And you forgave me! All my guilt is gone" (Psalm 32:5).

Truth is, there is not one confessed sin that God will not forgive and there is no wrong admitted that He will not blot out. Isaiah tells us that God even takes the stain of sin away. The only sin God cannot forgive and wipe clean is the one that is not confessed. "The LORD is slow to anger and filled with unfailing love, forgiving every kind of sin and rebellion" (Numbers 14:18).

My Prayer: Thank You that You are so merciful and forgiving of even the worst of my sins. I will not take advantage of Your willingness to forgive, for I always want to please You and do what is right. Your forgiving heart actually motivates me to live a life pleasing to You. You are an awesome God! Amen.

So Ready to Forgive

My Bible Reading:
O Lord, you are so good, so ready to forgive, so full of
unfailing love for all who ask for your help. (Psalm 86:5)

Yam ou and a few fellow students are at your friend's house for a
sleepover. Your friend's parents make it clear that all games and
activities are to be played in the basement rec room. The parents
explain they are running out for a few minutes to get some snacks.

Disregarding their instructions you and your friend make your
way upstairs. And while joking around you throw a couch pillow
across the room and it knocks over a very expensive vase. You sweep
up the broken vase and wait for the parents to return.

You apologize profusely and say you will pay for the broken vase,
which by the way costs a fortune. Your friend's mother says, "No need.
Your father came by yesterday and paid your debt even before you
broke the vase. You owe us nothing." That would be crazy, right?

Truth is, God was so ready to forgive you that Jesus paid your
debt before you ever committed a sin. "God showed how much he
loved us by sending his one and only Son into the world so that we
might have eternal life through him" (1 John 4:9). The price for your
forgiveness and eternal life was made before you were born. Your task
is to acknowledge your sins, confess them, and accept God's loving
forgiveness.

*My Prayer: Thank You, Lord, that You "are so good, so ready to
forgive" me. It is amazing that Your forgiveness and eternal life
were ready to be offered to me from the very beginning. I am so
glad I reached out in faith and claimed the relationship
You offered me. Thank You, thank You. Amen.*

Lingering Guilt

My Bible Reading:
Even if we feel guilty, God is greater than our feelings,
and he knows everything. (1 John 3:20)

Sometime in your life you may have hurt someone, felt guilty about it, and asked forgiveness. The person may have accepted your apology, but did your guilt hang around? Guilt does that sometimes. There is something about guilt that penetrates your feelings. And those feelings often don't go away immediately, even though in your head you know you have been forgiven.

Truth is, God is greater than your feelings. And your feelings will follow what you know is true about God and His promise to forgive. How? The Spirit of God will in fact confirm that truth. The Bible says, "There is no condemnation for those who belong to Christ Jesus. And because you belong to him, the power of the life-giving Spirit has freed you from the power of sin" (Romans 8:1-2). As you allow the truth of God's forgiveness to sink in, your feelings will get it—God's mercy and grace are real, and forgiveness is yours!

My Prayer: Thank You that You are greater than my lousy feelings. You are my Father and I am Your child. Guilt has no place in a relationship filled with love and acceptance. Thank You that You love me so. I love You. Amen.

Forgiving Yourself

My Bible Reading:
"Filled with love and compassion, he [the father] ran to his son,
embraced him, and kissed him. His son said to him, 'Father,
I have sinned against both heaven and you, and I am no longer
worthy of being called your son.' " (Luke 15:20–21)

You probably know the Bible story referred to as "The Prodigal
Son." The son tells his father he wants his inheritance so he can
move out and live like he wants. His father grants him his inheritance,
and the son blows through his money on partying and "good times."
Broke and disheartened, the boy makes his way back home in hopes
his father will take him back.

What's interesting in this story is that the boy no longer feels
worthy to accept the father-and-son relationship. He can't seem to
forgive himself for what he's done. He says, " 'Father, I have sinned
against both heaven and you, and I am no longer worthy of being
called your son.' " But the father, "filled with love and compassion,"
not only accepts the boy—he completely forgives him and organizes
a big feast of celebration to welcome his son home.

Truth is, sometimes you may be tempted to beat yourself up when
you've done wrong. You may refuse to forgive yourself. When you
face that temptation, be reminded that since the offended one (God)
freely forgives you, then you must agree with God. Because God, like
the boy's father says, " 'We must celebrate with a feast, for this [child]
of mine was dead and has now returned to life' " (Luke 15:23–24). If
God can forgive you, you can agree with God and forgive yourself.

My Prayer: *Thank You that You are so happy when I confess my
sins. Help me always accept Your forgiveness and forgive myself
for the wrong I have done. Let Your forgiveness sink so deep that I
too take myself off the hook. You are such a loving God. Amen.*

He Started It

My Bible Reading:
This is real love—not that we loved God, but that he loved us and sent his Son as a sacrifice to take away our sins. (1 John 4:10)

You look across the study hall and don't even notice the person. You've never even spoken to this individual. Then someone tells you that this particular, rather attractive-looking person, really likes you. What does that do to you? Most likely you're flattered and you start paying attention to that person. Maybe that even starts a boyfriend/girlfriend relationship.

Truth is, your relationship with God never began by you pursuing God. You didn't come to love God on your own. In fact, you would have never loved Him if He hadn't first loved you. His love for you is what drew you to Him. Jesus told His disciples, " 'You didn't choose me. I chose you' " (John 15:16). The same is true of you. God chose you. His Spirit reached out to you first in love and captured you. "When [you] were utterly helpless, Christ came at just the right time and died for [you]" (Romans 5:6). He is the one who started the relationship.

My Prayer: Thank You that You started it. Without You loving me I would not have had the life and power to love You back. Thank You that You came to me when I was helpless. You are such a compassionate and merciful God. Help me share Your amazing love with someone today. Amen.

Let Me Know

My Bible Reading:
Search me, O God, and know my heart; test me and know my
anxious thoughts. Point out anything in me that offends you,
and lead me along the path of everlasting life. (Psalm 139:23–24)

Your best friend comes to you and says, "Hey, if there's anything I
do that bugs you, let me know, okay? 'Cause I want our friendship
to continue and really be good." Would that seem weird? It shouldn't.
People that desire close relationships want others to let them know
when something offends them so they can seek forgiveness and
correct it.

King David wanted a close relationship with God. So he openly
invited God to search and know his heart. Obviously, an all-knowing
God already knew David's heart. But in David's prayer he was
welcoming God to reveal to him anything that offended his Lord.
He didn't want one thing to stand between him and God having an
intimate relationship.

Truth is, all healthy relationships require a willingness to be known
and have things pointed out so that all offenses can be addressed. A
transparency and teachable spirit are needed. David prayed, "Teach
me to do your will, for you are my God" (Psalm 143:10).

My Prayer: God, I want You to let me know if any part of my
life offends You, because I do want our relationship to deepen.
I do want You to teach me to do Your will and follow in Your ways.
You are the person I love, and I want to please You. Amen.

Forgiven People Forgive

My Bible Reading:

Jesus said, "If you forgive those who sin against you,
your heavenly Father will forgive you. But if you refuse to forgive
others, your Father will not forgive your sins." (Matthew 6:14-15)

When you were younger you may have heard someone say
something like, "If you don't stop that you can't play with us
anymore." You may have even uttered words like that. The point is
that it established a condition: if you do this or don't do that, then X
will follow.

At first, it may seem that Jesus was establishing a condition
that your own forgiveness is based on you forgiving others. But He
was not saying that. Other passages of scripture clearly state that
your forgiveness of sin is based solely on Christ and His atoning
sacrificial death on your behalf (Romans 3). So if Jesus wasn't setting
up a condition, then what does your forgiveness of others have to do
with God's forgiveness of you?

Truth is, if a person is unwilling to forgive others, it's a clear sign
he or she hasn't really experienced God's mercy and grace. When
people refuse to forgive those who wronged them, God knows that
any confession of their own sins is less than genuine and sincere.
How could anyone who truly experiences God's amazing grace
of forgiveness not also give mercy and grace to others? Jesus was
actually making the point that forgiven people forgive others.

---

*My Prayer: O God, let me always sense Your mercy and forgiveness
that I didn't deserve from You, so I can freely forgive others. I caused
You the pain of my sin and You forgave me. Because of You I can
forgive others who cause me pain. Thank You for Your mercy and grace
and help me always pass that mercy and grace on to others. Amen.*

How Many Times?

My Bible Reading:
Peter came to Jesus and asked, "Lord, how often should I forgive someone who sins against me? Seven times?" "No, not seven times," Jesus replied, "but seventy times seven!" (Matthew 18:21–22)

Since Jesus has forgiven you for all the wrong you have done, it's understandable that you would forgive those who do wrong against you, right? But what if someone keeps doing you wrong and keeps asking for your forgiveness? Surely there is a limit on this kind of thing. Peter, a disciple of Jesus, figured the limit was seven times. Yet Jesus had another perspective on the subject.

Jesus said that forgiving someone just seven times doesn't cut it. In fact, when He said to forgive someone seventy times seven He wasn't even saying to forgive someone a literal 490 times. He was saying to forgive others an unlimited number of times. Why? Because God's forgiveness is for an unlimited number of times.

Truth is, "the faithful love of the LORD never ends! His mercies never cease. Great is his faithfulness; his mercies begin afresh each morning" (Lamentations 3:22–23). Every morning when you get up, God's mercy and forgiveness begin all over again. Your forgiveness of others can follow that model—begin afresh every single morning!

My Prayer: *Thank You that Your mercies to me are endless. Let me begin this day and every day sensing Your mercies begin afresh with me so that I can extend mercy and forgiveness to others for an unlimited number of times. You are an awesome God. Amen.*

What Forgiveness Means

My Bible Reading:

Get rid of all bitterness, rage, anger, harsh words, and slander. . . .
Instead, be kind to each other, tenderhearted, forgiving one another,
just as God through Christ has forgiven you. (Ephesians 4:31–32)

Forgive like Jesus? What kind of forgiveness is that? It is a forgiveness that forgoes what is due, wipes the slate clean, cancels punishment, lets go, and gives up the right to get even no matter how much revenge is justified. That is Jesus' kind of forgiveness. It gives mercy rather than demands justice.

Truth is, that is precisely the kind of forgiveness you were given. You deserved punishment, but you were granted a pardon. You were due a death sentence, but you were given life eternal. You had a rap sheet a mile long, but your slate was wiped clean. And instead of anger, rage, and harsh words, which you deserved, Jesus was kind, tenderhearted, and forgiving. "He does not deal harshly with us, as we deserve" (Psalm 103:10). Since you have received that kind of forgiveness, give that kind of forgiveness to others.

My Prayer: I love Your kind of forgiveness. It motivates me to please You more when I think of how loving You are toward me. It also motivates me to show kindness and tenderness to others, forgiving them when they need it. Help me be more like You. Let me show Your kindness today to those who need to know they are loved. Amen.

What Sins?

My Bible Reading:

Let us go right into the presence of God with sincere hearts
fully trusting him. For our guilty consciences have been
sprinkled with Christ's blood to make us clean. (Hebrews 10:22)

"Let us go right into the presence of God." Imagine what that would be like. You drift out of consciousness and waken to see multicolor hues of light your eyes have never before seen. In the distance you see a glowing form coming toward you.

The colors and smells and feelings you have are new and unique, yet there is a strange familiarity about it all that comforts you. The form coming toward you takes shape and you see it's a person. As this person approaches, you clearly recognize Him as Jesus, though you've never seen Him in the flesh.

He smiles at you and reaches out to hug you. But a momentary fear grips you and you drop to your knees. With head down you begin nervously confessing, "I'm so sorry for my sins. Please forgive me, Jesus, for all those sins. . . ." You feel the touch of Jesus' hand under your chin as He gently lifts your head to gaze into your eyes. With a smile and a quizzical look on His face, your Savior responds, "What sins?"

Truth is, God has so thoroughly wiped away your sins that they are impossible to even recall. God's forgiveness goes so deep that your sins have been obliterated, totally wiped out and erased.

My Prayer: Thank You that Your sacrifice for me blotted out all my sins forever. You have cleared my guilty conscience. Thank You, thank You, thank You. Help me share that good news with others today. Amen.

How Rich?

My Bible Reading:
God is so rich in mercy, and he loved us so much, that even
though we were dead because of our sins, he gave us life
when he raised Christ from the dead. (Ephesians 2:4–5)

There are rich people in the world. There are some who year after
year have upwards of $75 billion in net worth. It is said that the
wealthiest five percent of people in the world control a staggering
portion of the world economy: an estimated $1.4 trillion. That's rich!

How do those riches compare to God's richness in mercy toward
us? No comparison! It is God's mercy that saves a soul from eternal
death. And the worth of one solitary soul is priceless! Jesus said,
" 'What do you benefit if you gain the whole world but lose your own
soul? Is anything worth more than your soul?' " (Mark 8:36–37). Jesus'
rhetorical question implies that possessing all the wealth in the world
has no comparison to having eternal life.

Truth is, God's mercy and love are infinite in wealth because God
grants a soul infinite life. You may experience God's love and mercy,
but you will never be able to comprehend their full value. "May you
experience the love of Christ, though it is too great to understand
fully" (Ephesians 3:19).

*My Prayer: Even though I may never fully comprehend Your mercy
to me, I will spend all eternity praising You for the richness of
Your love. Help me share Your love with someone today. Amen.*

Remember Me

My Bible Reading:

At the Last Supper Jesus said to His disciples, "This cup is the new covenant between God and his people—an agreement confirmed with my blood. Do this in remembrance of me as often as you drink it." [When you do] you are announcing the Lord's death until he comes again. (1 Corinthians 11:25-26)

It was the Passover meal (some call it the Last Supper). Jesus was breaking the bread and drinking the wine in remembrance of God delivering the children of Israel out of Egypt. But this Passover was different from any other Passover celebration held by Jewish families for over 1,300 years.

The traditional Jewish Passover meal celebrated the fact that the angel of death passed over the firstborn of every Jewish family if they had sacrificed an animal and smeared its blood on the sides and top of the doorframes of their homes. But instead of Jesus referring to the sacrificial lambs and goats in the first Passover, He was telling His disciples that it was His blood that would cause eternal death to pass over anyone who trusted in Him.

Truth is, Jesus wants you to remember Him often and what He did for you. You can do that when you take communion at church and when you let people know about Jesus' sacrifice. When you do, you are announcing that Jesus died for you and for all who trust in Him as their Savior.

My Prayer: *I never want to take for granted Your sacrifice on the cross for me. I always want to remember that You are a real person and You suffered, bled, and died a cruel death that I could live forever. You are an awesome Savior and You are worthy of my praise for all eternity. Help me share this truth with others today. Amen.*

JUNE

The Power to Save

Jesus Plus?

My Bible Reading:
No one can ever be made right in God's sight by doing what his
law commands.... We are made right in God's sight when we trust
in Jesus Christ to take away our sins. (Romans 3:20, 22 NLT)

What do you have to do on your part to convince God that you are worth forgiving? There's got to be something you can do, right? Maybe if the good you do on earth outweighs the bad, it will please God enough to allow you into heaven. You might call this kind of thinking "Jesus Plus."

"Jesus Plus" thinking is a reward system—if you follow God's commands, do good to others, read your Bible, pray, etc., God rewards you with points. It's like your good deeds earn you favor with Him. You still have to believe in Jesus, but you need to earn your way to being saved by the good things you do—Jesus plus good works.

Truth is, all your good works add nothing to your salvation. Your ability to have a relationship with God is not based on anything you can do. In fact, "when we display our righteous deeds," the Bible says "they are nothing but filthy rags" (Isaiah 64:6). The one and only thing that enables God to forgive you of your sins and give you life in relationship with Him *is Jesus.* Your faith in Jesus as your sacrifice for sin is all that God accepts.

My Prayer: God, when it comes to my salvation, Jesus is all I need. Sure, by loving You and following in Your ways I want to show my gratitude for You forgiving me. But I can't earn my forgiveness. That has already been earned by the death and resurrection of Your Son. Help me share that good news with someone today. Amen.

It's a Gift

My Bible Reading:
For the sin of this one man, Adam, caused death to rule over
many. But even greater is God's wonderful grace and his gift of
righteousness, for all who receive it will live in triumph over sin
and death through this one man, Jesus Christ. (Romans 5:17)

When did you get your last gift—at your birthday party or on
Christmas? How much did you pay for your gift? How long
did you work for it?

If you work or pay someone for a gift, it isn't really a gift, is it? By
definition, a gift is something given to another without compensation.
Gifts are meant to be free. They are not earned, or otherwise they are
not really gifts.

Truth is, when God made you righteous and gave you eternal life, it
was a gift. And you can't work for a gift. Scripture says, "When people
work, their wages are not a gift, but something they have earned.
But people are counted as righteous, not because of their work, but
because of their faith in God who forgives sinners" (Romans 4:4-5).
Wages for work done may be appreciated. But a pure gift that cannot
be earned produces a deeper sense of gratitude.

My Prayer*: I admit I didn't earn Your forgiveness or work for eternal
life. You gifted those to me. But what I can give You in return is my
praise and thankful heart. I am so grateful for Your gift of salvation.
"I will praise you every day; yes, I will praise you forever. Great is
the Lord! He is most worthy of praise!" (Psalm 145:2-3). Amen.*

Can't Boast

My Bible Reading:
Can we boast, then, that we have done anything to be accepted
by God? No, because our acquittal is not based on obeying
the law. It is based on faith [in Jesus]. (Romans 3:27)

Your team wins the championship. You win first prize in the competition. You are granted a scholarship for a high grade average. Accomplish those things and there is reason to be proud of yourself. You can boast.

Truth is, when it comes to your salvation you can't boast about any part of it. Why? Because you did nothing to obtain it except place your trust in Jesus. Now that's amazing. But if you tend to be performance-based, the whole idea that you can't earn God's love may be hard to grasp.

It may seem like you need to do something to gain God's favor. Yet God doesn't want you to focus on your efforts; He wants you to focus on His love and mercy toward you. "When God our Savior revealed his kindness and love, he saved us, not because of the righteous things we had done, but because of his mercy" (Titus 3:4–5). Keeping your focus on God's mercy will help keep you humble and grateful for a loving God.

My Prayer: *Let me always look to You so I will boast of Your mercy and love and saving grace. Help me continue to accept Your mercy even though I can't earn it and don't deserve it. You are such a merciful God. I love You. Amen.*

Saved by What?

My Bible Reading:

It is by grace you have been saved, through faith—and this is
not from yourselves, it is the gift of God. (Ephesians 2:8 NIV)

How are you saved—how have you gained a relationship with
God? Most people answer that question by saying, "By faith—I
am saved by faith."

Neither you nor anyone else is saved by faith. If you could be
saved by faith, then Jesus would not have had to die for you. You
could have saved yourself simply by exercising faith.

Truth is, faith and faith alone has no power. The power of faith is
in its *object*—it is what or whom you are putting your faith in that
has the power. It is God's grace (an unearned favor toward you)
that saved your soul as you reached out in faith to Jesus. "He [God]
generously poured out the Spirit upon us because of what Jesus
Christ our Savior did. He declared us not guilty because of his great
kindness" (Titus 3:6-7 NLT). The power of your faith is in Jesus and
what He did for you. And it is purely by God's grace that you are
forgiven and have eternal life.

*My Prayer: Thank You that I am saved by Your grace through faith
in Jesus. He and He alone has the power to get my death sentence
overturned by His sacrificial death and resurrection. My faith has
been placed in Him. And that was all made possible by Your grace—
Your kindness, Your mercy, and Your favor toward me—that was
totally unearned. Thank You, thank You, thank You. Help me tell
others about Your amazing grace. You are an awesome God. Amen.*

Need Evidence?

My Bible Reading:

Jesus said, "Don't believe me unless I carry out my Father's work. But if I do his work, believe in the evidence of the miraculous works I have done, even if you don't believe me." (John 10:37–38)

The skeptics of Jesus' time didn't believe He was God's Son. They insisted that He was just a mere man. So what did Jesus do to back up His claim? He pointed them to the evidences of His miraculous works.

Jesus had turned water into wine (John 2), made a crippled man walk (John 5), cleansed lepers (Luke 17), brought sight to the blind (Mark 10), fed more than five thousand people with just five loaves of bread and two fish (Matthew 14), healed a paralyzed man (Luke 5), raised a boy and man from the dead (Luke 7 and John 11), and much more. Who else but God's Son could do such things?

Truth is, Jesus' power to perform miracles simply reflects His identity as God. These miracles provide convincing evidence that He is the "'Lamb of God who takes away the sin of the world'" (John 1:29). At the end of John's writings he wrote: "The disciples saw Jesus do many other miraculous signs in addition to the ones recorded in this book. But these are written so that you may continue to believe that Jesus is the Messiah, the Son of God, and that by believing in him you will have life by the power of his name" (John 20:30–31).

My Prayer: Thank You for the evidence that confirms You are the Savior of the world who can rescue people from eternal death. You are the miracle worker who not only can heal the body, but can give everlasting life to the soul. Help me share this amazing truth with my friends. Amen.

Proof in the Experience

My Bible Reading:
A blind man who had been given sight by Jesus was questioned by the religious leaders. He replied to them, "Ever since the world began, no one has been able to open the eyes of someone born blind. If this man were not from God, he couldn't have done it." (John 9:32–33)

After Jesus healed the blind man, his neighbors took him to the religious leaders. They complained that Jesus performed the miracle on the Sabbath day. That would technically be working and working was not allowed on the Sabbath. So they called Jesus a Sabbath breaker.

The religious leaders couldn't make sense of Jesus. They refused to believe He was God's Son in spite of His miraculous power. When they told the healed blind man that Jesus was a sinner, what did the man say? " 'I don't know whether he is a sinner,' the man replied. 'But I know this: I was blind, and now I can see' " (John 9:25). No one could deny the man's personal experience!

Truth is, no matter what kind of accusations and objections people make about Jesus and Christianity, no one can discount what you have personally experienced. Jesus may not be real to unbelievers, but that doesn't take away the reality of your relationship with Him. Jesus provided outside evidence that He is the Savior of the world. But you have internal, experiential evidence He is your personal Savior. "For his Holy Spirit speaks to us deep in our hearts and tells us that we are God's children" (Romans 8:16).

My Prayer: Thank You, God, for the evidence You have given to confirm that Jesus is Your Son and Savior of the world. But thank You even more for the convincing evidence of Your Holy Spirit that tells me I am Your child. Give me strength to share my experience of You with those around me. Amen.

The Good News

My Bible Reading:
He [Jesus] brought this Good News of peace to you. . . .
Now all of us can come to the Father through the same Holy Spirit
because of what Christ has done for us. (Ephesians 2:17–18)

The Good News that Jesus brought was the message of salvation
(the Gospel) and that through Him you could have a personal
relationship with God. In fact, scripture points out that "he is a God
who is passionate about his relationship with you" (Exodus 34:14
NLT). He is so passionate that His Son died so you and anyone else
who is willing to trust in Him could have eternal life.

Truth is, that kind of news is worth sharing with a world that is dead
to God because of sin. The apostles of Jesus unashamedly spread that
Good News everywhere. "I am not ashamed of this Good News about
Christ," the apostle Paul wrote. "It is the power of God at work, saving
everyone who believes—the Jew first and also the Gentile. This Good
News tells us how God makes us right in his sight" (Romans 1:16–17).
Do you know how to share that Good News? Over the next number
of devotions you will see how scripture verses tell the Good News
message. It is a message you will want to share with your friends.

*My Prayer: Thank You that Your message of salvation reached
me and You have granted me eternal life in a relationship with
You. Help me share that message with others. You are an
awesome God worth telling people about. Amen.*

The Initiator

My Bible Reading:
"For God loved the world so much that he gave
his only Son so that anyone who believes in him
shall not perish but have eternal life." (John 3:16 TLB)

Have you ever been at an event where you were a total stranger? A place where you didn't know anyone at all? That's an awkward feeling. But perhaps someone across the room noticed you and took the initiative to smile and introduce himself or herself to you. It's great when someone takes the first step to get acquainted with you.

Truth is, God is the Great Initiator. You were not only a stranger to Him, but your sin put you in opposition to Him. But in spite of your sin, He loved you. "This is real love—not that we loved God, but that he loved us and sent his Son as a sacrifice to take away our sins" (1 John 4:10).

This is Good News to share with your friends. None of them loved God first. He was the initiator and it is His Spirit that stands at the door of their hearts and is knocking. He says, " 'If you hear my voice and open the door, I will come in' " (Revelation 3:20).

My Prayer: Your Spirit is calling people to believe in You so You can give them eternal life. Help me be a messenger of that Good News. Give me wisdom and strength to share with my friends how You have given me life in relationship with You. And how that same life can be theirs as they trust in You. Amen.

The Plan

My Bible Reading:
Jesus prayed to His Father, "Now this is eternal life:
that they know you, the only true God, and Jesus Christ,
whom you have sent." (John 17:3 NIV)

That's the plan! God's plan from the very beginning was that you would know God the Father and His Son in a deep relational way. Because knowing the God of life gives you eternal life.

Truth is, when God said, " 'Let us make human beings in our image, to be like us' " (Genesis 1:26), He was designing you and every human to enjoy life in a relationship as He did. God being Father, Son, and Holy Spirit, enjoyed a perfect relational oneness that defined the very meaning of joy, peace, fulfillment, and happiness. And His plan was for you and the whole of the human race to experience that kind of relationship for all eternity.

That's an incredible plan! That's a plan worth sharing. If your friends knew God really wanted that for them, they may very well be excited to explore what's involved in taking advantage of God's wonderful plan.

__My Prayer__: There are many who just don't understand how willing and ready You are, God, to give them eternal life in a relationship with You. You are a life-giving God who loves my friends. Help me share Your plan with them. Give me wisdom and courage to find the right time to reveal Your heart of love toward them. Amen.

The Future

My Bible Reading:
"For I know the plans I have for you," says the LORD.
"They are plans for good and not for disaster,
to give you a future and a hope." (Jeremiah 29:11)

God made a promise to Israel that you can claim as your own. He has a plan for your good that offers a bright future and a hope for tomorrow. Remember, every person born—past, present, or future—comes into this world with no hope of life beyond this one. We all have no hope apart from Christ's offer of eternal life.

Truth is, without Jesus sacrificing Himself for you, there is no hope of a lasting future. And He wants your future on this earth to be bright and then extend that future forever into eternity. That's why Jesus said, " 'Don't be so concerned about perishable things like food. Spend your energy seeking the eternal life that the Son of Man can give you' " (John 6:27).

It's easy to get caught up in the things of this earth. A lot of those things feel important, like getting a good education, having a car, a good job, maybe getting married, and having a family. But all those things will fade away—they won't last. The only real hope of a lasting future is in knowing Jesus and His eternal life. That's a great message to share with your friends.

My Prayer: Thank You that You have a lasting future for me. Help me remember the important thing in this life is knowing You and sharing with others that You are the true hope for this world. Amen.

The Problem

My Bible Reading:
The trouble [the problem] is not with the law, for it is
spiritual and good. The trouble is with me, for I am
all too human, a slave to sin. (Romans 7:14)

The real problem isn't that God doesn't love the world, because He does. He loves every person that was ever born. The problem is sin. It has caused a major separation between humans and God. And a holy God can't just reconnect with humans again because He "cannot allow sin in any form" (Habakkuk 1:13 NLT).

That creates a huge problem unless people can avoid sinning. But that's not a realistic solution at all. First, "everyone has sinned; we all fall short of God's glorious standard" (Romans 3:23) and second, everyone is born a sinner in the first place. "Adam's one sin brings condemnation for everyone" (Romans 5:18).

Truth is, many people don't think sinning is that big of an issue as long as their good deeds outweigh their bad deeds. This is only a formula for more disaster. "Those who live only to satisfy their own sinful nature will harvest decay and death from that sinful nature" (Galatians 6:8).

It is sin that creates a great gulf between a holy, loving God and humans. And no matter what people do in their own strength and abilities, their efforts can never close that gulf of separation. Your friends need to realize the problem in order to recognize the solution.

My Prayer: *I know the sin problem is a huge issue and it keeps people from looking to You as their solution. Help me reveal to my friends Your loving and compassionate heart for them and Your plan to resolve the sin problem. Amen.*

The Sentence

My Bible Reading:
The wages of sin is death. (Romans 6:23)

Sin is the big problem for humans, but what it causes is even more devastating. The sentence for being a sinner is spiritual death! And people simply don't recover from death. Spiritually dead people may be walking around now, but once they physically die, that's it; there is no hope.

Truth is, "when Adam sinned, sin entered the world. Adam's sin brought death, so death spread to everyone" (Romans 5:12). No one is immune to this death and there is no human solution. Good deeds are good. Being nice to people is nice. Helping the poor and needy is helpful. But it does nothing to reverse death. There is nothing dead people can do to raise themselves to life, because they're dead!

The apostle Paul knew how devastating the sentence for sin was for all humans, including himself. He wrote, "Oh, what a miserable person I am! Who will free me from this life that is dominated by sin and death?" (Romans 7:24). The Good News is that there is a solution for a life sentence of eternal death. But it is important for all sinners to realize that they cannot solve that problem alone. There must be a recognition that the solution to spiritual death rests in one and only one person, Jesus.

My Prayer: I pray for my friends who don't know You yet. Help them realize You, Jesus, are their only hope for life. Help me guide them in an understanding that You are the true Life Giver. Be with me as I share my own story of how I realized You are my only hope and how You gave me the real hope of eternal life when You forgave me of my sins. Amen.

The Solution

My Bible Reading:

Everyone has sinned and fallen short of God's glorious standard, and all need to be made right with God by his grace, which is a free gift. They need to be made free from sin through Jesus Christ. God sent him to die in our place to take away our sins. We receive forgiveness through faith in the blood of Jesus' death. (Romans 3:23–25 NCV)

God's solution went to the heart of the problem. Sin was the problem, and Jesus died as a sacrifice for sin so that every sin past, present, and future could be forgiven. Human efforts, no matter how good, could not erase the past deeds of sin. But Jesus' sacrificial death did.

Truth is, "God made Christ, who never sinned, to be the offering for our sin, so that we could be made right with God through Christ" (2 Corinthians 5:21). When God looks at you or your friends who have trusted in Christ, He sees you through the lens of Jesus. His sacrificial offering blots out all the sin of those who place their trust in Him for salvation.

God's plan of salvation was detailed and required a full satisfaction of God's holiness and justice that came at the high cost of Jesus' death. Yet receiving salvation is simple. It is as simple as people recognizing they are sinners, realizing Jesus is the solution to sin, and responding to Him in faith by placing their trust in Him as their Savior. That may not be easy for your friends to do, but God has made it clear and simple.

My Prayer: Thank You that Your death paid for my freedom and was the offering to forgive me of my sins. Help me share that amazing truth with those around me. This salvation of humans cost You so much and yet You offer it so freely. Thank You for Your mercy and love. You are an awesome God. Amen.

The Resurrection

My Bible Reading:
We died and were buried with Christ by baptism. And just
as Christ was raised from the dead by the glorious power of
the Father, now we also may live new lives. (Romans 6:4)

Let's say you really want a brand-new car, but you don't have the
money. Then your parents come to you and say, "We'll pay the
cost of a new car for you." As amazing as that would be, the fact that
your parents have the money to pay for the car does you no good
until the financial transaction has taken place and you actually have
the car in your possession.

Jesus' sacrificial death pays for your sins. But just as important,
your dead existence must be brought to life. Your sins have been paid
for, yet you must be given spiritual life.

Truth is, even though you were spiritually dead, "the Spirit gives you
life because you have been made right with God. The Spirit of God,
who raised Jesus from the dead, lives in you" (Romans 8:10–11). Jesus'
sacrifice paid for your sin, and because of His resurrection you are
given life through His Spirit.

---

*My Prayer: Thank You that Your power to forgive me includes the
power to give me spiritual life. Help me share this new life message
with my friends. Being alive in Jesus is exciting. Give me courage
and wisdom in sharing this wonderful message. Amen.*

The Exclusivity

My Bible Reading:
"I am the way, the truth, and the life. No one can
come to the Father except through me." (John 14:6)

Hey, Christianity isn't the only religion in the world. There are many paths to God, right? Doesn't it seem just a little arrogant to claim that your religion is the only true one that leads to God and eternal life?

To claim that Christianity is the one and only true religion does seem annoyingly exclusive and intolerant to most people. Consequently, many Christians today no longer claim that Christianity is exclusive.

Truth is, you don't need to make the claim that your religion is the only way to God, because that does tend to come across as arrogant. In fact, it would have been arrogant for Jesus to say He was the one true way if He hadn't been God in human form. But He was the God-man and He gave extensive evidence to back up His claim.

As a follower of Jesus you can avoid coming across as arrogant by making it clear it was Jesus who made the "one way—one truth" claim, not you. Jesus claimed He was sent to save the whole world, and as God He had the qualifications to do just that. When you explain that Jesus is the only way to God, you are simply sharing *His* message and what He claimed.

My Prayer: *Thank You that You made it clear You were my only way to eternal life. And thank You for all the evidences of prophecies that were fulfilled in You, Your virgin birth, all the miracles You performed, and Your resurrection. That gives me greater confidence as I share the message that You are our only hope of eternal life. Amen.*

The Relationship

My Bible Reading:

God sent him [Jesus] to buy freedom for us who were slaves to the law, so that he could adopt us as his very own children. (Galatians 4:5)

Think of the deepest, closest relationship a person can have with another human being. Would that be a classmate, a lover, or a married couple? Those could develop into deep relationships. But the closest possible connected relationship would have to be that tiny, yet growing, human inside the body of a mother.

All the warmth, nourishment, protection, and nurture of a newborn child come from the close and inseparable union with its mother. Those first hours and days of a new child are wrapped up in the close relationship with the parents that brought that baby into being. That close relationship is meant to continue throughout life.

Truth is, by trusting in Christ you become God's very own newborn child. The relationship God designed to have with you is one of a close child and parent relationship. Jesus said, " 'Humans can reproduce only human life, but the Holy Spirit gives birth to spiritual life' " (John 3:6). Jesus went on to refer to this as being "born again" into a new family with God as your heavenly Father.

My Prayer: Thank You that because of Jesus I can now call You my Father and know that I am Your child. Being part of a family is very important to me. Help me share with others that being a Christ follower makes a person a member of one big family with Almighty God as our Father. Amen.

No Self-Pay

Since it [salvation] is through God's kindness, then it is not
by their good works. For in that case, God's grace would not
be what it really is—free and undeserved. (Romans 11:6)

Purely trusting in Jesus for the forgiveness of sin without personally
earning that forgiveness is difficult for many people to accept.
Most feel that they should earn forgiveness by some form of penance
or self-punishment.

The entire legal system in America is based upon the concept of
laws and justice. If someone breaks the law, justice must be served. The
lawbreakers pay for their crimes by some sort of fine, an imprisonment,
or both. The point is that people have grown up with the idea that
lawbreakers (sinners) must pay for their own misbehaviors.

Truth is, God will not accept any amount of self-pay for sin by a
sinner. Payment for sin has been made by Jesus and that is the only
payment God will accept. That may be hard for your unbelieving
friends to grasp, but as undeserving as they may feel, they can't earn
forgiveness. It is a free gift out of God's pure kindness and grace.

*My Prayer: Thank You that salvation has been purchased by
Jesus' death and resurrection. Help me spread the message
that Your forgiveness is available to people by trusting in Your
Son as their Savior. Forgiveness and eternal life are free gifts
from a God of love and mercy. You are an awesome God
and I have an awesome message to share. Amen.*

The Invitation

My Bible Reading:
Hear me as I pray, O LORD. Be merciful and answer me!
My heart has heard you say, "Come and talk with me."
And my heart responds, "LORD, I am coming." (Psalm 27:7–8)

You have probably received a lot of invitations in your life. You may have been invited to birthday parties, winter dances, homecomings, proms, graduations, even weddings. Those are good invitations to receive.

Truth is, the greatest invitation you will ever receive is the Holy Spirit inviting you to have a relationship with God. Jesus said, " 'Look! I stand at the door and knock. If you hear my voice and open the door, I will come in' " (Revelation 3:20).

The whole idea of trusting in Jesus or receiving Christ is responding positively to His invitation to believe in Him as Savior. When you are leading someone to Christ, you are actually encouraging him or her to accept Jesus' invitation. Jesus says to " 'repent of your sins and turn to God' " (Matthew 4:17). This means a person must turn his or her back on the old life of doing wrong and turn to Jesus as the only hope of forgiveness and eternal life in relationship with God.

My Prayer: Thank You for inviting me to trust You as my Savior. Help me lead my unbelieving friends to You and explain that You are inviting them to have a relationship with You. Help them turn their backs on their old way of life and turn toward You. Help me share with others Your heart of compassion and love. Amen.

The Change

My Bible Reading:

He died for everyone so that those who receive his new life
will no longer live for themselves. Instead, they will live for
Christ, who died and was raised for them. . . . Anyone who
belongs to Christ has become a new person. The old life
is gone, a new life has begun! (2 Corinthians 5:15, 17)

M any caterpillars are not beautiful creatures. They are creepy-crawly gluttonous eaters. They will increase their weight ten-thousand-fold in less than a month. But at a certain point something deep inside them signals it's time to cocoon. During that time a radical change called metamorphosis takes place. And what emerges from the cocoon is a beautiful butterfly that spreads its wings to share its beauty with all of nature.

Truth is, every true child of God undergoes a supernatural "meta-morphosis" of the soul. Children of God are given a new nature that desires to please Him. "All this newness of life is from God, who brought us back to himself through what Christ did" (2 Corinthians 5:18 NLT).

The evidence that your friends have become true Christ followers is that they will exhibit a new nature that is thirsty for godly things. One of the writers of Psalms put it this way: "As the deer longs for streams of water, so I long for you, O God. I thirst for God, the living God" (Psalm 42:1-2).

*My Prayer: Thank You for the change You made in my life.
While I am far from perfect, I want to please You and follow
in Your ways. Help me live in a way that will reflect
honorably on You. I love You. Amen.*

The Result

My Bible Reading:
He [God] has given us eternal life, and this life is in his Son.
Whoever has the Son has life; whoever does not have God's
Son does not have life. I have written this to you who believe
in the name of the Son of God, so that you may know
you have eternal life. (1 John 5:11–13)

Did your parents read you fairy-tale stories when you were young?
Do you remember the ending phrase of almost every fairy tale?
They ended with "And they lived happily ever after."

That, of course, is the fairy-tale ending. Real life always ends in
death. But for those who place their trust in God's Son, even though
they pass through physical death, they enjoy a resurrected "happily
ever after" life as the result of their relationship with Jesus Christ.

Truth is, Jesus has eternal life and He is our only hope of a "forever
after life." Jesus said, "The Father has life in himself, and he has
granted that same life-giving power to his Son.... The time is coming
when all the dead in their graves [that know Christ] will hear the voice
of God's Son, and they will rise again" (John 5:26, 28–29). Because you
have a relationship with Jesus, you will have a life without end.

My Prayer: *Thank You that You have not only granted me the
forgiveness of my sins, but that You have gifted me with life
eternal with You. Help me share Your message of eternal
life in You with those around me. Amen.*

The Prayer

My Bible Reading:
Jesus said, "If any of you wants to be my follower, you must give
up on your own way, take up your cross daily, and follow me.
If you try to hang on to your life, you will lose it. But if you give
up your life for my sake, you will save it." (Luke 9:23–24)

You may have friends who have not yet turned from their selfish
ways (repented) and taken up their cross to follow Jesus (trusted
in Christ as Savior). There is a simple, but profound, prayer that can
lead a person to a relationship with God.

Truth is, a sinner's prayer is the heart of a person crying out to God
for grace and mercy, like this:

>*Jesus, I believe You are who You claimed to be, the
>Son of the living God.*
>
>*I recognize I am a sinner and I can do nothing in
>myself to earn Your forgiveness. Right now I turn my
>back on my selfish ways and place my trust in You and
>Your sacrificial death for me on the cross.*
>
>*I confess my sins to You and in faith I reach out
>to accept Your forgiveness and Your gift of salvation.
>Thank You that You have made me right with God so
>that I can call Him my Father. I pray all this in Your
>name, the name of Jesus. Amen.*

My Prayer: *Thank You that I have made that prayer my own
and that You have granted me eternal life in relationship
with You. Give me courage and wisdom in sharing this
sinner's prayer with someone who needs You. Amen.*

Your Light

My Bible Reading:
Jesus said, "You are the light of the world. . . . Let your good deeds shine out for all to see, so that everyone will praise your heavenly Father." (Matthew 5:14–16)

Have you ever hiked in the woods in the dark without a flashlight? It's hard to maneuver in darkness. You can get lost easily. That's when a flashlight really comes in handy. The light helps show you the way.

When Jesus said, " 'You are the light of the world,' " He was saying you are a messenger to show people the way to Him in order to find eternal life. God brought light to the world when Jesus took on human form. And when you became God's child, you too became part of that light.

Truth is, your kind and loving actions as a Christ follower are what shine out the brightest. Jesus even said that your love to other Christ followers would " 'prove to the world that you are my disciples' " (John 13:35). It is your Christlike life that is a living example—an advertisement of sorts—that attracts people to Jesus. Scripture encourages you to "live clean, innocent lives as children of God, shining like bright lights in a world full of crooked and perverse people" (Philippians 2:15).

My Prayer: Help me reflect Your nature of love and kindness today. Let those around me see Your light as it shines through me. I want my friends to come to know You. May the light I shine lead them to You. Amen.

Out of Place

My Bible Reading:
Jesus prayed to His Father, "I'm not asking you to take them [my followers] out of the world, but to keep them safe from the evil one. They do not belong to this world any more than I do." (John 17:15–16)

Jesus wanted His followers to live and serve as His ambassadors to the whole world. He wanted them to stand out as His witnesses to this world. He told His disciples that " 'you will be my witnesses, telling people about me everywhere' " (Acts 1:8). Jesus prayed to His Father, " 'Just as you sent me into the world, I am sending them into the world' " (John 17:18).

Truth is, you stand out as a Jesus follower and that helps you point people to a different world and a different way of life. Scripture says you are " 'temporary residents and foreigners' " (1 Peter 2:11) in this world but are "citizens of heaven" (Philippians 3:20). Like Jesus, you are directing people to God's heavenly kingdom, not to the kingdom of this world.

My Prayer: Thank You that You have made me a citizen of heaven. And thank You that I have the privilege as Your witness to point people to You and Your wonderful plan to give them eternal life in a relationship with You. You are an awesome God with an amazing message of life that I want to share. Amen.

The Scum

My Bible Reading:

Matthew invited Jesus and his disciples to his home as dinner guests, along with many tax collectors and other disreputable sinners. But when the Pharisees saw this, they asked his disciples, "Why does your teacher eat with such scum?" (Matthew 9:10-11)

Jesus really confused the religious leaders of His day in many different ways. And one of those ways was how Jesus treated sinners. He talked with them, ate with them, and made them His friends. You simply didn't do that if you were religious. Religious people felt associating with sinners and lowlifes would make them unclean.

Jesus, the holiest person who ever lived, was a friend to sinners. He didn't put people down, discriminate against them, or condemn them even though they weren't living right. Jesus said that His Father God "did not send his Son into the world to condemn the world, but to save the world through him" (John 3:17 NIV).

Truth is, Jesus accepts people for who they are and where they are. As His followers we are to do the same. Scripture says to "accept each other just as Christ has accepted you so that God will be given glory" (Romans 15:7). When you befriend those who are considered weird, outcasts, or scum by others, you are demonstrating the love of God to them. The result pleases and honors God.

My Prayer: Thank You that You accepted me even when I wasn't acceptable. Help me show kindness to those who may be considered "unacceptable" by some. I want them to know that You love all of us. Help me share Your message of love and acceptance. Amen.

Blessed

My Bible Reading:
Jesus said, "God blesses those who are humble, for they will inherit the whole earth. God blesses those who hunger and thirst for justice, for they will be satisfied. God blesses those who are merciful, for they will be shown mercy." (Matthew 5:5-7)

Most people spend the majority of their lives searching for happiness and joy—what the Bible calls *blessing*. Some people try to find happiness in wealth and material things; others might search for it in partying really hard, and/or using drugs or alcohol.

Jesus claimed that happiness and joy come out of being humble, seeking justice, showing mercy, and living pure—to name a few. The way Jesus pointed people to joy and blessing discouraged them from being self-absorbed or seeking self-serving pleasures.

Truth is, God designed humans to enjoy life, and so He ought to know the right way for people to maximize joy and fulfillment in life. Jesus summed it up this way: " 'Do for others what you would like them to do for you. This is a summary of all that is taught in the law and the prophets' " (Matthew 7:12). Being other-focused and looking for ways to help others is the key.

My Prayer: God, Your way of being and living is a way to enjoy life as it was meant to be lived. You came and died to save me from my sinful, selfish ways and give me life in You—a life of blessing, joy, and fulfillment. Thank You that You loved me that much. Help me share Your love with others today. Amen.

Not Ashamed

My Bible Reading:

Jesus asked, "Who do you say I am?" Simon Peter answered, "You are the Messiah, the Son of the living God." Jesus replied, "You are blessed, Simon son of John, because my Father in heaven has revealed this to you. You did not learn this from any human being." (Matthew 16:15–17)

Have you ever had someone ask you a pointed question that you weren't sure you wanted to answer? That's an uncomfortable position to be in, isn't it? A lot of people are not comfortable answering the key question about Jesus. Was He truly the Son of God or not?

When Jesus asked His disciples, " 'Who do you say I am?' " Peter didn't hesitate. He didn't shuffle his feet, lower his head, and in silence just stare at the ground. He had a deep belief about who Jesus was and he wasn't ashamed to speak up and let others know what he believed.

Truth is, Peter's belief in Jesus became a conviction that compelled him to tell others. That kind of conviction comes from God confirming to your heart that Jesus is truly your Savior and Lord. The apostle Paul had that kind of conviction. Even though he was persecuted for sharing his faith in Jesus, he wasn't ashamed. He said, "I am suffering now because I tell the Good News, but I am not ashamed, because I know Jesus, the One in whom I have believed" (2 Timothy 1:12 NCV).

My Prayer: *I believe that You, Jesus, are the Son of God and because I have trusted in You I am called a child of God. I never want to be ashamed to let others know that You are my Savior. Give me the courage and wisdom to express my convictions about You to those around me. Amen.*

Determined

My Bible Reading:

While he [Jesus] was preaching God's word to them, four men arrived carrying a paralyzed man on a mat. They couldn't bring him to Jesus because of the crowd, so they dug a hole through the roof above his head. Then they lowered the man on his mat, right down in front of Jesus. Seeing their faith, Jesus said to the paralyzed man, "My child, your sins are forgiven." (Mark 2:2–5)

As Jesus healed the sick, opened the eyes of the blind, made the lame to walk, cleansed the lepers, and even raised the dead, more and more people came to Him. They wanted to know more about this man and tap into His healing power.

Four friends of the paralyzed man desperately wanted to see him healed. And when the crowd kept them from getting close enough to Jesus, they improvised. They just climbed on top of the house, cut a hole in the roof, and lowered their friend down in front of Jesus. Consequently, Jesus met this man's spiritual need (forgave him) and his physical need (He also healed him).

Truth is, it took courage and ingenuity on the part of the four men to lead their paralyzed friend to Jesus. They knew he had a problem that only Jesus could solve. Their determination paid off. It will take determination, courage, and wisdom for you to also lead your friends to Jesus, the spiritual and physical Healer.

My Prayer: A number of my friends need You. Give me wisdom to know how to share that You are the solution to their sin problem. Help me tell them how You met my spiritual need for You. Thank You that You love my friends so much that You died for them. Help me lead them to You. Amen.

Solid Foundation

My Bible Reading:
Jesus said, "I will show you what it's like when someone comes to
me, listens to my teaching, and then follows it. It is like a person
building a house who digs deep and lays the foundation on solid
rock. When the floodwaters rise and break against that house,
it stands firm because it is well built." (Luke 6:47-48)

Have you ever watched a house being built? Once the ground
is graded rather level, the construction crew does a strange
thing. Rather than building the house from the ground up, they first
dig a hole. They dig a deep hole if there is going to be a basement,
otherwise a deep trench that matches the size of the house. They then
pour concrete into the trench to form the foundation. It is upon this
solid foundation that they build the house—a foundation that will
keep the house safe against the storms.

Truth is, Jesus is the solid foundation you can build your life upon.
Isaiah the prophet quoted God as saying, " 'I am placing a foundation
stone in Jerusalem, a firm and tested stone. It is a precious cornerstone
that is safe to build on. Whoever believes need never be shaken' "
(Isaiah 28:16). Jesus is that cornerstone. He is your solid foundation.

My Prayer: *Thank You that I can rely on You as my foundation
in this life and my solid rock for all eternity. I pray for my friends
who are building their lives on anything but a firm foundation.
Help me be a witness to them that You are the true foundation
for this life and the one to come. Amen.*

Joy of Forgiveness

My Bible Reading:

Oh, what joy for those whose disobedience is forgiven, whose sin is put out of sight! Yes, what joy for those whose record the LORD has cleared of guilt, whose lives are lived in complete honesty! (Psalm 32:1-2)

When were you the happiest? When you didn't have any homework? When you got a ton of money in a birthday card? When someone really special said, "I love you"? A lot of things in life can make people happy. But there is one thing that constantly brings deep joy to everyone who experiences it.

A person experiences joy, deep joy, when his or her sins are forgiven by God. A load is lifted. When guilt is removed, there is a wonderful sense of freedom, and that brings joy.

Truth is, that sense of freedom and joy of sins forgiven is one of the most attractive things that can draw a person to Christ. Guilt weighs heavy on a person's emotions. King David said, "My guilt overwhelms me—it is a burden too heavy to bear" (Psalm 38:4). Being free of guilt is not only a wonderful feeling, but also your testimony of sins forgiven can be a means of drawing your friends to Jesus.

My Prayer: Because of You I have experienced the joy of sins forgiven. Help me be a living witness before my friends to the joy of having the guilt of sin removed. Let my testimony point them to You. Amen.

What an Offer!

My Bible Reading:
Jesus said, "As the Father has loved me, so have I loved you. Now remain in my love. . . . I have told you this so that my joy may be in you and that your joy may be complete." (John 15:9, 11 NIV)

You were born spiritually dead. You were alone, abandoned, and without love because of sin. You were disconnected, without a true family connection. But now, because you have trusted in Jesus, you have a real family, and your joy has been made complete. "God has sent the Spirit of his Son into our hearts, prompting us to call out, 'Abba, Father [or Daddy]'" (Galatians 4:6).

Truth is, as a result of being made right with God by grace through faith, you are not only adopted into God's family, but "since we are his children, we will share his treasures—for everything God gives to his Son, Christ, is ours, too" (Romans 8:17 NLT). In effect Jesus is saying to you, "I have come to earth, demonstrated My love by giving My life for you, and I ask that you trust in Me as your only solution to life so My joy will be in you and your joy will be complete in this life and then forever in eternity with Me." What an offer! The apostle Peter put it this way: "We've been given a brand-new life and have everything to live for, including a future in heaven—and the future starts now!"(1 Peter 1:3-4 MSG).

My Prayer: Thank You for Your incredible offer! I have accepted Your offer and want to share it with others. Give me strength and courage to let others know how much You love them and how much You want to make their joy complete. You are an awesome God. I love You. Amen.

JULY

A New Person

July 1

Your Destiny

My Bible Reading:
For God knew his people in advance, and he chose them
[determined beforehand] to become like his Son. (Romans 8:29)

Have you ever planned out what you want to do in the future?
Maybe you said something like, "When I graduate I'm going
to. . ." or "When I get a job I'm going to. . ." or "When I'm really in
love with someone I'm going to. . ." In other words, you decided in
advance what you were going to do. Well God did that too.

God chose or decided beforehand that when you trusted in Christ
for the forgiveness of sin that He would literally change you. He
determined that He would not only raise you from death to new life
in Him, but He would mold you into the image of His Son, Jesus.

Truth is, as a follower of Christ you are destined to become Christlike.
Before He even created the world He "decided in advance to adopt us
into his own family" (Ephesians 1:5). He determined to give you a
spiritual DNA that would make you into a Godlike son or daughter
who would make Him proud. Scripture says, "This is what he wanted
to do, and it gave him great pleasure" (Ephesians 1:5).

My Prayer: *Thank You that You have given me a destiny to be a
son or daughter in the image of Your Son, Jesus. This means I will
have all the rights and privileges that come with being a member of
Your family. I can call You Father, enjoy that wonderful relationship,
and live forever with You. That blows my mind! Thank You for
choosing to give me such a great heritage. I will praise You forever.
Help me share my destiny story with someone today. Amen.*

Little Christ

My Bible Reading:

As we know Jesus better, his divine power gives us everything we need for living a godly life. . . . He has promised that you will escape the decadence all around you caused by evil desires and that you will share in his divine nature. (2 Peter 1:3–4)

Peter was a disciple of Jesus, and he understood that when a person trusted in Jesus, a miraculous change took place. The power of God personally changed him. He was once so frightened that he denied Jesus. Yet later, he became a mighty witness of Jesus. Peter was persecuted and eventually killed for his faith. What made the difference? He miraculously became a walking image of Jesus. God gave him Jesus' spiritual DNA—"his divine nature," and Peter became a bold witness for Christ.

This spiritual DNA transformation in Christ followers during the first century caused them to walk around thinking like, talking like, and acting like Jesus. In fact, these people were such replicas of Jesus that the ones persecuting the Christ followers tried to insult them by calling them "Christians" or literally translated, "Little Christs."

Truth is, it is an honor and a privilege to be given Jesus' nature and to become more and more like Him. Peter said to "be happy if you are insulted for being a Christian. . . . Praise God for the privilege of being called by his wonderful name!" (1 Peter 4:14, 16). Carry the Christian name as a badge of honor. He wants His divine nature to make you like Him. "The Lord—who is the Spirit—makes us more and more like him as we are changed into his glorious image" (2 Corinthians 3:18).

My Prayer: Thank You that You have forgiven me of my sins and given me Your nature. Help me know You better, read Your Word, and learn Your ways, so I can be more and more like You. Amen.

Proud Parent

My Bible Reading:
So you have not received a spirit that makes you fearful slaves.
Instead, you received God's Spirit when he adopted you as his
own children. Now we call him, "Abba Father." (Romans 8:15)

You may or may not have taken notice of how your parents
reacted to your various achievements as you were growing up.
It's interesting to watch parents when their kids do even the simplest
of things. A kid says, "Dada," and a father is ecstatic. The first step of
a baby produces parental applause. Then comes tying shoes, putting
on clothes without help, reading the first word, riding a bike, and the
list goes on. The point is that parents are proud of their children for
what they do and for who they are becoming.

Truth is, God is your spiritual parent. You are part of His family and
He too is proud of you. "For [you] are God's masterpiece. He has
created [you] anew in Christ Jesus, so [you] can do the good things
he planned for [you] long ago" (Ephesians 2:10). He made you in
His image and He is so proud of who you are and what you are becoming. "For once you were full of darkness, but now you have light
from the Lord. So live as people of light! For this light within you
produces only what is good and right and true" (Ephesians 5:8-9).

My Prayer: *Thank You that You are proud of me as Your child. I want
to continue to make You proud by not only being Your child, but also
by honoring You with my actions. Let Your light within me produce
good things in my life. Help me be kind, thoughtful, and considerate
of my parents, family, and those around me this very day. Amen.*

Freedom

My Bible Reading:
Christ has freed us so we may enjoy the benefits
of freedom. Therefore, be firm in this freedom,
and don't become slaves again. (Galatians 5:1 GWT)

The Fourth of July, 1776. That was the day the Congress of the thirteen colonies of the New World adopted the Declaration of Independence from Great Britain. Americans today not only celebrate that historic July of 1776, but also the reality that America has remained a free country. Other countries like Canada, France, Mexico, Peru, Australia, Poland, South Africa, and at least 150 other countries celebrate a freedom day.

Truth is, Jesus died and rose again so that you could be set free from sin and death and enjoy the benefits of spiritual freedom. That freedom is not a license to live however you want to live, but to live as God meant you to live. He has given you the freedom to enjoy a life of "love, joy, peace, patience, kindness, goodness, faithfulness, gentleness, and self-control" (Galatians 5:22–23). These are the fruits or expressions of God's Spirit who has set you free. When you live out and express Christlike attitudes and actions, you are celebrating the freedom for which Christ has set you free.

My Prayer: Thank You for setting me free to live as You designed me to live. You have destined me to live and be like You. I know that is when I am most content, at peace, and full of joy. You are the reason for my freedom. Thank You that You are such a merciful and loving God. Amen.

Your Purpose

My Bible Reading:
Whether you eat or drink, or whatever you do,
do it all for the glory of God. (1 Corinthians 10:31)

Whom do you resemble? Do you look like your dad or your mom? Maybe you have characteristics that reflect both of them. You no doubt have certain mannerisms that you got from your parents. When you exhibit a living resemblance or representation of those that birthed you and raised you, it gives them glory or honor. The same is true of God.

Truth is, God made you in His likeness and relational image and when you live out that image it honors and glorifies Him. In fact, that defines your purpose. "For everything comes from him [God] and exists by his power and is intended for his glory. All glory to him forever! Amen" (Romans 11:36).

You fulfill your purpose when you live out the Godlike life He has called you to live. When you think and talk and act according to His ways, it not only glorifies Him, but it also brings you joy and meaning. "Joyful are people of integrity, who follow the instructions of the LORD. Joyful are those who obey his laws and search for him with all their hearts" (Psalm 119:1-2).

My Prayer: *May my attitude, words, and actions honor You.
I want to reflect a Christlike life. I desire to forever give You honor,
for You are so deserving. Help me honor You today by the
way I treat others with kindness and respect. Amen.*

A Process

My Bible Reading:

Lazarus was dead and in the tomb. Then Jesus shouted, "Lazarus, come out!" And the dead man came out, his hands and feet bound in graveclothes, his face wrapped in a headcloth. Jesus told them, "Unwrap him and let him go!" (John 11:43–44)

L azarus was dead, but Jesus gave him life again. Yet it's interesting that the graveclothes didn't fall off of Lazarus immediately after he was raised to life. There was a *process* involved in getting him unwrapped from his "dead clothes."

Truth is, when Jesus raised you to new life, your old clothes of the "dead life" did not come off immediately either. It, too, requires a process. "You have stripped off your old evil nature and all its wicked deeds," Paul says. "In its place you have clothed yourselves with a brand-new nature." Yet Paul refers to the process when he concludes that your brand-new nature "is continually being renewed as you learn more and more about Christ, who created this new nature within you" (Colossians 3:9–10).

No one is ever finished with the process of becoming more and more like Christ in this life. You are on a continual journey of growth. "I am certain," Paul wrote, "that God, who began the good work within you, will continue his work until it is finally finished on the day when Christ Jesus returns" (Philippians 1:6).

My Prayer: Thank You for the process of being made more and more like You. Thank You for Your patience and love that don't give up on me when I fail. I am so thankful that Your "mercies begin afresh each morning" (Lamentations 3:23) because I need them. You are a faithful God! Amen.

How God Sees You

My Bible Reading:

I pray that your hearts will be flooded with light so that you can understand the confident hope he has given to those he called—his holy people who are his rich and glorious inheritance. (Ephesians 1:18)

When you look in the mirror, what do you see? Aside from your physical appearance, do you see the inner person that God sees? The truest statements about your relationship with God are revealed in His Word. The Bible is where God opens His heart about who you are and how He sees you. If what you think or feel about yourself doesn't line up with how the Bible describes you, then you have a case of mistaken identity.

It has been said that your self-concept is largely determined by what you believe the most important person in your life thinks about you. As a child, what your parents said and thought of you no doubt molded how you view yourself today. As other people came into your life that were important to you, they too have helped shape the concept you have of yourself.

Truth is, the most accurate image of yourself is the one that God sees. Since He is truly the most important One in your life, what He says is true about you should become your true identity as a Christ follower. Over the next couple of weeks of devotions you will discover just how God sees you.

My Prayer: *I confess that sometimes I don't have a healthy view of myself. I know You love me in spite of all my shortcomings. So help me see myself the way You see me. Let Your view of me become how I view myself. By doing so I can better reflect Your image through my life. Amen.*

I'm Forgiven

My Bible Reading:

So now there is no condemnation for those who belong to Christ Jesus. And because you belong to him, the power of the life-giving Spirit has freed you from the power of sin that leads to death. (Romans 8:1–2)

How many times have you failed in your life to do what was right? Ten times, twenty times, or more? Those failures and sins should logically build up to define you as a failure. But since you have received the power of the life-giving Spirit, you are by no means identified as a failure.

Truth is, because of what Jesus did, you belong to Him and you are no longer under condemnation. God the Father sees you as a forgiven child, pure and holy in His sight. "He [God] has enabled you to share in the inheritance that belongs to his people, who live in the light. For he has rescued [you] from the kingdom of darkness and transferred [you] into the Kingdom of his dear Son, who purchased [your] freedom and forgave [your] sins" (Colossians 1:12–14).

Don't believe the lie that you're guilty or a failure because of your past failings and sin. Since God sees you as forgiven, accept that as your new reality. What God says is true of you is absolutely true—you're forgiven!

My Prayer*: Thank You that I'm forgiven. Help me continue to confidently believe that Your life-giving Spirit has freed me from the power of sin. I belong to You. Help me share this wonderful truth with someone today. Amen.*

I'm at Peace

My Bible Reading:
Therefore, since we have been made right in God's
sight by faith, we have peace with God because of what
Jesus Christ our Lord has done for us. (Romans 5:1)

Have you ever offended someone in a serious kind of way? Perhaps afterward this person didn't even want to see you or ever talk to you again. That would be the definition of a person not being at peace with you. That was your situation with God. Your sin was an offense to Him and you were not able to be at peace with Him.

Truth is, there was nothing you could do to correct your enemy status with God. But because of what happened on a cruel cross, "Christ himself has brought peace to [you]" (Ephesians 2:14). The offense of your sin has been removed, and God sees nothing but peace between you and Him. In fact the word *peace* used in Romans 5:1 implies there was not even a prior conflict. It's as if you were never a sinner and at odds with God. That is how powerfully Jesus' death for you cleaned the slate and brought you peace with God.

Don't believe the lie that God has anything against you. Since God sees you at peace with Him, accept that as your new reality. What God says is true of you is absolutely true—you're at peace with Him!

My Prayer: Thank You that there is nothing between us and that we are at peace with each other. Thank You, Jesus, for making it possible for me to be at peace with Your Father—now my Father too. Amen.

I'm His Friend

My Bible Reading:
Jesus said to His disciples, "I no longer call you slaves, because a master doesn't confide in his slaves. Now you are my friends, since I have told you everything the Father told me." (John 15:15)

To whom do you tell your secrets? Do you tell them to the study hall monitor, the school janitor, or the grumpy person at the checkout counter of the grocery store? No, secrets and those things you really feel deeply about are reserved only for close friends—friends who are there for you no matter what.

Truth is, Jesus considers you His friend. He has revealed the heart of God to you. Wise Solomon understood what a true friend was and said that God "offers his friendship to the godly" (Proverbs 3:32). Sure, God is almighty, powerful, and perfectly holy. He knows everything and can do anything He wants. Yet He sees you, a mere human, as His friend.

Don't believe the lie that God is distant and too busy to be your friend. Since God sees you as His friend, accept that as your new reality. What God says is true of you is absolutely true—you're His friend!

My Prayer: Thank You that You are my God and my friend. Help me see Your Word as Your "friendship letters" to me that reveal Your heart and how You care for me. Help me open up more to You as a friend and share my heart, my dreams, and my desires to please You. Give me strength and courage to share with someone today how much a friend You are to me. Amen.

I'm His Branch

My Bible Reading:

Jesus said, "I am the vine; you are the branches. Those
who remain in me, and I in them, will produce much fruit.
For apart from me you can do nothing." (John 15:5)

Have you ever picked an apple off a tree? How about an orange
or a peach? It may appear that the branches they hang from are
the power source of their growth. But the branches are simply the con-
duits of the real power source—the tree.

What did Jesus mean when He said that He was the vine and His
followers were the branches? He was saying that He was the power
source for producing Christlike fruit, such as kindness, love, patience,
goodness, etc. In other words, you are to be a producer of good fruit,
but you must rely on Him to produce it through you.

Truth is, when you rely on Christ as your strength you can be a
powerhouse of goodness. Paul understood that when he said, "I can do
everything through Christ, who gives me strength" (Philippians 4:13).

Don't believe the lie that you can produce all kinds of Christlike
fruit in your own strength. Since God sees you as His branch or conduit of His power, accept that as your reality. What God says is true
about you is absolutely true—you are His branch!

---

*My Prayer: Thank You that You have made me Your branch.
Help me always remember my strength for godly living comes
from You. Today I want to rely on You and Your strength to
help me to bear the fruit of kindness to others. Amen.*

I'm His Home

My Bible Reading:
Don't you realize that all of you together are the temple of God and that the Spirit of God lives in you? (1 Corinthians 3:16)

Where do you mostly sleep, eat, and interact with people close to you? Where do you invite your friends to spend time with you? Home, right? That's the place where your life is lived and relationships are deepened. But does God live there?

Typically, people will say God lives in heaven. And that's true to a point. Yet God wanted to be with humans so He told Moses to " 'build me a holy sanctuary [temple] so I can live among them' " (Exodus 25:8). Then God showed up in human form (Jesus) and lived with humanity. Jesus told His disciples that the person of the Holy Spirit was living with them while He was on earth and that " 'later [He] will be in you' " (John 14:17).

Truth is, God through His Holy Spirit has made His home in you. When you trusted in Christ for the forgiveness of sin, His Spirit miraculously took up residence within the core of your life—your heart. Paul prayed that God "will give you mighty inner strength through his Holy Spirit. . .[and] that Christ will be more and more at home in your hearts as you trust in him" (Ephesians 3:16–17).

Don't believe the lie that God isn't around and has left you to make it on your own. He has made His home in your heart. Since God sees you as His place of residence, welcome Him and accept that He lives in you. What God says is true of you is absolutely true—you are where He lives!

My Prayer: Thank You that You have made Your home in my heart. Help me make You more and more at home by talking with You, reading Your Word, and following in Your ways. You are such a wonderful God! Amen.

I'm His Heir

My Bible Reading:

Since we are his children, we are his heirs. In fact,
together with Christ we are heirs of God's glory. (Romans 8:17)

It is common for parents to draw up what is called a "Last Will and Testament." The document normally lays out the inheritance of personal possessions, property, money, etc. that children will get once their parents pass away. Children become the heirs of what their parents own.

As an earthly heir you could receive something in this life that is passed on from your parents. That, of course, would be limited by whatever your parents had accumulated during their lifetime. Your inheritance as a child of God doesn't have that limitation.

Truth is, as a joint heir with Christ, you have become an heir to God's glory. That means you get God's presence in all of His splendor with all that He is and has and owns. Jesus said He would invite God's heirs to " 'enter into the joy of your master' " (Matthew 25:23 NASB). Whatever produces absolute joy is yours and it will last forever.

Don't believe the lie that you don't have a fantastic future. Since God sees you as His heir, accept the guarantee that you will receive an inheritance that is more fabulous than you can imagine. What God says is true of you is absolutely true—you are His heir!

__My Prayer__: Thank You that You have made me an heir to Your glory. And while I don't feel deserving of that, I am so grateful that I get to enjoy You and praise You—life without end. Help me share with someone today what You have promised me. Amen.

I'm a Member

My Bible Reading:

We have all been baptized into one body by one Spirit, and we all share the same Spirit.... All of you together are Christ's body, and each of you is a part of it. (1 Corinthians 12:13, 27)

Do you belong to some sports team, the school band, a glee club, or maybe you're a member in some other kind of group? You have probably belonged to some group most of your life. Being a member in good standing feels good. It gives you a sense of connection and belonging.

Truth is, because you trusted in Christ as your Savior, you are also made a member of His body—connected to all those who are God's children. With God as your Father, each Christ follower you meet is actually your spiritual brother or sister. As in a family, "we are many parts of one body, and we all belong to each other" (Romans 12:5). One of the greatest feelings of all is a sense that you belong. And because of Christ you certainly belong.

Don't believe the lie that you are alone and no one cares. Since Christ sees you as a member of His body, accept this as your new reality and realize that you are always wanted and very much needed. What God says is true of you is absolutely true—you belong to Christ's body!

My Prayer: Thank You that You have made me part of You, and I belong to a huge membership of other followers of Jesus. Help me connect better with other Christians around me to enjoy both the friendship and sense of belonging that comes with being a part of Your family. Amen.

I'm Secure in Him

My Bible Reading:

I am convinced that nothing can ever separate us from God's love. Neither death nor life, neither angels nor demons, neither our fears for today nor our worries about tomorrow—not even the powers of hell can separate us from God's love. (Romans 8:38)

Have you ever had someone say they really liked you (or even said they "loved" you)? But say that person broke up with you. Or maybe just a good friend started acting like a jerk and you are now no longer friends. Some people betray friendships and are even unfaithful to love relationships. With that going on all around you it's not difficult to feel a little insecure about relationships.

Truth is, your relationship with Jesus is not like any human relationship you have ever experienced. Jesus holds your relationship with Him secure, and even the devil himself can't touch you. "We know that God's children do not make a practice of sinning, for God's Son holds them securely, and the evil one cannot touch them" (1 John 5:18).

Don't believe the lie that you are not secure in your relationship with Jesus. Since God sees you in the secure arms of Jesus, accept that no outside force can ever overcome the power of Christ. What God says is true about your relationship with Jesus is absolutely true—you are secure in Him!

My Prayer: *Thank You that Your love for me is incredibly firm and secure. I love You and You love me, and that love will last forever. Help me share the power of Your love with someone today. Amen.*

I'm Set Apart

My Bible Reading:
Jesus prayed for His followers: "They are not of the world,
even as I am not of it. Sanctify them by the truth;
your word is truth." (John 17:16–17 NIV)

Have you ever worn something to school or to an event that made you feel out of place? Say you showed up to a formal dinner in a jogging outfit. You'd sort of feel out of place, right?

Normally it's uncomfortable to be seen as different or out of place. But as a Christ follower you are no longer a part of this world's evil system. Jesus prayed that you would be sanctified. That means you are "set apart" to live a life that is different from the lives of those who are not His followers.

Truth is, you are like what Peter called Christians in his day— " 'temporary residents and foreigners' " (1 Peter 2:11). You are marked by a new nature that causes you to think, talk, and act like a citizen of another world. Yet you have a mission to be a light to this world.

Don't believe the lie that you are to fit in and be part of this world's godless system. Since God sees you as "set apart" for another world, accept that as your new reality. What God says is true of you is absolutely true—you are "set apart" and a witness for Jesus.

My Prayer*: Thank You that You have set me apart from this world while still living in it. Help me be a shining witness for You so that people will want to know You. Please give me strength and courage to share You with someone today. Amen.*

I'm Yours

My Bible Reading:

For we are not our own masters when we live or when we die.
While we live, we live to please the Lord. And when we die,
we go to be with the Lord. So in life and in death,
we belong to the Lord. (Romans 14:7–8)

"Once I graduate and leave home, I'll be free. Then I can do whatever I want to do." Have you ever heard anyone say something like that? People who think like that generally feel they are in charge of their own lives.

Truth is, Christ followers don't believe they are in charge of their lives. In one sense they don't "own themselves." Scripture says, "You do not belong to yourself, for God bought you with a high price" (1 Corinthians 6:19–20). Rather, you are "God's very own possession. As a result, you can show others the goodness of God, for he called you out of darkness into his wonderful light" (1 Peter 2:9).

Don't believe the lie that you belong to yourself. Since God bought you and raised you from death to life, accept that you are His prized possession. What God says is true of you is absolutely true— you belong to God.

My Prayer: Thank You that You purchased me out of slavery to sin and death. I owe everything to You. Help me show others some of Your goodness today. I want to be gentle and patient and kind, especially to someone who is feeling low and discouraged. Lead me to that person. I'm Yours. Amen.

I'm His "Perfect" Example

My Bible Reading:

He [God] raised us from the dead along with Christ.... So God can point to us in all future ages as examples of the incredible wealth of his grace and kindness toward us. (Ephesians 2:6–7)

Do you have a trophy case at your school? Maybe pictures of teams or banners hanging somewhere indicate the championships won by your school. Schools like to put their trophies on display.

Truth is, you are one of God's trophies. "He chose to give birth to us by giving us his true word. And we, out of all creation, became his prized possession" (James 1:18). But instead of the focus being placed on you as the "perfect" example of Christlikeness (which would be a lot of pressure), scripture spotlights something else. You are not called on to be a perfect example of performance; rather, you are to spotlight God's mercy and grace. The trophy belongs to Christ for what He did for you as a sinner. You have the privilege and honor to be a showcase or example of His love and kindness.

Don't believe the lie that you are not an effective witness for Jesus. Since Christ loved you when you were still a sinner and died that you might live, accept that you are an example of His love and grace. What God says is true of you is absolutely true—you are a living example of what He can do for a person who is spiritually dead and without hope.

My Prayer: Thank You that You have such an incredible wealth of grace and love toward me. I am an example of what You can do for others. Help me share with someone today what You have done for me. You are worthy to be praised. Amen.

I'm Given Wisdom

My Bible Reading:
He has showered his kindness on us, along with
all wisdom and understanding. (Ephesians 1:8)

Do you know your IQ? Just how smart are you? Some people seem to be naturally smart and are perfect 4.0 students. Others have to really work to make good grades. So does becoming a Christ follower automatically make you smarter?

Truth is, the wisdom and understanding God grants His children are not things like math and science courses. Rather, they provide a new perspective on life. "In him [God] lie hidden all the treasures of wisdom and knowledge" (Colossians 2:3). Wise Solomon said, "The LORD grants wisdom! From his mouth come knowledge and understanding" (Proverbs 2:6). And when you seek to follow God and His ways you begin to see life from a new perspective. You begin to see life as God sees it. That is true wisdom.

"Trust in the LORD with all your heart; do not depend on your own understanding. Seek his will in all you do, and he will show you which path to take" (Proverbs 3:5-6). Don't believe the lie that wisdom and insight for living come from within you. Wisdom is from God. Since God sees you as His trusting child and grants you wisdom, look to Him and accept His direction and guidance. What God says is true of you is absolutely true—you are His child in whom He grants wisdom.

My Prayer: Thank You that You are my source of wisdom in life.
Help me resist looking to myself and depending on my own
understanding. I want to keep seeking Your will and following in Your
ways. You are such a remarkable and wise God. I love You. Amen.

I'm Made Complete in Him

My Bible Reading:

For in Christ lives all the fullness of God in a human body. So you also are complete through your union with Christ. (Colossians 2:9–10)

Have you ever felt like someone connected with you so deeply that it was like he or she completed you? Deep friendships can do that. Emotionally and relationally we need solid friendship to be there for one another and to feel that connected union.

Truth is, on a spiritual level we need a union—a oneness—with Christ in order to experience a fulfillment and completeness that only God can bring. Jesus prayed to His Father about His followers, " 'I have given them the glory you gave me, so they may be one as we are one. I am in them and you are in me. May they experience such perfect unity that the world will know that you sent me' " (John 17:22–23). Jesus, His Father, and the Holy Spirit live in a perfect circle of completeness. God wants you to enjoy the same kind of completeness with Him. In fact, your sense of feeling complete in Jesus is what will tell the world around you that Jesus is real and the true Savior of the world.

My Prayer: Thank You that You make me complete. You give me a sense of fulfillment and connectedness. I don't always feel that, so help me trust more in You, spend more time in Your Word, and stay better connected to You in prayer. You are a perfect God who is there to complete me. Thank You for that. Amen.

July 21

Heart and Actions Go Together

My Bible Reading:
Jesus said, "A good person produces good things from the
treasury of a good heart and an evil person produces evil
things from the treasury of an evil heart. What you say
flows from what is in your heart." (Luke 6:45)

In Jesus' day there was a group of leaders who preached strict
obedience to a lot of religious rules. They had a rule for just about
everything. Yet they themselves would speak evil of others, were
deeply prejudiced, and refused to help needy persons who weren't
a part of their religious group. Jesus called these leaders hypocrites
because even though they appeared to be good, in reality, their hearts
were full of evil.

Truth is, how a person consistently talks and acts reflects the true
nature of his or her character. If the consistent actions of a person
are good, you can trace it back to a good heart. If a person's fruit is
consistently bad, you can trace it back to a heart that isn't so good.
Jesus said, "'You can identify them by their fruit, that is, by the way
they act. . . . Yes, just as you can identify a tree by its fruit, so you can
identify people by their actions'" (Matthew 7:16, 20).

Think about your actions since you've been a Christ follower. What
are some of the things you've stopped doing or started doing? Your
different behavior reflects the heart change God made within you.

*My Prayer: Thank You that You gave me a new heart. Because
of my relationship with You, my life is being changed. Help me
keep growing and learning to become more like You. Amen.*

Direct Access

My Bible Reading:
Because of Christ and our faith in him, we can now come boldly and confidently into God's presence. (Ephesians 3:12)

Have you been given a key to your house? Are you able to unlock that door and go in anytime you want? Why is that? Your parents give you direct access to that house because you are their child and they want you to live there. That's what families do; they live together in the same place.

Truth is, because you have put your trust in Jesus as your Savior, you have direct access to God. Because God is all-powerful and perfectly righteous and holy, it might be a little scary to come into God's presence. But because of Jesus your sins are forgiven and you can go to God with boldness and confidence. "So let us come boldly to the throne of our gracious God. There we will receive his mercy, and we will find grace to help us when we need it most" (Hebrews 4:16).

Because of the faith you placed in Jesus, you have a key to unlock the door to God. He wants you to come to Him, to share about what's happening in your life, and for you to receive His help any time you need Him.

My Prayer: Thank You that You have given me direct access to You because of Your Son, Jesus. Without Jesus and what He did for me I could never know You and be able to live with You in eternity. I want to come to You in prayer more often and learn to better share my heart with You. Thank You for being there for me. In Jesus' name, amen.

I'm Blessed

My Bible Reading:
"All praise to God, the Father of our Lord Jesus Christ, who has blessed us with every spiritual blessing in the heavenly realms because we are united with Christ." (Ephesians 1:3)

Think a moment how you have been blessed. Maybe you've been blessed or rewarded with good looks because of your parents. Perhaps you've been blessed with a healthy body—maybe an athletic body to play sports, a graceful body to dance, a good singing voice, some gifted musical talent, or a sharp mind to study and learn. Think about the school you attend, the home you live in, the food you eat, the country you live in, and the freedoms you enjoy. You have been blessed.

Truth is, God has blessed you with every spiritual blessing because of Christ and you enjoy sins forgiven, access to God, and an eternal future of joy and happiness. That's quite a blessing. But sometimes things get tough in this life and you don't immediately feel like you're being blessed. Yet God still promises to bless you. "Don't retaliate with insults when people insult you," the scripture says. "Instead, pay them back with a blessing. That is what God has called you to do, and he will grant you his blessing" (1 Peter 3:9).

My Prayer: *Thank You for all You have blessed me with—my health, my home, my friends, and especially for giving me eternal life in a relationship with You. And even when things aren't going how I'd like them to, You are there to bless me as I continue to follow in Your way. Thank You for all Your blessings. Help me share with someone today how blessed I am. Amen.*

A Mind Change

My Bible Reading:
Don't copy the behavior and customs of this world, but let
God transform you into a new person by changing the way
you think. Then you will learn to know God's will for you,
which is good and pleasing and perfect. (Romans 12:2)

Have you ever changed your mind about something? Sure, every-one changes their mind many times. But what about changing
your mind to think in a whole new way? When you begin to think
differently, it can change you into a whole new person.

Truth is, God plans for you to understand and think like He does. "No
one can know a person's thoughts except that person's own spirit," the
scripture says, "and no one can know God's thoughts except God's
own Spirit. And we have received God's Spirit. . . . We understand
these things, for we have the mind of Christ" (1 Corinthians 2:11-12,
16). When you trusted in Jesus as your Savior, He gave you His Spirit.
"You have received the Holy Spirit, and he lives within you. . . . For
the Spirit teaches you everything you need to know" (1 John 2:27).
As you allow Him and His Word to teach you His ways, your mind
and your thought process become like His. And as you think like
Jesus, you begin to act like Jesus.

*My Prayer: Thank You that I have received Your Spirit. Help
me absorb Your Word more and more and yield to Your Spirit.
I want my mind to be like Your mind. I want to be transformed
into Your image. Thank You for what I am becoming. Amen.*

Love Grows

My Bible Reading:
God is love, and all who live in love live in God,
and God lives in them. And as we live in God,
our love grows more perfect. (1 John 4:16–17)

Have you ever heard someone say he or she "fell in love"? That's a common phrase for indicating that you are drawn to someone so deeply that you realize you love that person. That's not quite like it is when it comes to loving God. Because loving God isn't so much about "falling in love" with Him as it is about growing in love with Him.

Truth is, you don't know how to truly love God without God teaching you *how* to love. And He does that by demonstrating how He loves you. Before you loved God, He loved you with a sacrificing love. "This is real love—not that we loved God, but that he loved us and sent his Son as a sacrifice to take away our sins" (1 John 4:10).

As you learn to love God in return, your "love grows more perfect." That's what He wants your love to do: grow deep and strong. The Bible says, "May your roots go down deep into the soil of God's marvelous love" (Ephesians 3:17 NLT). God is pleased that you grow in love with Him more and more.

My Prayer: Thank You that You are my model of love and that You loved me first. Teach me to love like You love. Help me study Your Word to learn Your love qualities. Your love is amazing and I want my love for You to grow and grow. Amen.

Do What?

My Bible Reading:

Jesus said, "Since I, your Lord and Teacher, have washed your feet, you ought to wash each other's feet. I have given you an example to follow. Do as I have done to you." (John 13:14–15)

In the Jewish culture during Jesus' time it was common for servants to wash the feet of guests. Sandals were often worn and guests would have dusty feet. A common courtesy of hospitality was to have their feet washed—by the servants, of course.

When Jesus gathered for the Passover meal with His disciples, He did a very unexpected thing. He got up from the table, wrapped a towel around His waist, got a basin of water, and began washing the dust off His disciples' feet. He did what? Yes, this was Jesus, the Master Teacher and the disciples' Lord, and He washed people's feet. Why was He doing a servant's task of washing feet? He was setting an example for you to follow.

Truth is, Jesus gave you and everyone an example of a servant's heart of love. Jesus' kind of love is to serve the needs of others, and you are to follow that example. After Jesus washed His disciples' feet He said, " 'I am giving you a new commandment: Love each other. Just as I have loved you, you should love each other' " (John 13:34).

My Prayer: You have given me an example of how Your love is serving and sacrificial. I want to love others just as You love me. Help me serve someone today with Your kind of servant love. Amen.

Others & Self

My Bible Reading:
Jesus said, "Do to others whatever you would like them
to do to you. This is the essence of all that is taught
in the law and the prophets." (Matthew 7:12)

What does it feel like to have someone compliment you on what you're wearing? Or maybe someone pats you on the back and tells you what a nice person you are or perhaps takes notice that you're feeling low and is there to cheer you up. How does that make you feel? Pretty good, right?

Actually, you're a good judge of what feels good to you and what doesn't. In fact, you were wired to enjoy things like compliments, praise, recognition, appreciation, acceptance, respect, encouragement, etc. And you naturally want to protect yourself from experiencing things that aren't good like insults, disrespect, defeat, injury, and anything that could hurt you physically. It isn't selfish to want to be treated properly and avoid painful situations.

Truth is, you know instinctively how to treat others based on how you want to be treated. That's why Jesus said to " 'do to others whatever you would like them to do to you.' " After He said to love God with your everything, He said to " 'love your neighbor as you love yourself' " (Matthew 22:39 NCV). Again, the principle is the same: love others the way you want to be loved.

My Prayer: I do want people to treat me in a loving way. I want to be protected from harmful things too. Help me treat others in the same way as I want to be treated. Help me make that happen today. Let me engage in an act of kindness toward someone—expressing love to another as I would like to be loved. Amen.

Whose Interest?

My Bible Reading:
Don't be selfish; don't try to impress others. Be humble, thinking of others as better than yourselves. Don't look out only for your own interests, but take an interest in others, too. (Philippians 2:3–4)

Have you ever come across someone who is all about trying to impress others? He or she is thinking only about the interests of "number one" and no one else. You're probably not very attracted to people like that. What is attractive however, are people who are humble, not stuck on themselves, and who take an interest in other people.

Truth is, when you look beyond your own interest and take others into consideration, you are not only honoring God, but you become a more likable person. People like to hang around those who are unselfish and care about how others feel. Scripture says, "Don't think you are better than you really are. Be honest in your evaluation of yourselves, measuring yourselves by the faith God has given us" (Romans 12:3). Since you are to " 'love your neighbor as you love yourself' " (Matthew 22:39 NCV), you should evaluate yourself as lovable. That gives you the proper perspective to care about people and " 'do for others what you would like them to do for you' " (Matthew 7:12).

My Prayer: Help me, Lord, to have a healthy view of myself without being selfish. I want my mind-set to be one that looks out for the interest of others. Let me put that in practice today by saying and doing something special for someone. Amen.

July 29

Define It

My Bible Reading:
Love is patient and kind. Love is not jealous or boastful or proud or rude. It does not demand its own way. (1 Corinthians 13:4–5)

When you're being patient and kind with someone, you are showing love. When you resist being jealous, boastful, proud, or rude and instead don't demand your own way, you are expressing God's kind of love. That is the way love operates; it is other-focused. But what is a good definition of love?

The apostle Paul defined a Christlike love when he referred to how a man should love his wife as he does his own body. Then he said, "No one hates his own body but feeds and cares for it, just as Christ cares for the church" (Ephesians 5:29). To feed means to bring to maturity and *provide for* another person relationally, physically, spiritually, and socially. To care for means *to protect* another from anything that would cause harm to a person.

Truth is, *real love*, a love that provides for and protects, *makes the security, happiness, and welfare of another person as important as your own*. That's the definition of God's kind of love. It is a love that is giving and trusting, unselfish and sacrificial, secure and safe, loyal and forever.

My Prayer: Jesus, that is the kind of love I want to show to others. It's Your kind of love, the love You have shown me. Help me love people with Your love today. Guide me as I share this definition of love with a friend today. Amen.

The Identifier

My Bible Reading:
Jesus said, "Your love for one another will prove
to the world that you are my disciples." (John 13:35)

E very car has an emblem that identifies its manufacturer, schools
have names and symbols that identify their sports teams, and
countries have flags that identify their sovereign nations. These
identifiers are symbols or brands of what a product, a team, or a
nation stands for or represents.

For centuries people have dressed a certain way, worn symbols,
or had some outward markings to identify the religion they were a
part of. Can you think of some physical identifiers that people use to
brand Christianity?

Truth is, Jesus never pointed out physical markings like a cross,
a robe, or stained glass windows that could be identifiers of the
Christian religion. He said the world would know His followers by
the way they loved one another. Wearing a gold cross or a T-shirt
that indicates you're a Christian is by no means wrong. But that's
not the true indicator that you are God's child. "If we love our
Christian brothers and sisters, it proves that we have passed from
death to eternal life" (1 John 3:14). It is your Christlike love that
brands you as a Jesus follower. "If we love each other, God lives in
us, and his love is brought to full expression in us" (1 John 4:12).

*My Prayer: Thank You for loving me, living in me, and empowering
me to love others. Help me grow more and more in Your kind of love.
I want Your love in me and my love for others to mark me as Your
follower. Help me show that love to someone today. Amen.*

True or False

___

My Bible Reading:

Dear friends, do not believe everyone who claims to speak by the Spirit. You must test them to see if the spirit they have comes from God. For there are many false prophets in the world. (1 John 4:1)

Have you ever bought something you thought was authentic and found out later it was not? There are those who get rich running scams, selling rip-offs, and fooling people. It is not just dishonest salespeople who are trying to deceive others, but it's false religious leaders, too.

Truth is, you need to test what you hear and compare it to God's Word. There are those who will twist the truth and take scripture out of context. The apostle Paul talked about people like that. "They will act religious, but they will reject the power that could make them godly. Stay away from people like that!" (2 Timothy 3:5). He went on to challenge Christ followers to "be diligent [in]. . .accurately handling the word of truth" (2 Timothy 2:15 NASB). You can be certain that religious teachings are false if they aren't consistent with what scripture teaches.

___

My Prayer: Thank You that Your Word is true. Help me study and understand Your truth so I can discern what is genuine and false. Give me a greater love for Your Word so I can know You and Your ways. Thank You for the power of Your Word and Your Spirit that continues to change my life. You are a trustworthy and righteous God! Amen.

AUGUST

No End in Death

Your Faith Is Useless

My Bible Reading:

If Christ has not been raised [from the dead], then your faith is useless and you are still guilty of your sins. (1 Corinthians 15:17)

Can that be right? Aren't you forgiven of your sins because of Jesus' death on the cross? Believing that Jesus is God's Son and that He died for your sins is worth everything, isn't it? How can that kind of faith be useless?

Jesus' death was the sacrifice that allowed God to forgive you of your sins. But that's only half the story. The result of sin is spiritual death and eventual physical death. So you not only need to be forgiven, you also need to be brought to new life. Jesus' death allowed for your forgiveness, but it was His resurrection that gave you spiritual life. "God is so rich in mercy, and he loved [you] so much, that even though [you] were dead because of [your] sins, he gave [you] life when he raised Christ from the dead" (Ephesians 2:4–5).

Truth is, unless Jesus was literally raised from the dead, God's promise of forgiveness and an eternal relationship with Him is nothing but a fantasy. Jesus had to die and rise from the dead for your faith in Him to result in eternal life.

My Prayer: *Jesus, thank You, thank You, thank You for both dying for my sins and rising from the dead. I am so grateful that Your death and resurrection secure a place for me with You forever. Help me share that news with someone today. Amen.*

Offered by No One Else

My Bible Reading:
With his [Jesus'] own blood—not the blood of goats and calves—he entered the Most Holy Place once for all time and secured our redemption forever. (Hebrews 9:12)

Do you know your blood type? There are four major blood groups consisting of type A, B, AB, or O. But imagine if you were born with blood type XOXOXO (which doesn't exist). And because you inherit your blood type, there is only one person alive who could offer you blood for a transfusion—your dad.

Okay, keep imagining. Now you're in a hospital due to an accident and you need a blood transfusion right away. No blood bank in the world can save you because no one is XOXOXO except your dad. He is your only hope. Fortunately for you, he shows up at the hospital and quickly offers his blood to save you.

Truth is, Jesus' blood is the only sacrifice that a Holy God will accept because He is the only one who is sinless. "He [Jesus] is the kind of high priest we need because he is holy and blameless, unstained by sin" (Hebrews 7:26). If He doesn't show up and offer His own blood as your sacrifice, you can't be saved! Fortunately for you, He rose from the dead to enter the Most Holy Place in heaven "once for all time and secured [your] redemption forever" (Hebrews 9:12).

My Prayer: Jesus, no wonder Your resurrection was so important. Without it You would not have been able to give me eternal life. Thank You that Your love for me was so powerful that it enabled You to rise from the dead to secure my salvation forever. You are an extraordinary God! Amen.

Would Be a Lie

My Bible Reading:

If Christ has not been raised, then our preaching is useless. . . .
And we apostles would all be lying about God—for we have said
that God raised Christ from the grave. (1 Corinthians 15:14–15)

Jesus said a lot of good things. His teaching about treating one
another in love was excellent. And after Jesus' death His followers
continued to preach Jesus' message of how people ought to love God
and one another. So what's the big deal if Jesus didn't rise from the
dead? His message of love is still good, right?

The apostles and followers of Christ said their message about
Jesus would all be a lie if He hadn't risen from the dead. For Jesus'
message of love to be forever true, it needed to come from a forever
God. His love was about giving people new life in Him so they could
love like the eternal God, their Creator.

Truth is, because you were born into the human race of Adam, you
were born spiritually dead. A simple message of love for one another
spoken from a good teacher can't change that fact. But a risen Savior
can change all that. "Just as everyone dies because we all belong
to Adam, everyone who belongs to Christ will be given new life"
(1 Corinthians 15:22). The message that Jesus gives new life is not a
lie, because Jesus has risen from the dead.

*My Prayer: Thank You that You are a living God with a living
message that is true. You couldn't very well love me unless
You were alive. I am so thankful that You rose from the grave
and that I can live with You for eternity. Help me share
this message with those around me. Amen.*

How Miserable?

My Bible Reading:
If we have hope in Christ only for this life, we are the most
miserable people in the world. (1 Corinthians 15:19)

You're enjoying a really good movie or book. But you get to the
final scene or the last page and. . .it ends. You're at a great party
and everyone is enjoying it so much. But it's time to go home and. . .it
ends. You're eating your favorite sandwich and it really tastes good.
But you've swallowed the last bite and. . .it ends. You're on a fantastic
date. But the evening comes to a close and. . .it ends.

As Juliet says to Romeo, " 'Parting is such sweet sorrow.' " It's true
you may have another date. You can have another party, read another
book, go to another movie, or eat another sandwich. But sooner or
later everything must come to an end.

Truth is, if your only hope is in what this life can bring, then there is
reason to really feel miserable. Why? Because nothing lasts, everything ends, and all is gone in a matter of years. That is, unless "Christ
has been raised from the dead" (1 Corinthians 15:20). The resurrection
means that in Christ true joy can last forever.

*****

*My Prayer: Thank You that You are my reason for living.
You allow me to enjoy so much in this life. And I am so thankful
for that. But what is so amazing is that because You rose from
the dead I will enjoy a new life with You forever and ever.
You are such a marvelous forever God. Amen.*

He Escaped Death

My Bible Reading:
It is God who saved us.... And now he has made all of
this plain to us by the coming of Christ Jesus, our Savior,
who broke the power of death and showed us the way to
everlasting life through the Good News. (2 Timothy 1:9–10)

The famous magician Harry Houdini was a master escape artist. He could free himself from jails, handcuffs, chains, and ropes. Perhaps his most famous escape was the "Chinese Water Torture Cell." Houdini was suspended upside down in a locked glass-and-steel cabinet full of overflowing water. He escaped every time even though it required him to hold his breath for more than three minutes. But one thing Houdini could not escape was death.

Truth is, no normal human can escape death. Scripture says that "each person is destined to die once" (Hebrews 9:27). But there is one not-so-normal human who broke the power of death. That was the God-man, Jesus, and He "showed us the way to everlasting life." Because of His resurrection the power death has over you is broken. Jesus said, " 'Anyone who believes in me will live, even after dying' " (John 11:25).

My Prayer: *Thank You that You have shown me the way to
everlasting life. Death may be inevitable, but because of You
and Your resurrection my death is not final. Help me share the
news with others that You offer everlasting life to all those who
place their trust in You. You are a merciful Savior. Amen.*

The Resurrection Starts Now

My Bible Reading:
For you were buried with Christ when you were baptized. And with him you were raised to new life because you trusted the mighty power of God, who raised Christ from the dead. (Colossians 2:12)

God told the first human beings that they could eat of all the fruits of the garden, except one. And if they disobeyed Him and ate from that tree, a terrible consequence would follow. " 'If you eat its fruit,' " God said, " 'you are sure to die' " (Genesis 2:17).

Both Adam and Eve ate the fruit, but they didn't die right then. In fact "Adam lived 930 years, and then he died" (Genesis 5:5). Yet as soon as the first couple disobeyed God, they did die spiritually and then eventually died physically.

Truth is, because you were born dead spiritually, you will die physically. But since you have trusted Jesus, you have been resurrected spiritually and once you die you will be resurrected physically. So your resurrection really starts now. That's because "the Spirit of God who raised Jesus from the dead, lives in you" (Romans 8:11). The Holy Spirit has made you alive now and will later make your life permanent and forever.

My Prayer: Thank You that my resurrection has started now. You have made me alive to You. I can talk to You, and You can give me strength to live for You and tell others about Your life-giving plan. Help me share Your plan of salvation with someone today. Amen.

When & Where

My Bible Reading:
There is an order to this resurrection: Christ was raised
as the first of the harvest; then all who belong to Christ
will be raised when he comes back. (1 Corinthians 15:23)

You probably knew some people who were Christians that died, right? If they aren't going to be resurrected until Jesus returns, then where are they now? And if they're in heaven, do they have new, transformed bodies?

The Bible gives all the answers people need in order to trust in Christ and know how a Christian ought to live and treat others. But there are questions that aren't fully answered. God has not explained all of the details about what happens after death.

Truth is, God's Word has explained that once a person who has trusted in Christ dies, he or she is with Him. "To be absent from the body," Paul wrote, is "to be at home with the Lord" (2 Corinthians 5:8 NASB). Scripture also says that once a person dies "the spirit will return to God who gave it" (Ecclesiastes 12:7).

It may not be clear just what kind of form people might have while they are with God waiting for Jesus to return. But you can be assured they are filled with joy and are at home in the presence of God.

My Prayer: Thank You that You have worked out all the details of me living for eternity with You, even though I don't know all those details. I do know that You love me and all my loved ones and that together we will enjoy eternity with You. Thank You for being such a faithful God. Amen.

Sin Not Allowed

My Bible Reading:
"We have already shown that all people, whether Jews or Gentiles, are under the power of sin. As the Scriptures say. . . 'All have turned away from God; all have gone wrong. No one does good, not even one.' " (Romans 3:9–10, 12)

S in is a big problem. Everyone who has ever lived has sinned (except Jesus). Think of it, the selfish nature of sin has caused dishonesty, fighting and wars, murder, and every kind of evil you can imagine. Sure, Jesus came to die and rise again to forgive sin, but it's still around.

Wouldn't it be great if everyone would accept Christ's sacrifice for sin, be forgiven and never sin again? That would allow everyone to enjoy peace and harmony in the world. That's what the apostle Paul wrote that we all want: "For we long for our bodies to be released from sin and suffering" (Romans 8:23).

Truth is, there will be a day when sin will be done away with and there will be a world without dishonesty, wars, or evil of any kind. That will take place when God raises His children from the dead and gives every child of God a new body. "We, too, wait with eager hope," Paul wrote, "for the day when God will give us our full rights as his adopted children, including the new bodies he has promised us" (Romans 8:23). We will then live in a world where "nothing evil will be allowed to enter" (Revelation 21:27).

My Prayer: *Thank You that one day You will destroy sin and all its effects on me and the world around me. You are a Holy God without sin and I'm so glad You forgave me of my sins and plan to let me enjoy all eternity with You in a place without sin. Amen.*

A Life without End

My Bible Reading:
Our earthly bodies, which die and decay, will be different when they are resurrected, for they will never die. (1 Corinthians 15:42)

The words "All good things must come to an end" were written by poet Geoffrey Chaucer over six hundred years ago. And it seems to be true. You will finish school, friendships will fade, parties will end, your clothes will wear out, your body will wear down—it certainly seems that all good things will eventually come to an end.

The idea that something, anything, can last forever is almost impossible to grasp. Everything from recorded time has an end. Stars cease to shine, the sun will someday burn out, and everything on earth is continuing to decay. So to think that you will one day be made to live forever is mind-blowing.

Truth is, God is eternal. "You are always the same," the Bible declares about God, "you will live forever" (Psalm 102:27). And what is incredible is that the eternal God is willing and happy to grant you eternal life. "And this is what God has testified: He has given us eternal life, and this life is in his Son. Whoever has the Son has life. . . . He is the only true God, and he is eternal life" (1 John 5:11–12, 20).

*****My Prayer:*** *I can't comprehend the idea of life without end. Yet I don't like the idea of good things coming to an end. I'm glad You have all the answers. As hard as it is to embrace the idea that I will live forever, I will gladly accept it because I trust You, my eternal God. Thank You that You will raise me up with a new body that will never die. Amen.*

What's Glory?

My Bible Reading:
Our bodies are buried in brokenness,
but they will be raised in glory. (1 Corinthians 15:43)

What's glory? Glory is something that secures praise; it is a distinguished quality or asset; it is magnificence, a state of great gratification or exaltation. To be raised from death to a state of glory is a big deal.

You get straight A's and you will be placed on the honor roll. You win all your games and you will become a champion. You work hard at your job and you will be rewarded. You achieve great things at a company and you might even advance to become CEO. You win the national election and you will become president. But when you are given a resurrected body by God, you will experience the ultimate promotion, a magnificent advancement. In fact, it will be the most important and greatest gift you will ever receive—you "will be raised in glory."

Truth is, when you are given a new body you receive the same magnificent status that Jesus received when He was raised from the dead. "He [God] called you to salvation when we told you the Good News; now you can share in the glory of our Lord Jesus Christ" (2 Thessalonians 2:14). You will receive God's glory—the most distinguished quality of eternal life that God has. You will be made immortal!

My Prayer: You are magnificent. You are to be exalted and praised. You are to receive glory because of who You are. Yet in Your mercy and kindness You are going to allow me to share in Your glory of everlasting life. That leaves me speechless. All I can do is lift up my heart in praise and thanksgiving for Your love and mercy to me. You are a phenomenal God and I will forever love and praise You. Amen.

Powerful

My Bible Reading:
Our bodies now disappoint us. . . . They are weak now, but when they are raised, they will be full of power. (1 Corinthians 15:43)

Superman can bend steel with his bare hands, see through solid rock, and fly faster than the speed of sound. Wonder Woman can skillfully use her Amazon bracelets to stop bullets and wield a golden lasso to defeat the strongest of men. The powers of superheroes are fictional, of course. But it might feel fun to think of one day being mighty and powerful.

Truth is, when you are raised up to receive a spiritual body, you will be full of power. You will have power over death and sin. Nothing can harm you. You will have power over suffering, pain, and heartache because you will be with those who make their home with God. Scripture says, " 'God himself will be with them. He will wipe every tear from their eyes, and there will be no more death or sorrow or crying or pain. All these things are gone forever' " (Revelation 21:3–4).

In this life your body may experience sickness. You feel pain when you are injured. Your body has limits and will eventually wear out. So it's natural to want to experience the power of a resurrected body. Paul wanted that when he wrote, "I want to know Christ and experience the mighty power that raised him from the dead" (Philippians 3:10). One day you will experience that mighty power.

My Prayer*: Thank You that You will someday grant me the mighty power of Your resurrection. Thank You for being with me now to strengthen and comfort me. And thank You for the future You have in store for me. My total hope is in You. Amen.*

A Body like Jesus

My Bible Reading:
He [Jesus] will take our weak mortal bodies and change them into glorious bodies like his own, using the same power with which he will bring everything under his control. (Philippians 3:21)

What would it be like to have a resurrected body like Jesus had after His resurrection? People could recognize Him because He looked like Himself. Yet when He wanted, He "kept them [two of Jesus' followers walking to the village of Emmaus] from recognizing him" (Luke 24:16). He was able to appear before people and disappear from them at will (Luke 24:31, 36). He ate with His followers (Luke 24:41-42) and revealed Himself to a lot of other people (1 Corinthians 15:6).

Truth is, no one really knows all you will be able to do with your resurrected body. Yet scripture does make it clear that "every human being has an earthly body just like Adam's, but our heavenly bodies will be just like Christ's. Just as we are now like Adam, the man of the earth, so we will someday be like Christ" (1 Corinthians 15:48-49). Whatever incredible things you will be able to do with your heavenly body, you can be sure it will be amazing and a lot of fun!

My Prayer: I don't really know all You have in store for me when You give me a heavenly body, but I know You have incredible plans for me. Thank You for dying for me and rising from the dead so I can live with You in a heavenly body just like Yours. Help me share this wonderful news with someone today. Amen.

August 13

A Secret

Let me reveal to you a wonderful secret. We will not all die,
but we will all be transformed.... [When Jesus returns] those
who have died will be raised to live forever. And we who are
living will also be transformed. (1 Corinthians 15:51–52)

When Jesus was on earth He told His followers He was going back to His Father in heaven to prepare a place for all those who trusted in Him as Savior. And He would return to get them. "'When everything is ready, I will come and get you,'" Jesus said, "'so that you will always be with me where I am'" (John 14:3). So there is no secret that Jesus is returning. But the apostle Paul revealed a wonderful secret about Jesus' plans for those who are living at the time of His return.

Truth is, scripture tells us that not everyone will die a natural death. Those who are alive when Jesus returns will go through a transformation to receive a heavenly body but won't actually die a natural death. "The Lord himself will come down from heaven with a commanding shout. . . . First, the believers who have died will rise from their graves. Then, together with them, we who are still alive and remain on the earth will be caught up in the clouds to meet the Lord in the air" (1 Thessalonians 4:16–17). Dead or alive, because of Jesus' resurrection, all those who have placed their faith in Him will be transformed and receive a heavenly body.

My Prayer: *Thank You for Your wonderful plan to give all of Your followers new bodies. You are the God of resurrection and transformation so that all who trust in You can live with You forever. You are so incredible! Amen.*

Assurance of Eternal Life

My Bible Reading:

For we know that when this earthly tent we live in is taken down (that is, when we die and leave this earthly body), we will have a house in heaven.... God himself has prepared us for this, and as a guarantee he has given us his Holy Spirit. (2 Corinthians 5:1, 5)

The summer is coming to a close and you're fresh out of money. You need gas money for a trip you want to take, cash for new clothes you want to buy, and money for those times you want to go out to eat with friends. Then out of the blue a stranger tells you to watch for a check in the mail. What do you make of that? How assured are you that money is going to show up from nowhere? You would probably have doubts, because "who can trust a stranger?"

But suppose your grandfather calls and says, "I've heard that you're in need of some extra cash. So I've just dropped a check in the mail to you." Now how assured are you that money is coming your way? You would probably be confident you're going to get some money because someone you know and trust told you so. You're assured of getting something when you're confident in the one who has made the promise.

Truth is, a very trustworthy person has promised that you have been given eternal life. And that person is the Holy Spirit. "For his Spirit joins with our spirit to affirm that we are God's children.... We have the Holy Spirit within us as a foretaste of future glory" (Romans 8:16, 23). The Holy Spirit is your guarantee that you have a home in heaven.

My Prayer: Thank You that Your Holy Spirit is within me to give me assurance that I am Your child. Because of Your resurrection, I too will be raised from the dead to live with You and have life without end. Help me share this truth with someone today. Amen.

I Want Proof

My Bible Reading:

After Jesus' resurrection He showed Himself at a meeting of His disciples, but Thomas wasn't present. They told him [Thomas], "We have seen the Lord!" But he replied, "I won't believe it unless I see the nail wounds in his hands, put my fingers into them, and place my hand into the wound in his side." (John 20:25)

Thomas wanted proof that Jesus had risen from the dead. You can hardly fault him. The rest of the disciples didn't believe the report from the women who saw Jesus alive at the tomb. They didn't believe until Jesus revealed Himself personally to them. It just seemed too amazing to actually believe Jesus was resurrected.

Eight days after Jesus had shown Himself to the disciples, He showed up again. This time Thomas was there. Jesus offered to let the doubting disciple put his fingers in the wounds in His hand and side. Jesus said, " 'Don't be faithless any longer. Believe!' 'My Lord and my God!' Thomas exclaimed" (John 20:27–28).

Truth is, the reliable eyewitness accounts of Jesus' resurrection are evidence that He literally rose from the grave. Jesus told Thomas, " 'You believe because you have seen me. Blessed are those who believe without seeing me' " (John 20:29). The disciple John concludes his written testimony in chapter 20 by saying, "These are written so that you may continue to believe that Jesus is the Messiah, the Son of God, and that by believing in him you will have life by the power of his name" (John 20:31).

My Prayer: I have never seen You with my physical eyes. But You have opened my spiritual eyes and heart, and I believe You are my resurrected Lord and God. Thank You for giving me the accurate and reliable report of scripture that deepens my faith in You as the true Messiah. Help me share Your story with those around me. Amen.

Body Stolen?

My Bible Reading:
Some of the guards went into the city and told the leading priests what had happened. A meeting with the elders was called, and they decided to give the soldiers a large bribe. They told the soldiers, "You must say, 'Jesus' disciples came during the night while we were sleeping, and they stole his body.'" (Matthew 28:11–13)

Some people don't believe Jesus actually rose from the dead. Of course Jesus' dead body was never found to prove He remained dead. To address that issue they claim the body was stolen by His disciples. But this stolen-body theory creates more problems than it solves. For example,

- If the guards were sleeping, how did they know the disciples—or anyone—stole the body?
- Roman soldiers were executed for sleeping on duty. Would all those guarding the tomb decide to take a nap, knowing it would cost them their lives?
- The stone sealing the tomb weighed between one and two tons! How plausible is it that thieves could sneak past the guards, roll the stone away, enter the dark tomb, and exit with the body without waking up a single guard?

Truth is, there is more credible evidence for Jesus' resurrection than there is for any stolen-body theory. According to historical accounts, the disciples were skeptical themselves when they heard the news of the empty tomb. After the women reported they saw the resurrected Jesus, "the story sounded like nonsense to the men, so they didn't believe it" (Luke 24:11). The body of Jesus wasn't stolen by His disciples, because He in fact was risen!

My Prayer: Thank You for the historical account of Your resurrection found in scripture. You are the risen Christ who secured my salvation. Thank You for loving me enough to die and rise again to give me life eternal. You are a trustworthy God. Amen.

Didn't Really Die?

My Bible Reading:

Joseph of Arimathea took a risk and went to Pilate and asked for
Jesus' body. . . . . Pilate couldn't believe that Jesus was already dead,
so he called for the Roman officer and asked if he had died yet.
The officer confirmed that Jesus was dead, so Pilate told
Joseph he could have the body. (Mark 15:43–45)

Some people claim that Jesus never rose from the dead because
He really didn't die in the first place. They say once Jesus was
taken off the cross—after being beaten almost to death and suffering
a bloody crucifixion—that He actually revived. They claim He wasn't
quite dead yet; He was only in shock. And once He was placed in the
tomb, the cool damp air of the tomb resuscitated Him.

The problem with this theory—aside from the fact that it is
unrealistic—was the death certification that Pilate required. He was
surprised that Jesus was reportedly dead after some six hours on
the cross. Normally death on a cross takes much longer than that.
So only after receiving a firsthand report did Pilate release the body,
thus fully verifying the fact that Jesus was dead before He was placed
in the tomb.

Truth is, Jesus died on the cross. And to be absolutely sure, one of
the soldiers at the crucifixion "pierced his [Jesus'] side with a spear,
and immediately blood and water flowed out. (This report is from an
eyewitness giving an accurate account. He speaks the truth so that
you also may continue to believe)" (John 19:34–35). There is sufficient
evidence to verify that Jesus truly died and truly rose from the dead.

*My Prayer: Your death was real, but the grave could not hold You. It was
by Your mighty power that You broke the chains of death to purchase
my salvation. Thank You that Your love for me was that powerful.
Help me share the power of Your love with someone today. Amen.*

A Ghost?

My Bible Reading:
Two men were telling their story of seeing the resurrected
Jesus, and just as they were telling about it, Jesus himself
was suddenly standing there among them. "Peace be with you,"
he said. But the whole group was startled and frightened,
thinking they were seeing a ghost! (Luke 24:36–37)

Imagine being at a reception of friends and family after a funeral.
You are all saddened and talking about your departed friend. Then
all of a sudden, the one who was dead appears in front of all of you
and says, "I'm here, don't be afraid." Even with your friend saying not
to be afraid, you would probably be freaked out, right?

Some skeptics accept the reality that many people thought they
saw Jesus after His death. But they claim everyone was just hallu-
cinating. It was like everyone was seeing a ghost that wasn't real. The
problem with this line of thinking is that hallucinations are highly
individualized and extremely subjective. It is unreasonable to think
that hundreds of people hallucinated the same thing at the same time.

Truth is, Jesus wasn't a ghost or a hallucination. He said, " 'Look at
my hands. Look at my feet. You can see that it's really me. Touch me
and make sure I am not a ghost, because ghosts don't have bodies,
as you see that I do' " (Luke 24:39). Jesus was a real person who really
rose from the dead. He wasn't some hallucination.

*My Prayer: God, I am so thankful that Your Son really lived,
really died, and really rose again. Your Holy Spirit is real even
though I can't see Him. He lives within me and has let me know
I am Your child. Thank You that I'm serving a living God who
has given me eternal life. You are so worthy of my praise! Amen.*

Not Seeing yet Believing

My Bible Reading:

Paul reports: Christ died for our sins, just as the Scriptures said. He was buried, and he was raised from the dead on the third day, just as the Scriptures said. He was seen by Peter and then by the Twelve. After that, he was seen by more than 500 of his followers at one time, most of whom are still alive, though some have died. Then he was seen by James and later by all the apostles. (1 Corinthians 15:3–7)

The apostle Paul wrote 1 Corinthians about twenty years after Jesus' resurrection. At the time, every teenager could have only *heard* about Jesus because they weren't alive when Jesus was on earth. But Peter and hundreds of others who saw the risen Jesus could tell them firsthand what they had seen. That must have been powerful evidence because it was eyewitness testimony from men and women who had seen Jesus die and later saw Him alive.

Truth is, so many people were eyewitnesses to Jesus' resurrection it makes it impossible for an open-minded person to deny. And when Jesus' followers told others about Jesus dying for sin and His power over death, many believed in Him as their Savior. Peter wrote, "You love him even though you have never seen him. Though you do not see him now, you trust him. . . . The reward for trusting him will be the salvation of your souls" (1 Peter 1:8–9). Jesus is real. He really died and rose again so that you can experience the reality of being given eternal life.

My Prayer: Thank You for appearing to so many people to show that You conquered death. That message has been passed down over all the centuries and now I have heard it and believed in You. Even though I have never seen You, I have trusted in You. Thank You for being the living Christ who has forgiven me and entered my life through the power of Your Holy Spirit. You are so awesome! Amen.

Put It in Perspective

My Bible Reading:

We know that God, who raised the Lord Jesus, will also raise us with Jesus and present us to himself together with you. All of this is for your benefit.... That is why we never give up. Though our bodies are dying, our spirits are being renewed every day. (2 Corinthians 4:14–16)

Y ou fail a test, lose a game, get cut from the team, or get snubbed by your "friends." Life hands you stuff that's just tough sometimes. And that can naturally cause you to feel both disappointed and discouraged. So what do you do?

Put it in perspective. Back up a minute and see the bigger picture. Things may at times seem messy and you might wonder how things are going to turn out. But God is really in charge and He isn't surprised or taken back by anything that happens.

Truth is, "despite all these things, overwhelming victory is ours through Christ, who loved us" (Romans 8:37). *Because He lives* you can face anything and everything in life. For in the end you will be raised to live with Him forever. That is reason to never give up in the midst of discouraging times. God will turn even the most disastrous of times into a glorious future with Him. "He is God, the one who rules over everything and is worthy of eternal praise! Amen" (Romans 9:5).

__My Prayer__: Thank You that You are ultimately in charge of everything. I can look to You and You are always there for me. You will never leave me or let me down. You have a purpose for me. Help me share Your love and mercy with someone today. Amen.

A Confident Faith

My Bible Reading:
Because God raised Christ from the dead and
gave him great glory, your faith and hope can
be placed confidently in God. (1 Peter 1:21)

You studied hard and know the material. You're confident you'll do well on the test. You've memorized every line so you're confident you'll do well in the play. Your dad said he'll cosign the papers, therefore you're confident you'll get the car loan. Confidence is born out of certainty.

Truth is, *because He lives* you can have complete confidence that God has forgiven you and will give you eternal life. Knowing that God raised Christ from the dead gives you confidence that He will raise you from the dead. His resurrection puts in motion a whole harvest of resurrections. "Christ has been raised from the dead. He is the first of a great harvest of all who have died" (1 Corinthians 15:20).

Because Jesus was victorious over death you will be victorious over death. Because He lives forever you can have faith that in Him you will live forever.

My Prayer*: It's true—all my hopes and dreams for a forever future depend upon You. Everything really centers around You. Jesus, You are the beginning and end of my faith. All of my hope is in You. I'm glad You are the powerful Savior who rose from the grave. Help me share that good news with someone today. Amen.*

A Fearless Faith

My Bible Reading:
Even though I walk through the valley of the shadow
of death, I fear no evil, for You are with me; Your rod
and Your staff, they comfort me. (Psalm 23:4 NASB)

A re you afraid of the dark? A lot of people are and for good reason. The dark hides your surroundings and keeps you from knowing what's there. So it's natural to fear the unknown. And what unknown is greater than death?

What does it feel like to die? What happens immediately after you pass from this life to the next? What actually goes on? No one on earth really knows—it's an unknown experience. And many people really fear death.

Truth is, *because He lives* your faith in the risen Jesus gives you a fearless faith, even when it comes to death. The apostle Paul wrote: "When our dying bodies have been transformed into bodies that will never die, this Scripture will be fulfilled: 'Death is swallowed up in victory. O death, where is your victory? O death, where is your sting?' For sin is the sting that results in death, and the law gives sin its power. But thank God! He gives us victory over sin and death through our Lord Jesus Christ" (1 Corinthians 15:54-57).

My Prayer: Thank You that Your victory over death is my victory too. I don't have to fear death (although it does seem creepy) because You will be there to lead me safely through it when the time comes. In the meantime, I will rejoice in the life You have given me. Amen.

A Peace-Giving Faith

My Bible Reading:

Jesus tells His followers about His pending death. Then He says,
"I have told you all this so that you may have peace in me.
Here on earth you will have many trials and sorrows. But take
heart, because I have overcome the world." (John 16:33)

Have you ever gotten in a war of words with someone? It generally produces a lot of tension and hostility. That's not a very comfortable feeling. Sometimes a person can feel a tension within himself or herself without even fighting with anyone. It's that sense of uneasiness within, and not feeling at peace in mind or spirit.

Truth is, *because He lives* Jesus is the "Prince of Peace." He overcame the world and gives peace to the troubled soul. And scripture gives a formula to keep receiving His peace. "Don't worry about anything; instead, pray about everything. Tell God what you need, and thank him for all he has done. Then you will experience God's peace, which exceeds anything we can understand. His peace will guard your hearts and minds as you live in Christ Jesus" (Philippians 4:6–7).

My Prayer: Thank You for being the God of peace. My faith in You has given me peace in my soul. Help me keep receiving Your peace of mind and heart. I want to always come to You about everything and I do thank You for all You have done for me. Remind me when I'm tense and uneasy to be grateful and keep praising You for being my Savior and friend. Amen.

A Giving Faith

My Bible Reading:

God will generously provide all you need. Then you will
always have everything you need and plenty left over to
share with others. . . . Yes, you will be enriched in every way
so that you can always be generous. (2 Corinthians 9:8, 11)

When you were growing up, did your parents try to teach you to
share your toys? Those kids who never shared always seemed
to be the ones who were the most discontented. Those who never
shared were those who never experienced the joy of giving.

Truth is, *because He lives* Jesus always generously gives enough to
you so that you can give to others. And that's when you really benefit.
Passing your blessings through to others actually keeps you blessed.
If you focus on the giving, you'll keep on receiving. Jesus said, " 'Give,
and you will receive' " (Luke 6:38). But that requires a faith and trust
in a living God who will keep giving as you give to others.

"Taste and see that the LORD is good," King David wrote. "Oh the
joys of those who trust in him! . . . Even strong young lions sometimes
go hungry, but those who trust in the LORD will never lack any good
thing" (Psalm 34:8, 10). A giving faith produces an enriched life.

---

*My Prayer: Thank You for giving me so much. You died for me, You
rose for me, and You meet my needs. Help me always share what I
have with others. I want Your generous and loving heart to be mine.
Help me give of what I have received to someone today. Amen.*

My God of Hope

My Bible Reading:
"For I know the plans I have for you," says the LORD.
"They are plans for good and not for disaster,
to give you a future and a hope." (Jeremiah 29:11)

A re you an optimistic person? Is a glass half full of water or half empty? Optimistic and hopeful people are generally happier people. To believe you have a bright future gives you hope. And there is reason for hope when you place your trust in the living God.

Truth is, *because He lives* Jesus does have a wonderful plan for your life. The prophet Jeremiah told the children of Israel that God had plans for their lives to give them hope. And He has a plan for you too. There is a reason you are here and Jesus will guide you to fulfill your purpose as you continue to keep your trust in Him.

"I pray that God, the source of hope, will fill you completely with joy and peace because you trust in him. Then you will overflow with confident hope through the power of the Holy Spirit" (Romans 15:13).

My Prayer: *Jesus, I know that my ultimate purpose is to honor and glorify You by becoming more and more like You. Help me do that each day, and in doing so, please make it clearer and clearer to me how I can best fulfill my specific purpose in honoring You. You are the God of hope and I put all my hope in You. I love You. Amen.*

How God Sees It

My Bible Reading:
For you were buried with Christ when you were baptized. And with him you were raised to new life because you trusted the mighty power of God, who raised Christ from the dead. (Colossians 2:12)

When your parents see you, whom do they actually see? Do they see a student, a musician, a sports player, a house guest—just whom do they see? You may play an instrument or a sport, and you may study courses and live in their home. But your parents look beyond all the things you do and see the person you are—their very own child.

When God sees you He sees you as His child too, but for a different reason. You are a child of your parents because you were physically born into their family. They are the ones who conceived you. But spiritually you were born dead to God because of sin. Scripture says, "Adam's sin brought death, so death spread to everyone" (Romans 5:12). So how is it that God can see you as His child?

Truth is, *because He lives* God saw you and your sins buried with Jesus when He was buried. And because you trusted in Jesus, You are now alive to God and are His child, all because of your identity with Christ and His resurrection. "For when we died with Christ we were set free from the power of sin. . . . We are sure of this because Christ was raised from the dead" (Romans 6:7, 9).

My Prayer: Thank You that my identity as a risen child of God is in You. Without Your death and resurrection I could never be seen by God as His child and I would have never received Your life—eternal life. I am so glad I put my trust in You. Thank You for dying and rising from the dead. Help me share Your story of life with someone today. Amen.

August 27

Give Worries Away

My Bible Reading:
Give all your worries and cares to God,
for he cares about you. (1 Peter 5:7)

When you focus a lot on the problems of life, you tend to worry and fear what might happen. By looking on the dark side of things most of the time, it's hard to see the bright side. That's why Paul said to "fix your thoughts on what is true, and honorable, and right, and pure, and lovely, and admirable. Think about things that are excellent and worthy of praise" (Philippians 4:8).

Truth is, *because He lives* Jesus has an answer for worries. He wants you to give them away to Him. "Give your burdens to the LORD," King David said, "and he will take care of you" (Psalm 55:22). Giving away your worries to Jesus means you no longer hold on to them—it means you trust in Him to take care of you. David went on to say, "I trust in God, so why should I be afraid?" (Psalm 56:11).

My Prayer*: Help me avoid worry. I know You care about me, and I know that because You are the resurrected Jesus. You can lead me where You want me to go. Today I give You my worries and my fears. Help me keep my trust in You for my life and my future. Thank You for loving me. Amen.*

God Never Fails

My Bible Reading:

We are pressed on every side by troubles, but we are not crushed and broken. We are perplexed, but we don't give up and quit. We are hunted down, but God never abandons us. We get knocked down, but we get up again and keep going. (2 Corinthians 4:8–9)

Have you ever failed at something? You're not alone; every human fails. Thomas Edison was a brilliant inventor, but most of his over one thousand inventions were failures. It is said that the genius Albert Einstein failed an entrance exam and consequently was not accepted into the prestigious Federal Polytechnic Academy. Fifteen-year-old Michael Jordan tried out for a high school varsity basketball team and failed to make the team. Some of the greatest achievers and achievements were at first fraught with failure.

Truth is, *because He lives* you can take heart in a God who never fails. He will always be there for You no matter what. "If you are suffering in a manner that pleases God, keep on doing what is right and trust your lives to the God who created you, for he will never fail you" (1 Peter 4:19). He is the Almighty God who through Jesus conquered death. " 'You [Jesus] made the heavens and earth by your strong hand and powerful arm. Nothing is too hard for you!' " (Jeremiah 32:17).

My Prayer: Thank You that You are always there for me as a God who has failed at nothing. You are perfect. There is no one like You. That You are so interested in me and the details of my life blows my mind. I love You and want to love You more each day. Amen.

The Unchanging God

My Bible Reading:
Jesus Christ is the same yesterday, today, and forever. (Hebrews 13:8)

Life is full of change. Seasons change as summer turns to fall and fall turns to winter. You are changing from one grade to another and possibly heading off to college. Friendships go through change and many may even fade away. Your body is changing as it matures and grows older. And with all the change going on around you, sometimes it's hard to know whom you can trust and count on.

Truth is, *because He lives* there is only One you can count on who has never changed and will never change—God Himself. For God has "bound himself with an oath, so that those who received the promise could be perfectly sure that he would never change his mind. So God has given both his promise and his oath. These. two things are unchangeable because it is impossible for God to lie" (Hebrews 6:17–18).

Jesus as your God and Savior does not change. His character, in all its holiness, mercy, and justice, never changes. His truth is eternal. His love lasts forever. His mercy has no end. He always forgives the repentant heart. He never breaks a promise and you can count on Him no matter what. " 'God is not a man, so he does not lie. He is not human, so he does not change his mind. Has he ever spoken and failed to act? Has he ever promised and not carried it through?' " (Numbers 23:19).

My Prayer: Change can be scary. Life can be uncertain. But I am so glad You are the risen and unchanging God that I can count on. I can rest secure in Your love, Your care, and Your guiding hand on my life. Help me always to look to You and Your Word as I navigate through this changing world. Amen.

Content

My Bible Reading:

True godliness with contentment is itself great wealth. After all, we brought nothing with us when we came into the world, and we can't take anything with us when we leave it. So if we have enough food and clothing, let us be content. (1 Timothy 6:6–8)

Have you ever run across people who are always wanting more? They are never quite satisfied with what they have—they are simply discontented. These people have come to expect things, and when they don't get them they are not content.

A great way to live a life of contentment is to lower your expectations for material things. That way if you receive little, you'll be satisfied with little. That doesn't mean you shouldn't have lofty goals. It simply means your goals should be focused on things that bring God honor.

Truth is, *because He lives* you can be content in Jesus. He said, "Don't worry about these things, saying, 'What will we eat? What will we drink? What will we wear?' These things dominate the thoughts of unbelievers, but your heavenly Father already knows all your needs. Seek the Kingdom of God above all else, and live righteously, and he will give you everything you need" (Matthew 6:31–33). Seek to please Jesus by following in His ways and be grateful for what He provides, and you will experience a sense of inner contentment.

My Prayer: Help me seek You first in my life. I want to be content with what I have. You have already given me so much by forgiving me of my sins, making me a child of God, and giving me eternal life. You are such a generous God. I love You. Amen.

A Courageous Faith

My Bible Reading:

Be on guard. Stand firm in the faith. Be courageous.
Be strong. And do everything with love. (1 Corinthians 16:13–14)

Courage is the quality of persevering through danger, fear, or pain. In scripture you can read about a group of men who lacked courage when they found their lives in danger.

Jesus' disciples were on a boat in the middle of a lake without Jesus. It was night when a storm suddenly swept in. The Gospel of Mark tells us that Jesus "saw that they were in serious trouble, rowing hard and struggling against the wind and waves" (Mark 6:48). So He made His way out to them by walking on the water. " 'Don't be afraid,' he said. 'Take courage! I am here!' Then he climbed into the boat, and the wind stopped" (Mark 6:50–51).

Truth is, *because He lives* you can have a courageous faith. When you have Jesus you can be strong. Jesus is with you to strengthen you in whatever you are facing. "The LORD is a shelter for the oppressed, a refuge in times of trouble" (Psalm 9:9). "The LORD is my strength and shield. I trust him with all my heart. He helps me, and my heart is filled with joy" (Psalm 28:7).

My Prayer: *Thank You that You are with me. When I am facing difficulty remind me that You are here with me. At those times help me call upon You and rely on Your strength as my strength. I can be courageous and stand strong in my faith because of You. I love You. Amen.*

SEPTEMBER

Empowered

The Eternal Spirit

My Bible Reading:
In the beginning God created the heavens and the earth.
The earth was formless and empty, and darkness covered
the deep waters. And the Spirit of God was hovering
over the surface of the waters. (Genesis 1:1-2)

When you think of God, what picture comes to mind? You might picture a majestic being seated on a throne beaming with such radiant light that you can't make out His face. But you call Him God the Father. Or, you might picture a bearded man in a robe and sandals seated on a rock teaching His followers. You call Him Jesus, the Son of God. Yet there is another person of God that some may not picture—the Holy Spirit.

Truth is, the Holy Spirit is the third person of what is called the Trinity. He has coexisted as an eternal equal member of the Godhead. The Spirit of God was there at creation hovering over the earth when Jesus "created everything in the heavenly realms and on earth" (Colossians 1:16). All three persons of the Godhead made themselves known the day John the Baptist baptized Jesus. "As Jesus came up out of the water, the heavens were opened and he [John] saw the Spirit of God descending like a dove and settling on him. And a voice from heaven said, 'This is my dearly loved Son, who brings me great joy' " (Matthew 3:16-17). The Father, Son, and Holy Spirit have always existed together as the Almighty, eternal God.

My Prayer: I may not call You by name when I pray, but You, Holy Spirit, are the one who speaks to me and tells me that I am a child of God. Thank You that You are with me every day to strengthen me and help me become more and more like Jesus. You are a majestic God. Amen.

A Real Person

My Bible Reading:

Jesus said, "When the Spirit of truth comes, he will guide you into all truth.... All that belongs to the Father is mine; this is why I said, 'The Spirit will tell you whatever he receives from me.'" (John 16:13, 15)

Some people say the Holy Spirit is simply the influence of good and not a separate entity or third person of the Trinity. So when scripture speaks about the Holy Spirit, they say it is only God's influence. Yet when Jesus referred to the Holy Spirit He used the pronoun "he." You don't call an influence "he."

Truth is, the Holy Spirit is a real person who acts in unity with God the Father and God the Son. Paul the apostle knew that the Holy Spirit was a real person when he indicated He had a mind, saying, "He who searches our hearts knows the mind of the Spirit" (Romans 8:27 NIV). Also, Peter told Ananias, "'You lied to the Holy Spirit'" (Acts 5:3). Ananias wasn't lying to an influence; he was lying to a person. Peter said to him, "'You weren't lying to us but to God!'" (Acts 5:4).

The Holy Spirit is a real person who reveals the heart of God to you. He is in you to speak to you and "guide you into all truth."

My Prayer: Thank You that I have the Spirit of Truth with me, guiding me to follow in Your ways. I am moved that You, the mighty Creator of the universe, care for me so and help me in my everyday life. You are such a loving God. Help me let others know how faithful and caring You are and that You want everyone to know You and have eternal life in You. Amen.

In Perfect Oneness

My Bible Reading:
"Understand that I alone am God. There is no other God—
there never has been, and there never will be. I, yes, I am
the LORD, and there is no other Savior." (Isaiah 43:10–11)

O ver and over Moses and the prophets declared that there was only
one Almighty God of the universe, who was eternal, all-knowing,
and the ever-present Deity. And while scripture clearly states there is
but one God, it repeatedly explains that He coexists as three divine
persons.

Truth is, there is such infinite love within the three-person Godhead
that it produces a oneness beyond comprehension. In their infinite
love, the three persons of the Trinity are so intent on pleasing one
another that they become one.

Jesus said, " 'The Father and I are one' " (John 10:30). He goes
on to say what this infinite love does to their relationship. " 'I am in
the Father and the Father is in me' " (John 14:11). He's talking about
a perfect oneness, a bonded relationship that actually fuses them
together to the point that Jesus can accurately say, "Anyone who has
seen me has seen the Father!" (John 14:9). And the Holy Spirit is so
in oneness with the Son that Jesus says, " 'He [the Holy Spirit] will
bring me glory by telling you whatever he receives from me' " (John
16:14). The incomprehensible oneness of the Godhead is not so much
a result of God's awesome power as it is the amazing love shared
within the Trinity.

*My Prayer: Thank You for Your love. You show me that it is
Your love for one another that makes You such a unified One
God in three persons. I am so glad You love me with such an
amazing relational love. I want to love You in return with
that same kind of love. You are an astounding God! Amen.*

God as a Verb

My Bible Reading:
Jesus told his disciples, "You will receive power when the
Holy Spirit comes upon you. And you will be my witnesses,
telling people about me everywhere." (Acts 1:8)

L eading up to the death of Jesus, His disciples were frightened
and cowardly. Yet they became bold preachers of Jesus and His
message. The message they declared and those that came after them
resulted in millions of lives being transformed. This didn't happen
just because Jesus' followers decided it was time to stand up for Jesus.

Truth is, God the Holy Spirit was the power at work in the lives of
His followers. As a child of God, you can be sure that He is alive and
at work in your life too. Once Jesus ascended into heaven, the Holy
Spirit became the interactive agent of God to His believers. Jesus said,
" 'The Father sends the Counselor [Holy Spirit] as my representative' "
(John 14:26). Someone has suggested that when God sent His Holy
Spirit, the word *God* was not only a noun—it also became a verb.

The Holy Spirit is the active, moving nature of God that impels you
to action. He is about living, loving, responding, enjoying, embracing,
comforting, supporting, accepting, encouraging, respecting, discipl-
ing, growing, etc. The Holy Spirit is the dynamic, inspiring, and
ever-present One who enables you to experience God in your everyday life.

*My Prayer: Thank You that You sent Your Holy Spirit so that
I can experience You in my life. Help me tell others, even today,
that You are real and alive and that You want people to experience
Your love and forgiveness. You are a God who lived on this earth
and died for sinners, a God who sits in heaven, and a God who is
in this world right now drawing people to You. Help me share
that truth in the power of the Holy Spirit. Amen.*

God in You

My Bible Reading:
If we love each other, God lives in us, and his love is brought
to full expression in us. And God has given us his Spirit
as proof that we live in him and he in us. (1 John 4:12–13)

When you were young, did anyone tell you that you needed to "ask Jesus into your heart"? Some little kids take that literally and think that Jesus lives in their physical hearts. While God the Holy Spirit does not live inside of you physically, He does live in your spiritual heart which is the center of your spiritual being.

Truth is, Jesus said, " 'When I am raised to life again, you will know that I am in my Father, and you are in me, and I am in you' " (John 14:20). And it is God giving you His Holy Spirit that becomes the proof that Jesus lives in your spiritual center or heart. The disciple John wrote how "God's word lives in your hearts" (1 John 2:14). He then said, "You have received the Holy Spirit, and he lives within you" (1 John 2:27).

There is only one way that you can be forgiven of your sins, become a child of God, and have eternal life. The Holy Spirit must enter your life spiritually and make you alive to God. And He can do that because of Christ's death and resurrection on your behalf. The Holy Spirit is like Christ without a body. When you have the Holy Spirit in you it is like having Christ in you. That is why Paul could say, "Christ lives in you, and this is your assurance that you will share in his glory" (Colossians 1:27).

My Prayer: Thank You that You live in my heart! I have trusted in Your death as my sacrifice. I have been buried in Your death and raised to life through Your resurrection. Your Holy Spirit resides within me. And now I am Yours! Help me share this incredible message that a spiritually dead person can be made alive by the power of the Holy Spirit. Amen.

He's the Identifier

My Bible Reading:
When you believed in Christ, he identified
you as his own by giving you the Holy Spirit,
whom he promised long ago. (Ephesians 1:13)

You're going to a concert and stop by the will call window to pick up your tickets. What does the ticket window attendant ask for? Your ID. You're taking a trip and you're going through security at the airport. What does security ask for? Your ID. That laminated piece of paper identifies you as the person you are. But that's not your only ID.

Truth is, you have a spiritual ID that is not a physical laminated piece of paper. Your ID is the Holy Spirit. He is the one who identifies you as God's child. "You received God's Spirit when he adopted you as his own children.... For his Spirit joins with our spirit to affirm [to identify] that we are God's children" (Romans 8:15–16). "He [the Holy Spirit] has identified you as his own" (Ephesians 4:30).

You can wear cool T-shirts that let people know you belong to Jesus. You can put on jewelry that indicates you're a Christian. You can even tell people you are a Christ follower. But your true identity as God's child is within you—He is the Holy Spirit who has given you spiritual life and empowers you to live a godly life.

My Prayer: Thank You that You live in me and have become my spiritual ID. I want Your Spirit to show through my life so that those around me can tell I am Your child by my attitudes and actions. I want my life to be molded into the image of Jesus. Let Your Holy Spirit be at work in and through me today as I show kindness and love to others. Amen.

September 7

He's the Relational Connector

My Bible Reading:
Jesus said, "I am praying not only for these disciples but also for
all who will ever believe in me. . . . My prayer for all of them is that
they will be one, just as you and I are one, Father—that just as you
are in me and I am in you, so they will be in us. . .I in them and
you in me, all being perfected into one." (John 17:20-21, 23)

W hat creates a close, loving connection with another person? Is it
being compatible, or liking the same things, or being attracted
to another's looks? What really makes a relational connection with
another is much deeper than that. Deep relational connections are
about truly knowing another and allowing someone to truly know
you. It's about discovering a person for who he or she truly is and
growing to love that person.

Truth is, having a deep relational connection with God is about
getting to know Him for who He is and inviting Him into every
aspect of your life. Jesus prayed to His Father, " 'This is the way to
have eternal life—to know you, the only true God, and Jesus Christ,
the one you sent to earth' " (John 17:3). God said, " 'I want you to show
love, not offer sacrifices. I want you to know me more than I want
burnt offerings' " (Hosea 6:6). And King David prayed, "Search me,
O God, and know my heart; test me and know my anxious thoughts"
(Psalm 139:23).

The Holy Spirit of God enters your life to reveal the heart of Jesus
to you and He also wants you to open your life to Him. That will
deepen your relationship with God like nothing else will. The Holy
Spirit is your relational connector to God.

*My Prayer: Help me come to know Your true heart. Open Your
Word to me so I can know You. And I really do want to reveal
myself to You. I don't want to try and hide any aspect of myself
from You. I want to know You and I want to allow You to know
the real me. You are such a merciful and loving God. Amen.*

He's Sensitive

My Bible Reading:
Do not bring sorrow to God's Holy Spirit by the way you live.
Remember, he has identified you as his own, guaranteeing that
you will be saved on the day of redemption. (Ephesians 4:30)

Have you ever made someone mad at you for what you've done
or not done? Being human, people may get a little emotional
when you blow it. God has emotions too, like anger. But God's anger
isn't like human anger. His anger is holy, with a holy purpose. Instead
of God striking out at you when you do wrong, He feels sorrow for
what you've done because He knows wrong actions bring painful
consequences.

Truth is, God loves you and doesn't want to see you suffer the consequences of wrong choices. The Holy Spirit is sensitive. The sorrow
He feels when you do wrong motivates Him to correct or discipline
you so you will learn to make right choices. " 'The LORD disciplines
those he loves,' " the scripture says. "God's discipline is always good
for us, so that we might share in his holiness" (Hebrews 12:6, 10).

My Prayer: *That is what I want—I want to share in Your holiness
by thinking and living like Jesus. I want to be like You, and when
I'm not I am honored that You grieve for me. That really tells
me You care and want what is best for me. I want to please You.
I want to follow the leadings of Your Holy Spirit. "Make me walk
along the path of your commands, for that is where my
happiness is found" (Psalm 119:35). Amen.*

September 9

He Prays

The Holy Spirit helps us in our weakness. For example, we don't
know what God wants us to pray for. But the Holy Spirit prays for us
with groanings that cannot be expressed in words. (Romans 8:26)

What do you pray for? There are many kinds of prayers. You
might pray over a meal and thank God for the food you eat.
You might pray that God would help others when they need help.
There are prayers seeking personal forgiveness, prayers for specific
people to come to know Christ, and prayers of thanksgiving to God.
There are many different kinds of prayers.

Truth is, God prays too. Jesus prayed often. He would slip away from
His disciples and spend long periods of time praying to His Father.
Those prayers were not only for His followers at the time He was on
earth; Jesus said they were also for " 'all who will ever believe in me' "
(John 17:20). That includes you. Scripture says, "We have an advocate
with the Father—Jesus Christ, the Righteous One" (1 John 2:1 NIV).
And in your weakness, even when you don't know how to pray or
what to pray for, the Holy Spirit prays for you.

---

*My Prayer: You are not a distant God who is far from me. You are
not a distracted God who is too busy to take notice of me. You are
a caring God who is interested in the details of my life to the point
Your Holy Spirit prays for me. When I think of all You have done for
me, it motivates me to love and serve You more. Help me share with
someone today how grateful I am that You are my God. Amen.*

He's the Gift Giver

My Bible Reading:
There are different kinds of spiritual gifts, but the same Spirit
is the source of them all. There are different kinds of service,
but we serve the same Lord.... It is the one and only Spirit
who distributes all these gifts. He alone decides which gift
each person should have. (1 Corinthians 12:4–5, 11)

What do you look forward to on your birthday? How about Christmas? What do you look forward to on that special day? Gifts! Everyone loves to get gifts. And who gives you the gifts? You probably receive gifts from parents, siblings, grandparents, friends, and maybe even from a special friend. But your loved ones are not the only gift givers.

Truth is, God is the greatest giver of all and it is the Holy Spirit who distributes spiritual gifts. "A spiritual gift is given to each of us so we can help each other" (1 Corinthians 12:7). Those gifts include the gift of encouragement (Romans 12:6, 8), discernment (1 Corinthians 12:7, 10), evangelism (Ephesians 4:7–11), faith (1 Corinthians 12:7, 9), leadership (Romans 12:6, 8), teaching (Romans 12:6–7), administration (1 Corinthians 12:28), and more. Do you know which gifts God has given to you? "God has given each of you a gift from his great variety of spiritual gifts. Use them well to serve one another" (1 Peter 4:10). Right now you may not be able to identify all the gifts the Holy Spirit has given you, but you can rest assured that whatever they are, they are to be used to serve others.

My Prayer: Jesus, help me discover all the gifts the Holy Spirit has given me so I can serve and help those around me. Help me serve someone in my special way through the power of Your Spirit. Let me bring a blessing to someone in need of it this very day. Amen.

He's the Life Changer

My Bible Reading:
The Lord—who is the Spirit—makes us more and more like him
as we are changed into his glorious image. (2 Corinthians 3:18)

One of the things that is fascinating and maybe even frustrating at times, is the process of physically growing into an adult. Your body changes in so many ways. Over a few short years you not only grow taller, but you actually change into a different-looking person. You no longer look like a little kid; you are being shaped into a man or woman.

Truth is, you are being changed spiritually by the Holy Spirit from a person who selfishly lives to please yourself to a person who unselfishly pleases God. "He [Jesus] died for everyone so that those who receive his new life will no longer live to please themselves. Instead, they will live to please Christ" (2 Corinthians 5:15). One of the reasons the Holy Spirit takes up residence in you is so you can get to know Jesus and live an unselfish life like Him. "As we know Jesus better," Peter wrote, "his divine power gives us everything we need for living a godly life" (2 Peter 1:3). Growing up to think like and live like Jesus begins to happen as you live in the power of the Holy Spirit.

My Prayer*: Thank You for Your Holy Spirit that lives within me. I want You to make me more and more like You. Teach me to know You. Teach me to have a Christlike attitude and serve others unselfishly. Let me serve someone today by showing your kind of generous and loving spirit. Amen.*

Who Wants to Drive?

My Bible Reading:
Those who are dominated by the sinful nature think about sinful things, but those who are controlled by the Holy Spirit think about things that please the Spirit. (Romans 8:5)

What's the great thing about being able to drive your own car or truck? It's that you get to go where you want to go and when you want to go! It's about being in control. When you're in the driver's seat you control the place and time of your choosing. That's a great feeling!

Truth is, whoever is in the spiritual driver's seat determines whether you follow the direction of your sinful nature or your spiritual nature. "So I say, let the Holy Spirit guide your lives. Then you won't be doing what your sinful nature craves" (Galatians 5:16). If the Holy Spirit is not in the driver's seat, you cannot very well please Jesus. "But you are not controlled by your sinful nature. You are controlled by the Spirit if you have the Spirit of God living in you.... For all who are led by the Spirit of God are children of God" (Romans 8:9, 14).

It is great to drive a physical car. But when it comes to driving spiritually, it's great to let the Holy Spirit do the driving on a road that leads to a life of joy and fulfillment.

My Prayer: You created me and know best where I was meant to go and what I was meant to be. I want You to do the driving. Help me stay out of the spiritual driver's seat and let You guide me in every aspect of my life. I want to be a true Christ follower. Please keep guiding me. Amen.

He's the Teacher

My Bible Reading:

No one can know a person's thoughts except that person's own spirit, and no one can know God's thoughts except God's own Spirit. And we have received God's Spirit (not the world's spirit), so we can know the wonderful things God has freely given us. (1 Corinthians 2:11–12)

Have you ever had a really great teacher? A great teacher is someone who inspires you with what he or she teaches and motivates you to learn more. Learning is especially a wonderful thing when it unlocks new insights that impact your life in positive ways. When you learned to walk as a child, you were able to get around on your own. Being taught how to read, or mastering a skill, or learning how to be a close friend enhances your life. You can gain so much from those who teach you.

Truth is, you have received the greatest teacher of all—the Holy Spirit. Jesus told His followers that the Holy Spirit would come to live within them and lead them " 'into all truth. . . . He will teach you everything and will remind you of everything I have told you' " (John 14:17, 26). And what is so great is that the Holy Spirit has a language and a vocabulary. He only speaks to you with thoughts and truths that are consistent with God's Word. Scripture "is useful to teach us what is true and to make us realize what is wrong in our lives. It corrects us. . .and teaches us to do what is right" (2 Timothy 3:16). The Holy Spirit is your personal tutor, and the more you know His vocabulary of the Word, the more He can teach you those truths that will positively impact your life.

My Prayer: Thank You that You are my Teacher. I want to hear more from You and follow in Your ways. I want to learn more of Your vocabulary that makes up scripture. Help me be ever sensitive to Your voice and learn from You. Amen.

Be Filled

My Bible Reading:
Jesus said, "Now I will send the Holy Spirit, just as my Father
promised. But stay here in the city until the Holy Spirit
comes and fills you with power from heaven." (Luke 24:49)

Jesus' disciples were not a very brave group. When Jesus was
taken away to be crucified, all of them scattered. They were afraid
and confused. Even after Jesus rose from the dead, they still didn't
understand God's plan. That's why Jesus told them to wait, because
" 'you will receive power when the Holy Spirit comes upon you. And
you will be my witnesses, telling people about me everywhere' "
(Acts 1:8). It wasn't long after Jesus ascended to heaven that the
Holy Spirit came and filled His disciples.

Truth is, God has sent His Holy Spirit to dwell in every Jesus follower.
Paul told Christ followers not to "be drunk with wine, because that
will ruin your life. Instead be filled with the Holy Spirit, singing
psalms and hymns and spiritual songs among yourselves. . . . And
give thanks for everything to God" (Ephesians 5:18–20).

As a child of God you have the Spirit of Christ in you. Inviting
Him to fill every part of you will assure "that Christ will be more and
more at home in your hearts" (Ephesians 3:17 NLT). He wants you to
feel His presence every day in every circumstance of your life.

My Prayer: *Lord, I want all of You and I want You to have all
of me. Fill me afresh today. I don't want to hold any of my life
from You. Fill me with Your Holy Spirit and live through me so
that I can be a shining witness of Your love to those around
me. Thank You for the great gift of Your Spirit. Amen.*

He Produces Good Fruit

My Bible Reading:
Jesus said, "Remain in me, and I will remain in you. For
a branch cannot produce fruit if it is severed from the vine,
and you cannot be fruitful unless you remain in me." (John 15:4)

Did you ever have someone treat you nicely and then find out later he or she wasn't being nice at all—that, in fact, you were being used? Someone invites you to a party and asks you to also bring your brother or sister with you. Then you find out that all the person really wanted was for your sibling to show up. When good works (what can be called good fruit) are selfishly motivated they turn out to be bad fruit.

Truth is, it is human nature to be selfish. And left to your own devices you are bound to produce bad fruit. Jesus was saying that apart from Him you can't really produce His kind of good fruit. He's the vine and when you allow Him to remain in you and you in Him, through the power of the Holy Spirit He produces good fruit. That's what He wants you to do. " 'I appointed you,' " Jesus said, " 'to go and produce lasting fruit' " (John 15:16).

My Prayer: I confess, I do tend to think I can do a lot of good things on my own. Help me see You as the vine through which all my strength comes to produce good fruit. You are right; I can't really do anything unselfish apart from You. Let Your unselfish love and care for others flow through me today. Help me give of myself to encourage, strengthen, or lift someone up. Let Your unselfish goodness become my unselfish goodness so that I can produce lasting, good fruit. Amen.

You Complete Me

My Bible Reading:
Jesus said, "As the Father has loved me, so have I loved you.
Now remain in my love. . . . I have told you this so that my joy may
be in you and that your joy may be complete." (John 15:9, 11 NIV)

There was a mystery to their attraction. She sensed an indefinable longing to know more than what she could physically see. . .and so did he. They were both drawn to a deeper relationship that would connect and bond them together. It seemed as though they were both created with half a heart that was meant to become one. When he proposed marriage to her, she looked deeply into his eyes and said, "Yes, for you complete me!" When two people truly love one another, they do emotionally complete each other.

Truth is, God sent the Holy Spirit not only to give you spiritual life, but also to complete you. You were created in God's image, and as you become intimate with God through His Holy Spirit, you begin to live as God intended and you become the person God designed. Paul said, "It's in Christ that we find out who we are and what we are living for" (Ephesians 1:11 MSG). Through the power of the Holy Spirit, He puts you on a journey to discover your true meaning and purpose in life.

My Prayer*: Thank You for creating me in Your image and loving me. It is like I have become spiritually married to You because You are the great "completer" to life. Help me keep discovering You more and more each day. You bring true meaning and completion to my life. Amen.*

A Never-Ending Conflict

My Bible Reading:
The Spirit gives us desires that are opposite from what
the sinful nature desires. These two forces are constantly
fighting each other, and your choices are never free
from this conflict. (Galatians 5:17)

Y ou realized you were a sinner and you asked God to forgive you. You trusted in Jesus as your sacrifice for sin and accepted Him as your Savior. You received His Holy Spirit who confirmed you were now a new person, alive to God and one of His children. So does that make you perfect? Do you no longer struggle with your sinful, selfish nature?

Truth is, since you have trusted in Christ and received the Holy Spirit, you have been given a spiritual nature. But your selfish, sinful nature is still around. The apostle Paul was one of the most mature Christians to ever live. He said he had come to spiritually know Christ and experienced the power of His resurrection. Yet he said, "I don't mean to say that I have already achieved these things or that I have already reached perfection! But I keep working toward that day when I will finally be all that Christ Jesus saved me for and wants me to be" (Philippians 3:12).

Paul wasn't perfect, but he knew whom he was following. He continually sought to follow his spiritual nature rather than his sinful nature. You will always have your sinful nature to contend with, but the Holy Spirit is in you to empower you to follow your spiritual nature.

My Prayer: Thank You that You have given me a spiritual nature. I need Your constant help to resist my selfish nature and follow You. Help me keep looking to You and Your Word for guidance and strength. I want to keep yielding to Your Spirit and become more and more like You. Amen.

Deny Yourself

My Bible Reading:
Jesus said, "Whoever wants to be my disciple must deny themselves and take up their cross daily and follow me." (Luke 9:23 NIV)

Every athlete who wins, every Olympic gold medalist, or every body builder knows this one thing. They must deny themselves to become winners. There are diets to maintain. There are strict regimens to be kept. There are disciplines to follow. Denying themselves certain foods and pleasures is part of the price to achieve success. No pain, no gain.

Truth is, following Jesus and your spiritual nature requires denying your selfish nature. But just like with physical discipline there is great reward for denying your selfishness. Jesus said, " 'If you try to keep your life for yourself, you will lose it. But if you give up your [selfish] life for me, you will find true life' " (Luke 9:24). Saying no to your selfish nature doesn't feel good at the moment. There is pain in not getting what you want when you want it. But as you follow Jesus, the One who loves you more than you can fathom, you discover what true living is all about.

My Prayer: I know my selfish desires don't get me what I need or really want. Selfish living isn't fulfilling in the long run. Help me sense that when I start to be selfish. Prompt me with Your Holy Spirit and remind me that by denying my selfishness I find the way of true life. You gave so much for me. I want to give my life back to You. Jesus, You are so worthy of my devotion and praise. Amen.

Crucified

My Bible Reading:

Those who belong to Christ Jesus have nailed the passions and desires of their sinful nature to his cross and crucified them there. Since we are living by the Spirit, let us follow the Spirit's leading in every part of our lives. (Galatians 5:24–25)

The powerful God of the universe cannot be defeated by anyone or anything. He is invincible! So as a human being, didn't Jesus have that kind of power? Men arrested Him, beat Him, mocked and spat on Him, and then crucified Him. Where was His power when He needed it? Couldn't He have resisted them?

Yes, He had that kind of power, but He didn't use it. Jesus' followers drew their swords to resist His arrest. Yet Jesus told them to put their swords away. He said, " 'Don't you realize that I could ask my Father for thousands of angels to protect us, and he would send them instantly?' " (Matthew 26:53). He also said, " 'No one can take my life from me. I sacrifice it voluntarily' " (John 10:18).

Truth is, a powerful and almighty Jesus sacrificed Himself voluntarily because He loved you. He gave His life so you could live. That's what love does—it sacrifices itself for others. When you crucify your selfish nature for Jesus and for others, you are demonstrating real love too. "Live a life filled with love," Paul wrote, "following the example of Christ. He loved us and offered himself as a sacrifice for us" (Ephesians 5:2). When you follow the Spirit's leadings and give up yourself for others, He is honored and you are blessed.

My Prayer: Thank You for sacrificing Yourself for me. I want to follow in Your steps and nail my selfish desires to Your cross and love others unselfishly. Help me do that today. Help me give unselfishly of my time, energy, and finances to those in need. Amen.

Dead yet Alive

My Bible Reading:
My old self has been crucified with Christ. It is no longer I who live, but Christ lives in me. So I live in this earthly body by trusting in the Son of God, who loved me and gave himself for me. (Galatians 2:20)

Before the apostle Paul miraculously met Jesus he put all his energy in just being a rule keeper. He strictly followed the Jewish laws of scripture. He thought that following the law and doing good deeds was the way to heaven. But once he met Jesus he realized that his old self, even all his good work efforts, had to be nailed to the cross. That is when he came alive in Christ and it was the Spirit of Christ that empowered him to live like Jesus.

Truth is, it takes dying to your selfish nature, even to your good works, to begin to live. As you die to your selfish ambitions, desires, and dreams, the power of selfishness loses its grip over you—and that's when you really begin to live. "We know that our old sinful selves," Paul said, "were crucified with Christ so that sin might lose its power in our lives. We are no longer slaves to sin. For when we died with Christ we were set free from the power of sin" (Romans 6:6–7).

My Prayer: Thank You that You live in me. I know that as I continually die to my selfishness, You empower me to live and love like You. The power to live like You comes from Your Spirit. Help me go to Your Word for strength and understanding of You. You are a merciful and loving God. I love You. Amen.

September 21

When You Fail

My Bible Reading:
You do not desire a sacrifice, or I would offer one. You do not want
a burnt offering. The sacrifice you desire is a broken spirit. You will
not reject a broken and repentant heart, O God. (Psalm 51:16–17)

Die to your selfishness. Don't rely on your good works. Focus on
Jesus. Yield to the Holy Spirit and allow Him to control you.
These may all be the right things to do, but who can do them all the
time? No one is perfect, right? People are bound to fail in allowing
the Holy Spirit to empower them to live more and more like Jesus.

Truth is, when you fail, God is not looking for you to make it up by
doing more good works. That's what King David meant when he said
that God didn't want "sacrifices" and "burnt offerings." What God
wants when you fail is a broken spirit. He wants a heart that says "I'm
sorry." Scripture says, "If we confess our sins to him, he is faithful and
just to forgive us our sins" (1 John 1:9). God loves a repentant heart
and He will never fail to forgive. "Your unfailing love will last forever.
Your faithfulness is as enduring as the heavens" (Psalm 89:2).

---

*My Prayer: You are a God of love and mercy. When I fail,
help me see You as a compassionate Father who wants to
pick me up, love me, forgive me, and empower me to live more
like Jesus. Keep my heart tender and help me seek Your
forgiveness when I blow it. Thank You for loving me so. I love You. Amen.*

The Way to Worship Him

My Bible Reading:
Give your bodies to God because of all he has done for you.
Let them be a living and holy sacrifice—the kind he will find
acceptable. This is truly the way to worship him. (Romans 12:1)

You may think of worship as singing and praising God in a group setting and that is true. Yet true worship is giving all of yourself—your talents and gifts and abilities—to God to be used for His glory. But what if you feel you don't have a lot of that to give? What if you think you have more limitations than anything else?

Truth is, giving God whatever you are and have, even all of your limitations and weaknesses, is good enough for God. The apostle Paul was struggling with his weaknesses and God told him, "'My grace is all you need. My power works best in weakness.' So now I am glad to boast about my weaknesses, so that the power of Christ can work through me. . . . For when I am weak, then I am strong" (2 Corinthians 12:9-10).

God wants you to rely on Him. He wants to be needed. When you rely on yourself, it's like telling Him you're strong enough and you really don't need Him that much. He loves it when you admit your own weakness and ask for His help. "'God blesses those who are poor and realize their need for him'" (Matthew 5:3).

My Prayer: Lord, I guess I have a combination of strengths and weaknesses. But I give them all to You. I want Your power to work through me. I do realize my need for You. Help me keep sensing that so I can keep depending on You as my power source. You are such an exemplary and loving God. Amen.

Learn from Me

My Bible Reading:
"Come to me, all you who are weary and burdened,
and I will give you rest. Take my yoke upon you and
learn from me, for I am gentle and humble in heart,
and you will find rest for your souls." (Matthew 11:28–29 NIV)

Back in Jesus' day farmers used oxen or horses to plant their fields. They would often hitch two animals together in a yoke for plowing the ground. The yoke was made of two U-shaped attachments fastened side by side to a contoured wooden crossbar. This formed a harness that fit over the necks of the two animals so they would be linked together. That's the picture Jesus had in mind when He said, " 'Take my yoke upon you and learn from me' "

Truth is, Jesus, through the power of the Holy Spirit, is inviting you to be yoked with Him. He wants you to be joined, connected, and so bonded together that you learn from Him. As a Christ follower you have a new nature, but you need to be taught how to think, feel, and act. And the Spirit of Christ is yoked with you to teach and empower you to be like Him. "You have stripped off your old evil nature," Paul wrote. "In its place you have clothed yourselves with a brand-new nature that is continually being renewed as you learn more and more about Christ" (Colossians 3:9–10). As you know Jesus more intimately, His "divine power gives [you] everything [you] need for living a godly life" (2 Peter 1:3).

My Prayer: I accept Your invitation. I want to be yoked with You so closely that I learn how to be patient, kind, gentle, forgiving, caring, and loving like You are. Let some of Your kindness flow through me to someone today. Amen.

First from Him

My Bible Reading:
We know how much God loves us, and we have put our trust in him.
God is love, and all who live in love live in God. . . . We love each
other as a result of his loving us first. (1 John 4:16, 19)

How did you learn to talk? You didn't create sounds that formed words out of nowhere. Today you are able to speak because your parents or someone else taught you by speaking to you.

How did you learn to read? You didn't just look at words on a page and figure out what they meant by yourself. You read today because someone taught you how.

How do you learn to be and act like Jesus? How do you become patient, kind, forgiving, good, gentle, and loving to others like Jesus? Do you just read the Bible and try hard to be like Him?

Truth is, you can love like Jesus does when you have received Jesus' love through the power of the Holy Spirit. When you experience God's forgiveness, you are empowered to forgive others. When you experience Jesus' patience, comfort, kindness, and gentleness, you are empowered to be patient, comforting, kind, and gentle to others. As you receive and experience all the goodness from God the Holy Spirit, you become a conduit of His goodness to others. That is how Paul could say, "I can do everything through Christ who gives me strength" (Philippians 4:13).

*My Prayer: Lord, I want to be more of a conduit of Your love
and goodness to others. Help me openly receive more
from You so I can give more to others. I can truly love others
because You loved me first. Thank You for that. Amen.*

September 25

His Comfort—My Comfort

My Bible Reading:
God is our merciful Father and the source of all comfort.
He comforts us in all our troubles so that we can
comfort others. (2 Corinthians 1:3-4)

Imagine that one of your friends is really hurting emotionally. This person's parents just divorced and the parent who has custody is moving out of the area. This means the student must leave the only friends he or she has and move to a strange place. How do you feel toward your friend? This person needs comfort. Do you have comfort to offer?

Truth is, when you experience God's comfort, you are empowered to offer comfort to others. When you've been down and in need of comfort, God has been there for you. And because God has comforted you, Paul explains that when other people need comfort, "We will be able to give them the same comfort God has given us" (2 Corinthians 1:4).

Jesus was known for His compassionate heart. Time after time He was moved with compassion. Today He is there for you with compassion to comfort you when you're down. And He is also there to empower you to comfort others with a compassionate heart. Paul asked Jesus' followers, "Are your hearts tender and compassionate? Then make me truly happy by agreeing wholeheartedly with each other, loving one another, and working together with one mind and purpose" (Philippians 2:1-2).

My Prayer: You are the God of compassion and comfort.
Thank You for being there for me when I've so needed You.
And thank You for empowering me with Your compassion and
comfort so that I can be there for someone in need. You are my
source of comfort. Let me be Your channel of comfort for others. Amen.

His Patience—My Patience

My Bible Reading:
The Holy Spirit produces this kind of fruit in our lives:
love, joy, peace, patience, kindness, goodness, faithfulness,
gentleness, and self-control. (Galatians 5:22–23)

You're waiting on your friend to pick you up for an important meeting. You don't want to be late, yet your friend has been late on more than one occasion. And today is no different. Do you get impatient? Being patient with people, especially with those who repeatedly fail to keep their commitments, is not easy. Yet the Holy Spirit is there in your life to produce patience. How?

Truth is, when you experience Jesus' patience, you are empowered to be patient with others. "May the Lord lead your hearts into full understanding and expression of the love of God," Paul wrote, "and the patient endurance that comes from Christ" (2 Thessalonians 3:5). You have no doubt failed more than once. And how does Jesus respond to you in your failures? With a compassionate and understanding heart He says, *"I know it's hard and you're not perfect. But you love Me and you're becoming like Me even though it's taking some time. I'm a patient God and I love you so."*

As you receive Jesus' patience, you are empowered to pass that patience on to others. "May God, who gives this patience and encouragement, help you live in complete harmony with each other" (Romans 15:5).

My Prayer: Thank You that You are so patient with me. I blow it and yet You don't give up on me. Help me make Your patience toward me my patience toward others. You are my source of patience. Lead me to someone who needs patience and let me demonstrate the patience I've received from You. Amen.

His Forgiveness—My Forgiveness

My Bible Reading:
Make allowance for each other's faults, and forgive
anyone who offends you. Remember, the Lord forgave you,
so you must forgive others. (Colossians 3:13)

Someone lied about you and as a result you didn't get invited to
a party. When you found out, it angered you a little. And to top
it off, this person has not apologized to you at all. It's hard to make
allowances for someone like that. So do you forgive that person
anyway or do you hold a grudge?

Truth is, when you experience God's forgiveness, you are empowered
to forgive others even before they ask for it. Before you were born,
before you ever sinned, Jesus died for you. So as soon as you sinned
and before you asked for it, Jesus' forgiveness was available to you.
That is the kind of God He is. The prophet wrote, " 'You are a God of
forgiveness' " (Nehemiah 9:17). The Psalmist said, "O Lord, you are so
good, so ready to forgive" (Psalm 86:5). Because you have experienced
Jesus' forgiving heart, you can offer forgiveness to those who don't
even ask for it.

God forgiving you and you forgiving others sets up a cycle of forgiveness. Jesus said, " 'Forgive others, and you will be forgiven. Give,
and you will receive' " (Luke 6:37–38). And since you have received
forgiveness, you can keep on forgiving others.

---

*My Prayer: Thank You that You have such a willing heart to
forgive. When others offend me, help me remember I have
experienced Your forgiveness over and over again. Allow
Your power of forgiveness to become my source of forgiveness.
Help me maintain a heart of forgiveness like Yours. Amen.*

His Kindness—My Kindness

My Bible Reading:

Be done with all deceit, hypocrisy, jealousy, and all unkind speech. Like newborn babies, you must crave pure spiritual milk so that you will grow.... Cry out for this nourishment, now that you have had a taste of the Lord's kindness. (1 Peter 2:1–3)

Words can hurt. The hateful and mean words of a bully can emotionally scar a person. Have you ever been tempted to say mean things to someone? Maybe you've felt the sharp sting of hateful and unkind words thrown at you by others.

Truth is, when you experience God's kindness, you are empowered to express kindness toward others. You have sinned. You have fallen short of God's standard of rightness. But through Jesus, "God in his gracious kindness declares [you] not guilty" (Romans 3:24). At the core of God's heart you will find pure kindness. It is a heart that is warm, full of grace and caring. In loving kindness God "cares about what happens to you" (1 Peter 5:7).

It may seem at times that some people don't deserve kindness. But as you experience Jesus' kindness that wasn't deserved—which is grace—you discover that you are able to express His kindness to others.

My Prayer: You have been so kind to me, so loving and full of grace. I haven't deserved it, yet You have shown me nothing but love. Allow that truth to soak into my mind and heart so it will empower me to show kindness and grace to all those around me. You are my source of kindness. Help me be kind today, even to those who are unkind. Amen.

His Gentleness—My Gentleness

My Bible Reading:
For jealousy and selfishness are not God's kind of wisdom. . . . But
the wisdom from above is first of all pure. It is also peace loving,
gentle at all times, and willing to yield to others. (James 3:15, 17)

Have you ever run into a person who is critical, insensitive, harsh, and abrasive? When a person like that expresses his or her opinion it is often in a belligerent tone that expresses disrespect for others. Maybe you've met some people like that. Do you tend to listen carefully to them and want to learn more of what they have to say? Not likely.

Truth is, when you experience God's gentleness, you are empowered to express gentleness to others. Actually, you learn best from those who show respect for you and are gentle at heart. As Jesus invites you to take His yoke upon you, He says, " 'Learn from me, for I am gentle and humble in heart' " (Matthew 11:29 NIV). He is the master teacher. His Holy Spirit never pushes but leads you into all truth with a gentle and humble heart.

As you experience the Holy Spirit's gentle leading you are not only empowered to express gentleness with others, but you are also able to share effectively your hope in Jesus. Peter said, "If someone asks about your hope as a believer, always be ready to explain it. But do this in a gentle and respectful way" (1 Peter 3:15–16). God's truth is most powerful when it is shared with conviction from a gentle and respectful heart toward others.

My Prayer*: Your gentle and humble heart humbles me.
Thank You that You are a gentle Savior. You are my source
of gentleness. Help me share Your truth with others with
gentleness and respect. Let me do that even today. Amen.*

Better than Life Itself

My Bible Reading:
Your unfailing love is better than life itself; how I praise you!
I will praise you as long as I live, lifting up my
hands to you in prayer. (Psalm 63:3-4)

What can be better than life itself? Living is everything, isn't it? What King David was saying is that mere living isn't enough. No one can truly find meaning, purpose, and fulfillment in life just by living. It takes relationships, and the highest quality of life is found in a deepening relationship with God.

Truth is, the only way a close relationship with God is possible is through the power of the Holy Spirit that He has given you. He has made His home in you to reveal Himself to you and to give you everything necessary to be made complete in Him. That is why Paul said, "I pray that Christ will be more and more at home in your hearts . . .as you trust in him" (Ephesians 3:17 TLB).

My Prayer: I want You to be more and more at home in my heart. I make Paul's prayer for all the followers of Jesus my personal prayer. May my roots "grow down into God's love and keep [me] strong. And may [I] have the power to understand, as all God's people should, how wide, how long, how high, and how deep his love is. May [I] experience the love of Christ, though it is too great to understand fully. Then [I] will be made complete with all the fullness of life and power that comes from God" (Ephesians 3:17-19). You, O Lord, are my true source of power and loving relationships! I love You. Amen.

OCTOBER

How You View the World

October 1

An Alien

My Bible Reading:
Jesus was asked if he was the King of the Jews. He said,
"My Kingdom is not an earthly kingdom. If it were, my followers
would fight to keep me from being handed over to the Jewish
leaders. But my Kingdom is not of this world." (John 18:36)

The saucer-shaped aircraft lands on your front lawn. Highly
intelligent alien life-forms step out and begin asking you questions. They want to know all about you—what you do and why you
do it. As aliens they have a totally different view of your world than
you do.

Truth is, Jesus too had a totally different view of this world than those
around Him. He saw this world through His Godly spiritual nature.
What He saw was a sinful world doomed to death and destruction.
And He had come to make it known "that everyone who believes in
him will not perish but have eternal life" (John 3:16). That singular
truth gave Jesus a totally different worldview than everyone else. So
when a Roman leader asked, " 'So you are a king?' Jesus responded,
'You say I am a king. Actually, I was born and came into the world to
testify to the truth. All who love the truth recognize that what I say is
true' " (John 18:37).

Because you have accepted Jesus as the Truth and follow Him, you
too see the world differently. You see life through a spiritual lens that
makes you sort of like an alien. As Jesus said, " 'They [His followers]
do not belong to this world any more than I do' " (John 17:16).

---

*My Prayer: You have made me alive to You and I do see life
differently. You have changed my value system. I want You
to be first in my life so I can love and accept others as You
have loved and accepted me. Help me to live this out even
today as I make others a priority in my life. Amen.*

At War

My Bible Reading:
We are not fighting against flesh-and-blood enemies,
but against evil rulers and authorities of the unseen world,
against mighty powers in this dark world, and against evil
spirits in the heavenly places. (Ephesians 6:12)

D o you know of anyone who has fought in a war? Maybe a family member years ago served in the armed forces. Wars have been fought over the centuries for many reasons resulting in millions and millions of deaths. War has been a part of this world from almost the beginning of civilization.

Truth is, you are in a war right now. It isn't a physical war with guns or fighter jets, drones and bombs. It is a spiritual war between God and His ways and Satan and his ways. And as a follower of Jesus you are fighting this war alongside Christ. "We know that we are children of God," John wrote, "and that the world around us is under the control of the evil one" (1 John 5:19). And together with Christ this spiritual war will be won. "For Christ must reign until he humbles all his enemies beneath his feet. . . . Then, when all things are under his authority, the Son will put himself under God's authority, so that God, who gave his Son authority over all things, will be utterly supreme over everything everywhere" (1 Corinthians 15:25, 28). With Christ you are on the winning side.

My Prayer: Thank You that You will one day defeat Satan for good. And help me engage in this spiritual battle by being a witness for You and allowing Your love for others to be part of my life. Let me this very day show love and kindness to someone and strike a blow against the enemy. Amen.

Confused about the Kingdom

My Bible Reading:
After Jesus rose from the dead, he proved to them [his followers]
in many ways that he was actually alive. And he talked to them
about the Kingdom of God. . . . So when the apostles were with
Jesus, they kept asking him, "Lord, has the time come for you
to free Israel and restore our kingdom?" (Acts 1:3, 6)

When Jesus was on earth, the Jewish people were under the
rule of the Romans. They were looking for their Messiah to
break the power of Roman domination and restore their kingdom.
And it must have been a bit confusing when Jesus didn't establish
an earthly kingdom before or even after He rose from the dead. They
had their hearts set on being free of Roman oppression.

Truth is, Jesus did come to set people free from oppression—the
oppression of sin. "Once you were slaves of sin," Paul wrote. But
because Christ came, died, and rose again, "you are free from your
slavery to sin, and you have become slaves to righteous living"
(Romans 6:17-18). Jesus was the Messiah who came to free all who
trust in Him from the slavery of sin. And instead of an earthly kingdom Jesus focused His followers on a heavenly Kingdom. That's why
Jesus said, " 'Don't store up treasures here on earth where moths eat
them and rust destroys them. . . . [Instead] store your treasures in
heaven' " (Matthew 6:19-20).

---

*My Prayer: Thank You for coming to establish Your Kingdom of
heaven in my life by dying for me and setting me free from sin and
death. Help me keep focused on the relational and spiritual treasures
that are truly valuable and will last forever. Let me build up some
treasures today by sharing Your love with those around me. Amen.*

The Kingdom Message

My Bible Reading:
On the first day of Jesus' public ministry he began to preach, "Repent of your sins and turn to God, for the Kingdom of Heaven is near".... [And from that point on] Jesus traveled throughout the region of Galilee, teaching in the synagogues and announcing the Good News about the Kingdom. (Matthew 4:17, 23)

The Kingdom truth Jesus spread was truly radical. It wasn't about power and politics, earthly authorities and thrones, or a permanent homeland and occupied territories. His Kingdom message was about the heart and the sin nature, attitudes and actions, love and relationships. Jesus said love your enemy. He explained you must die to live, give in order to get, bow down in order to rise up, be last in order to be first. It didn't make sense to a lot of people then, and it doesn't make sense to a lot of people now.

Truth is, Jesus' Kingdom message is a whole new way to see God, yourself, life, and relationships. It is a view of the world defined by Jesus and His Word. He said, " 'You must love the LORD your God with all your heart, all your soul, and all your mind.... [And] love your neighbor as yourself' " (Matthew 22:37–39). Loving God and making Him the first priority in your life develops a Kingdom mindset that brings everything into perspective—love God and those around you as you love yourself.

My Prayer: Thank You for Your Kingdom message that is all throughout Your Word. Help me study and know Your Word so I can better live out Your Kingdom message of loving unselfishly just as You do. Help me love others that way today. Amen.

Not Understood

My Bible Reading:

We have received God's Spirit (not the world's spirit), so we can know the wonderful things God has freely given us. . . . But people who aren't spiritual can't receive these truths from God's Spirit. It all sounds foolish to them and they can't understand it, for only those who are spiritual can understand what the Spirit means. (1 Corinthians 2:12, 14)

Have you ever tried to speak to someone who didn't speak your language? Your words didn't make sense to the person, did they? And that's understandable.

People who have not trusted in Christ and received God's Spirit may not make sense of the Kingdom truths that you share with them. What you believe and how you live may actually seem foolish to some. And that's understandable too. Because it takes a person who is spiritually in tune with God to understand what the Spirit means.

Truth is, Jesus wasn't understood by most of the people He spoke to either. In fact "he came into the very world he created, but the world didn't recognize him. He came to his own people, and even they rejected him" (John 1:10–11). When you're not understood by those who are not spiritual, take heart; you're in good company. Jesus said, " 'If the world hates you, remember that it hated me first. The world would love you as one of its own if you belonged to it, but you are no longer part of the world' " (John 15:18–19).

My Prayer: Thank You that You have given me Your Spirit and I have a spiritual view of life. When people reject me or don't understand me because I am Your follower, help me remember that it is because I belong to You and not to this world. And also help me return love in the face of ridicule and give out kindness in the face of rejection. Thank You for loving me and always being with me. Amen.

Kingdom Come Soon

My Bible Reading:
Jesus said, "Pray like this: Our Father in heaven, may your name be kept holy. May your Kingdom come soon." (Matthew 6:9–10)

Someone very wise once stated that all misunderstandings are a result of differing assumptions. And one of the most significant misunderstandings Jesus' disciples had about Him was because of a differing assumption. They assumed that Jesus was going to establish His earthly kingdom right then and there. However, His plan was for His followers to establish His kingdom in the hearts of men and women once He went back to His Father.

Truth is, you are helping to establish God's Kingdom on a spiritual level here and now as you live a godly life and become a witness for Christ. You are "Christ's ambassadors; God is making his appeal through [you]" (2 Corinthians 5:20). It is your life of goodness and love that draws others to Jesus. Your words to others about Jesus are important, but it is your Christlike life that makes those words powerful. "For the Kingdom of God is not a matter of what we eat or drink [or religious rules], but of living a life of goodness and peace and joy in the Holy Spirit" (Romans 14:17).

Jesus' next words to His Father following His prayer that God's "Kingdom come soon," were "May your will be done on earth, as it is in heaven" (Matthew 6:10). As you do God's will, you become a living example of the Kingdom of God to all those around you. That means you are helping to fulfill Jesus' prayer to advance God's Kingdom.

My Prayer: Thank You for making me a part of helping to bring Your Kingdom to the hearts and minds of those around me. Let Your will be done in my life today as I live "a life of goodness and peace and joy in the Holy Spirit" in front of my friends (Romans 14:17). Help me let others know I really care about them. Amen.

How Do You View God?

My Bible Reading:
Long ago you [God] laid the foundation of the earth and
made the heavens with your hands. They will perish,
but you remain forever. (Psalm 102:25–26)

Your view of God affects how you view yourself, others, and what you consider to be real and valuable in life. There are some who believe that God does not exist, or if He does, He doesn't concern Himself with human beings. Their view of themselves and life is drastically different from yours.

Truth is, because you believe in God, you see life and relationships coming out of the nature and character of a relational God who created you as a relational being. Your world of reality then exists because of God. As a Christian you believe that "Christ is the visible image of the invisible God. . . . Everything was created through him and for him. He existed before anything else, and he holds all creation together" (Colossians 1:15–17).

Because you view a relational God as Creator of all, your view of the world is uniquely a biblical worldview. This means you see a God who honors you enough to give you the right to choose Him and His ways. He is a God who values your creativity and sense of responsibility. He has given you relationship with others and a world to nurture and care for. He loves you and gives you the capacity to love Him and other human beings.

My Prayer: You are a gracious God who has given me so much. Thank You for life, this wonderful planet, and the capacity to love You and others. Thank You for giving me that reality. Amen.

Why We Worship

My Bible Reading:
"You must worship no other gods, for the LORD,
whose very name is Jealous, is a God who is jealous
about his relationship with you." (Exodus 34:14)

Have you ever felt jealous? Maybe someone was jealous of you. Jealousy is normally not thought of as a good thing. But when it comes to God being jealous, it's really a good thing. God said of Himself, " 'I, the LORD your God, am a jealous God' " (Exodus 20:5). The word *jealous* denotes passion and zeal. It conveys the idea of a passionate caring that wants only the best for another person.

Truth is, God wants you to worship Him and only Him because that is what is best for you. God " 'himself gives life and breath to everything, and he satisfies every need. . . . For in him we live and move and exist' " (Acts 17:25, 28). He is the only one who can truly satisfy your soul. He knows that when you love and worship Him exclusively—with all your heart, soul, and strength—it allows you to experience the joy and meaning you are looking for in life. And when God allows you to experience negative consequences for not loving Him exclusively, that is His discipline of love. He wants you to delight in all the joy that comes with putting Him first and worshipping Him and only Him. That is more than a good reason to worship God.

My Prayer: *You are the Almighty God who created me and loved me enough to send Jesus to die so that I could live. You are worthy of my worship. I know Your command for me to worship You is because You want me to be filled with the joy of the Lord. Your love is beyond my comprehension. I bow down in worship of You, not out of fear, but out of love and devotion to You. Amen.*

The Domino Effect of Worship

My Bible Reading:
If someone says, "I love God," but hates a fellow believer, that person
is a liar; for if we don't love people we can see, how can we love God,
whom we cannot see? And he has given us this command: Those who
love God must also love their fellow believers. (1 John 4:20–21)

Have you ever seen someone set up rows of dominoes for the purpose of watching them topple one by one until all have fallen over? Maybe you've done that yourself. Well, there's a domino effect in worshipping God too.

Truth is, if you truly love and worship God, it will spill over into loving yourself and others. Worshipping and loving God naturally lead to caring for yourself. "Your body is the temple of the Holy Spirit. . . . So you must honor God with your body" (1 Corinthians 6:19–20). That's why you avoid such things as sexual immorality and illegal drugs. Worshipping and loving God also lead to loving " 'your neighbor as yourself' " (Matthew 22:39). That means promoting things like social justice, taking care of the sick, meeting the needs of the less fortunate, defending the God-given rights of others, and protecting the innocent. Your worship and love of God have a domino effect in loving and caring for others. That is why the disciple James wrote, "Pure and genuine religion in the sight of God the Father means caring for orphans and widows in their distress and refusing to let the world corrupt you" (James 1:27).

*My Prayer: Because I love and worship You, I want Your love
to overflow from my life to those around me. Give me more of
Your compassionate heart to meet the needs of the needy.
Let me care more for those who are hurting. Even today let me
touch a life with the kind of love You have given me. Amen.*

How Do You View Scripture?

My Bible Reading:
Above all, you must realize that no prophecy in Scripture ever
came from the prophet's own understanding, or from human
initiative. No, those prophets were moved by the Holy Spirit,
and they spoke from God. (2 Peter 1:20–21)

There are thousands of religions in the world. Demographic studies show that less than one-third of the world's population is Christian. The rest of the world is Muslim, Hindu, Buddhist, Jewish, and a myriad of other religions. That means that over half the world's population turns to some source other than the Judeo-Christian scriptures for teaching about their religion. So isn't it rather narrow-minded to think that the Christian Bible is the only reliable source to know God?

Half of the world's population doesn't even believe in the God of the Christian Bible, so do you claim that the Bible reveals the only one and true religion?

Truth is, you don't have to make that claim, because the Creator God has already done so. The Bible isn't so much a book about a specific religion. It is a written revelation to all humanity from the Creator of the universe. " 'I alone am God!' " He stated to the prophet Isaiah. " 'I am God, and there is none like me' " (Isaiah 46:9). The Bible is a historically reliable document that gives you a complete narrative of the story of humanity, what went wrong, and how a loving God set forth a plan to redeem the fallen human race and restore everything to His original design. The one and only Almighty God has revealed Himself to you through His reliable Word, the Bible. Accept that and you are on your way to fully embracing the biblical worldview.

My Prayer: You are the God of Abraham, Isaac, and Jacob. You spoke through Moses, the prophets, and the apostles to compile Your Word. And I believe Your Word is alive today to speak to me through Your Holy Spirit. Thank You for miraculously preserving the holy scriptures so that I could know You. You are an awe-inspiring God! Amen.

God Says, "Know Me"

My Bible Reading:

Jesus said to His followers, "You are permitted to understand the secrets of the Kingdom of Heaven, but others are not. To those who listen to my teaching, more understanding will be given, and they will have an abundance of knowledge." (Matthew 13:11–12)

The Bible is like no other book. True, it records historical events accurately, so on one level it is a history book. It tells the sweeping saga of a family, so you could also call it a series of biographies. It is a narrative of Jesus' life, His teaching, and the impact He had on His followers, so you could also call it a life story. But the Bible is a much deeper and more profound book than that.

Truth is, the Bible is a love story that reveals the loving heart of God to those who spiritually seek Him. It reveals a relational God who "would speak to Moses face to face, as one speaks to a friend" (Exodus 33:11). Moses said to God, " 'If you are pleased with me, teach me your ways so I may know you' " (Exodus 33:13 NIV). It is a revelation of " 'a God who is passionate about his relationship with you' " (Exodus 34:14). From the first words Moses penned in the book of Genesis to the last word John wrote in Revelation, it reflects the loving heart of a God who wants you to know Him and be in right relationship with Him so that you can enjoy all the benefits that relationship offers.

The Bible is a spiritual book that can be understood by spiritually-minded people who are hungering to know God. " 'If you look for me wholeheartedly,' " God says, " 'you will find me' " (Jeremiah 29:13). Seeing God's Word as an accurate revelation of God is a foundational piece of your biblical worldview.

My Prayer: I want to know You more deeply. Help me discover You within the words of scripture. Let Your Holy Spirit open my spiritual mind to better know Your heart and experience Your love more and more each day. Thank You for loving me. I love You. Amen.

On the Right Road

My Bible Reading:
The LORD is good and does what is right; he shows the
proper path to those who go astray. He leads the humble
in doing right, teaching them his way. (Psalm 25:8–9)

Have you ever taken the wrong turn and gotten lost? Even when
you use your GPS, that doesn't guarantee that you'll take the
ideal route to get you where you want to go. But there is a spiritual
"GPS" that you can count on to always take you down the right path.

Truth is, God has given you His Word as a revelation of both Himself
and His ways. Because God is perfectly right, the way He acts is
perfectly right. And when His Word directs you to do this or don't
do that, God is actually instructing you to follow down the road He
takes—to live according to His ways. When you do, you are living in
His image, just as He designed for you to live. And that's how you
enjoy life to the max. "The LORD will withhold no good thing from
those who do what is right. O LORD of Heaven's Armies, what joy for
those who trust in you" (Psalm 84:11–12).

There is a worldview that advocates that you may do what you
want to do because you are in charge of your own life. A biblical
worldview says that God is in charge and His Word has been given to
you, in part, to direct you down the right road—God's road that leads
to real joy and everlasting life.

My Prayer: Thank You that You're there to instruct me
and guide me with Your reliable Word. Help me continue to
know You and Your ways so that I can be all I can be for You.
I love You. Help me share with someone today how wonderful
a God You are and how much You love all of us. Amen.

How Do You View Sin?

My Bible Reading:
I know that nothing good lives in me, that is, in my
sinful nature. I want to do what is right, but I can't.
I want to do what is good, but I don't. (Romans 7:18–19)

You know quite a few people, right? What kind of people are they—
thieves, drug dealers, murderers, and violent criminals? Probably
not. Most of the people you know are no doubt good people who on
occasion may do some things that aren't so good. But overall their
good deeds probably outweigh their bad deeds.

That's the way most people see themselves. They consider themselves basically good and believe they should be graded fairly by the
amount of good they do against the bad. That's the way most people
in the world see it.

Truth is, everyone alive is born with a sinful nature that makes them
spiritually separated from God or dead to God. That's what sin does;
it separates everyone from God and no amount of good deeds by
humans can reverse that spiritual death. That's why Paul wrote, "Oh,
what a miserable person I am! Who will free me from this life that is
dominated by sin and death?" (Romans 7:24). The answer, of course,
is Jesus Christ. He died for sin and rose again to give eternal life to
each person who trusts in Him.

The prominent worldview today is that the good a person does
will make up for any bad he or she does. The biblical worldview is
that sin brings spiritual death and the only remedy for death is a
spiritual resurrection through Jesus Christ.

My Prayer: *Thank You that You are the world's solution to
spiritual death. Help me take Your message of life and hope
to those around me. Let Your mercy and love for a lost world
flow through me to others. Help me represent Your heart of
compassion to my friends. You are such a loving God. Amen.*

Two Models of Truth

My Bible Reading:
You [God] know everything I do. You know what I am going to
say even before I say it, LORD. . . . Such knowledge is too wonderful
for me, too great for me to understand! (Psalm 139:3–4, 6)

Who is to say what's right for you and what's wrong for you?
What's true for you may not be true for another person. Everyone has the right to determine her own values according to her own
truth, right? No one else has the right to dictate someone else's moral
values.

The above thinking is what most people today accept as a tolerant
view of morality. Truth is defined by the individual, and the person
chooses for himself what is morally right or wrong. In this model,
truth is subjective and created by the individual.

Truth is, God knows all and is the definer of all that is right and wrong
based on His character and nature. He is the Creator of humans, and
as such He and He alone establishes a universal morality. "O LORD,
you are our Father," the prophet Isaiah wrote. "We are the clay, and
you are the potter. We all are formed by your hand" (Isaiah 64:8). In
God's model, truth is objective; it is outside yourself. When you adopt
this biblical worldview, you are saying that God as your Creator
defines what is true and right, and you discover that truth in His
Word. God and His Word become your standard of morality.

My Prayer: *You are my standard of truth. I look to You to define what
is right for me. And I know that whatever You tell me is right is for my
best interest. You are the Almighty God of the universe who loves me
and wants what is best for me. Thank You. I love You. Amen.*

A Long-Term View

My Bible Reading:
God's way is perfect. All the LORD's promises prove true.
He is a shield for all who look to him for protection. (Psalm 18:30)

Every truth, every rule, and every guideline coming from God's Word originates from the loving heart of God for your own good. God knows that when you follow in His ways, you will reap the benefits of right living. Yet those benefits are not always immediate.

Truth is, sometimes doing the right things doesn't bring immediate rewards and wrong choices don't always result in immediate negative consequences. The prophet Jeremiah asked, "Why are the wicked so prosperous? Why are evil people so happy?" (Jeremiah 12:1). People can and do experience satisfaction out of sinful ways. Following in God's ways isn't right because His ways are beneficial to a person. They are right because they come from a right and perfect God and in the end they will prove beneficial.

King David understood this and had a long-term view—a biblical worldview. He said, "I have seen wicked and ruthless people flourishing like a tree in its native soil. But when I looked again, they were gone! Though I searched for them, I could not find them! Look at those who are honest and good, for a wonderful future awaits those who love peace. But the rebellious will be destroyed; they have no future" (Psalm 37:35–38).

My Prayer: I follow You and Your ways because You are a good and perfect God. Your ways are true. Even if my reward is not realized until the next life, I will follow You. In the end Your love for me and my love for You will win out big time. You are a faithful God! I love You. Amen.

How Do You View Jesus?

My Bible Reading:
Jesus asked His disciples, "Who do people say I am?"
"Well," they replied, "some say John the Baptist, some say Elijah,
and others say you are one of the other prophets." Then he
asked them, "But who do you say I am?" (Mark 8:27–29)

There are certain things in life that are true and factual—they are undeniable. You are the son or daughter of two people. Those two people are your parents. People could deny it, give you another name or claim you are an alien, but the facts remain. You are who you are no matter what others say. The same is true of Jesus. No matter what others think or say, Jesus is who He is.

Truth is, Peter's answer to Jesus' question about His identity is the right one: "Peter answered, 'You are the Messiah, the Son of the living God'" (Matthew 16:16). Seeing Jesus as the Son of God changes everything. It means there is a real God who created you, wants a relationship with you, and offers you eternal life. He died and rose again to make that happen. And this offer isn't just for you, but for the entire human race. "'There is salvation in no one else,'" Peter stated. "'God has given no other name under heaven by which we must be saved'" (Acts 4:12).

Your view of Jesus affects your view of human destiny. Death is humanity's destiny, unless people trust in Jesus. "'Anyone who believes in me,'" Jesus said, "'will live, even after dying'" (John 11:25). That is a foundational truth that makes up your biblical worldview.

My Prayer: *Thank You that You entered this world to save me from a life of sin and eternal death. You are my only hope and I have placed my trust in You. Thank You for making me Your child with an eternal future in Your family. Amen.*

What's in a Name?

My Bible Reading:
God elevated him [Jesus] to the place of highest honor and gave
him the name above all other names, that at the name of Jesus
every knee should bow, in heaven and on earth and under the
earth, and every tongue declare that Jesus Christ is Lord,
to the glory of God the Father. (Philippians 2:9–11)

How much is your name worth? Say you ask a friend for a loan of
$25. "I'll pay you back next week," you explain. If your friend gives
you the money, you might say that your honorable and trustworthy
name is at least worth $25. The more honorable and trustworthy your
name becomes, the more it rises in value and worth.

Truth is, there is a name above all names that is more valuable than
all others. That is the name of Jesus. It is in His name that sins can
be forgiven, a life can be set free of sin, and a person can receive the
hope of eternal life. That is a truth worth sharing with the world. And
you have the honor and privilege to share it.

"For God is working in you," Paul wrote, "giving you the desire
and the power to do what pleases him. . . . Live clean, innocent lives as
children of God, shining like bright lights in a world full of crooked
and perverse people" (Philippians 2:13–15). You are a shining light to
a dark world. Your message about Jesus is the hope for a world that
is lost without Him. What an honor to share His trustworthy name
with others.

*My Prayer: You are the hope for all the world. Thank You that I
have the incredible privilege to share Your wonderful name
with those around me. Give me courage and wisdom today to
share with someone how You have changed my life. Amen.*

It's All about Relationships

My Bible Reading:
Don't be selfish; don't try to impress others. Be humble, thinking of others as better than yourselves. Don't look out only for your own interests, but take an interest in others, too. (Philippians 2:3–4)

What are the best things in life? You might answer: good grades, winning at sports, popularity, a car, a nice home, money, etc. But are those things the best things? The late American humorist and syndicated columnist Art Buchwald was quoted as saying, "The best things in life aren't things." The statement, of course, begs the question: "If the best things in life aren't things, then what matters the most?"

Truth is, the best things in life are all about relational connections. Good grades, achievements, popularity, and material things don't really mean much without someone with whom to share them. Jesus was all about unselfish relational connections. He taught that everything boils down to having other-focused relationships. " 'Do to others,' " He said, " 'whatever you would like them to do to you. This is the essence of all that is taught in the law and the prophets' " (Matthew 7:12).

The world may say you've got to look out for "number one." The idea of focusing on yourself and what you want out of life may be popular. But a biblical worldview takes others into consideration and treats people as you would want to be treated. That creates relational connections that result in finding true purpose and meaning in life.

My Prayer*: Thank You that You are a giving God who is focused on giving me life in relationship with You. Help me follow Your example and be other focused. I want to be more unselfish and develop better relational connections that bring real purpose and meaning to life. Help me be unselfish toward someone today. Amen.*

A Sense of Justice

My Bible Reading:
God said, "He [Jesus] is my chosen one, who pleases me. I have put my Spirit upon him. He will bring justice to the nations. . . . He will bring justice to all who have been wronged." (Isaiah 42:1, 3)

Have you ever witnessed someone being bullied? Those who are a little different, odd, or even those who are perceived to be a little weak are sometimes made fun of. It seems that some think it's enjoyable to humiliate, ridicule, and put down a weaker and more vulnerable person. And when that happens, how do you feel? What does it stir within you? Do you sense an injustice is taking place?

Truth is, the conviction that people deserve humane treatment and that every person has value comes from somewhere. Human dignity is derived from the character and nature of God. Human beings are created in the image of a just God. The scriptures declare that " 'The Lord is just!' " (Psalm 92:15). And because He is just, "He will help the oppressed, who have no one to defend them. He feels pity for the weak and the needy, and he will rescue them" (Psalm 72:12–13).

When you stand up for the weak and defend the defenseless you are reflecting a biblical worldview. You are acting on behalf of a just and righteous God who is working through you to someday " 'bring justice to all who have been wronged.' "

My Prayer: Thank You that You are a just God who cares about those who have been mistreated and wronged. Help me take a stand against those who would ridicule or try to humiliate others. Let Your compassion and courage flow through me to help bring greater justice to the world around me. Amen.

Giving It Up for Others

My Bible Reading:
Jesus said, "This is my commandment: Love each other in
the same way I have loved you. There is no greater love
than to lay down one's life for one's friends." (John 15:12–13)

How much time and energy was required of your parents to care
for you in the first year of your life? You couldn't feed yourself.
Someone had to do that for you. You couldn't provide shelter from the
outside elements. Someone had to provide you a safe place to live.
You couldn't bathe yourself or clothe yourself. In fact, you were so
helpless that people had to sacrifice a great deal of time and energy
24/7 in order for you to make it beyond a year. But for those who loved
you and cared for you, it was worth it!

Truth is, anything of true value requires a sacrifice, especially caring
for others. If you really want to make a difference in people's lives,
it means giving up a significant measure of your time and energy.
Real love and true caring for others comes at a price—but it's worth
it. Jesus gave up so much, but it resulted in the salvation of so many.
Scripture says, "You must have the same attitude that Christ Jesus
had. Though he was God. . .he gave up his divine privileges; he took
the humble position of a slave and was born as a human being. . .and
died a criminal's death on a cross" (Philippians 2:5–8).

*My Prayer: You gave Yourself for me. And Your Spirit
empowers me to give myself to others. It is because of You
that I can make a difference to others. Help me care for
someone in need this very day. It will be worth it. Amen.*

Helping Those in Need

My Bible Reading:

Jesus said, "For I was hungry, and you fed me. I was thirsty, and you gave me a drink. I was a stranger, and you invited me into your home. I was naked, and you gave me clothing. I was sick, and you cared for me. . . . 'I tell you the truth, when you did it to one of the least of these my brothers and sisters, you were doing it to me!'" (Matthew 25:35–36, 40)

Have you ever given food to someone who was really hungry? Maybe you helped pack up meals for hungry children to be sent to a foreign country. Have you ever given clothes to a group that helped clothe the poor? Or maybe you saw someone who was really in need and you took the time to help that person. But you also helped someone else.

Truth is, whenever you unselfishly help or minister to the needs of others, you are also ministering to Jesus. He so cares and feels for those people in need that when you help the needy, He feels it Himself. And what happens if you refuse to help those in need? Jesus says, "'When you refused to help the least of these my brothers and sisters, you were refusing to help me'" (Matthew 25:45).

It's a great motivator to know that you are ministering to Jesus as you minister to the needs of others. That biblical worldview gives you a sense of responsibility to the world around you to share what you have with those in need.

My Prayer: I am so privileged. I am moved when I think of those who have so little. Help me give readily to those in need. And when I do, remind me that I am also giving to You. Help me bless someone today. Amen.

A God of Second Chances

My Bible Reading:
"This is what the LORD of Heaven's Armies says: Judge fairly, and show mercy and kindness to one another." (Zechariah 7:9)

You fail to come to a complete stop. The driving instructor sitting beside you in the car shakes his head slowly. To compound the problem, on your last turn you were slow to turn on your blinker. You're sure that he's going to fail you. This is the second time you've taken the driver's test and you know you're going to fail it again.

"Please pull the car to the side of the road," the instructor says softly, but firmly. You comply. He turns toward you and says, "I sense you're really nervous. I think you can do better than this. How about I give you a second chance?" He smiles and directs you to try again.

Truth is, God is a God of second chances. He is a God whose "mercy endures forever" (Psalm 107:1 NKJV). He is one who "delight[s] to show mercy" (Micah 7:18 NIV). Peter asked Jesus, " 'Lord, how often should I forgive someone who sins against me? Seven times?' 'No, not seven times,' Jesus replied, 'but seventy times seven!' " (Matthew 18:21–22).

God has shown mercy on you. He has forgiven you, probably more than just once. And you are to in turn show mercy to others over and over again. Compassion, mercy, and forgiveness are essential elements of the biblical worldview. They are distinguishing marks of Christianity.

My Prayer: Mercy is part of who You are, so let mercy be part of who I am. Let Your mercy flow through me to others. Let Your forgiving heart be my forgiving heart. You have treated me with mercy and forgiveness over and over again; let me treat others continually with mercy and forgiveness. Amen.

October 23

The Power of Love

____

My Bible Reading:
Jesus said, "You have heard the law that says, 'Love your neighbor'
and hate your enemy. But I say, love your enemies! Pray for
those who persecute you! In that way, you will be acting as true
children of your Father in heaven." (Matthew 5:43–45)

Get criticized—criticize back. Get pushed—push back. Get kicked—
kick back. If you don't, people will run over you, right? You live
in a "dog-eat-dog" world and you've got to stand up for yourself.

That's the viewpoint of the world. You can love your family and
friends, but you must push back and resist your enemies. It doesn't
pay to love them.

Truth is, loving others, even loving your enemies, does pay off. You
may think that your enemies don't deserve your love. Yet loving
the unlovable is rewarded. That's the power of Godlike love. Jesus
said, " 'God blesses those who are persecuted for doing right, for the
Kingdom of Heaven is theirs'" (Matthew 5:10). Peter wrote, "Don't
repay evil for evil. Don't retaliate with insults when people insult you.
Instead, pay them back with a blessing. . .and he [God] will grant you
his blessing" (1 Peter 3:9).

When you love those who hate you and pray for those who would
do you harm, you are living out a biblical worldview. God's way is
showing mercy, forgiving others, and treating people fairly even
when they treat you unfairly. It's a powerful way to live that reaps
eternal benefits.

____

My Prayer: *Your way is a way of love and mercy. I am glad You
expressed that to me. Keep empowering me to express that to everyone
around me. Help me show love and mercy to someone today. Amen.*

You Get What You Give

My Bible Reading:
Jesus said, "God blesses those who are merciful,
for they will be shown mercy." (Matthew 5:7)

Have you heard the saying, "What goes around comes around?" That means if you treat people badly, it will come back to you in people treating you badly. Live a life of deceit and dishonesty, and it will pay dividends of ruined relationships, guilt, and a bad reputation. If you disrespect others, expect disrespect in return. Show no mercy to others and look for retribution as a result.

Truth is, you will get back whatever you give out. Scripture puts it this way: "You will always harvest what you plant. Those who live only to satisfy their own sinful nature will harvest decay and death .... But those who live to please the Spirit will harvest everlasting life from the Spirit" (Galatians 6:7–8). Jesus said, " 'Whatever measure you use in giving—large or small—it will be used to measure what is given back to you' " (Luke 6:38).

Be merciful and you'll be shown mercy. Forgive others, and you'll be forgiven. Live a life of love, generosity, and integrity and you will reap a wonderful harvest in return. "The generous will prosper; those who refresh others will themselves be refreshed" (Proverbs 11:25).

My Prayer: Thank You that You are a fair and just God. You allow me to reap what I sow. Help me continue to sow a life of honesty, faithfulness, peace, mercy, and love toward my friends and my enemies. You are a remarkable God. Amen.

Who You Are

My Bible Reading:

A Samaritan woman questioned why Jesus was asking her for a drink of water. Jesus replied, "If you only knew the gift God has for you and who you are speaking to, you would ask me, and I would give you living water." (John 4:10)

During the time of Jesus the Samaritans were a group of people that Jews wanted nothing to do with. They actually considered them like scum. They avoided them continually and even took long detours to avoid walking on their land. They would only accept those who converted to Judaism and followed the strict laws of their own religion. But Jesus not only walked through Samaria, He talked openly with a Samaritan woman, accepting her for who she was. He even offered her salvation.

Truth is, God doesn't accept you or anyone else based on your religious beliefs or what you do. Acceptance by God is based upon the fact that you are His creation and He considers you worth saving. He accepts you for who you are, not for what you've done. Even though you were a sinner and a lost child of God, He died to restore you. " 'God sent his Son into the world not to judge the world, but to save the world through him' " (John 3:17).

A common worldview is that people are what they do. Their identity is in their doing. A biblical worldview affirms that a person's real value is based upon being made in the image of God with dignity and worth.

My Prayer: Thank You that You created me in Your image and that You accepted me even when I was a lost sinner. You have restored me as Your child in a relationship with You. I am so glad I belong to You. Help me share this wonderful message with others today. Amen.

Becoming

My Bible Reading:
I pray that your love will overflow more and more, and that you will keep on growing in knowledge and understanding. (Philippians 1:9)

How much did you know and understand about the world around you when you were in the first grade? How much more have you learned in the last year? Once you graduate from high school or college will your learning stop? People may receive multiple degrees that indicate they have higher degrees of learning, but is there always more to learn?

Truth is, when you are made a child of God in a relationship with Christ, you have begun an exciting journey. Yet you are only at the beginning of the process of knowing Jesus and becoming more like Him. Peter wrote that "you must grow in the grace and knowledge of our Lord and Savior Jesus Christ" (2 Peter 3:18). As a follower of Jesus you are ever becoming more like Him. You are in an ever-growing relationship with Him. That is what is so exciting about love and relationships—they are never standing still, but rather forever growing deeper and deeper.

My Prayer: You are the eternal God who has infinite love and knowledge and understanding of all things. While I can never know You exhaustively and understand everything You know, I can learn more and more about You each day. Thank You for the process of becoming like You. I'm excited for what You are going to teach me this year, this week, and this very day. I'm glad I'm on an ongoing journey with You. Amen.

You Belong to Truth

My Bible Reading:
Dear children, let's not merely say that we love each other;
let us show the truth by our actions. Our actions will show
that we belong to the truth, so we will be confident
when we stand before God. (1 John 3:18–19)

What do you belong to? You may be in the school band, on a team, in a drama club, or in a youth group. Chances are you belong to something. Belonging is a big deal.

Truth is, being a follower of Jesus means you belong to the truth. But that means a lot more than believing there is only one God and that Jesus is His Son. "Good for you!" James wrote. "Even the demons believe this, and they tremble in terror" (James 2:19). Belonging to the truth means believing and acting in accordance with those beliefs. Scripture says, "We must believe in the name of his Son, Jesus Christ, and love one another, just as he commanded us" (1 John 3:23).

Jesus said, "'I am the way, the truth, and the life'" (John 14:6). When you belong to the truth, you also belong to a person. Believing in Jesus isn't just a way of thinking; it is a way of living. When you belong to Jesus, who is the Truth, you become His living representative to all those around you. That's an exciting privilege.

My Prayer: *Because I have believed in You, my life belongs to You and Your truth. Help me better make Your truth a lifestyle of loving You and loving those around me as I love myself. You are everything to me. Help me express that by the way I show kindness and love to someone today. Amen.*

Children of Light

My Bible Reading:

For you are all children of the light and of the day; we don't belong
to darkness and night. So be on your guard, not asleep like the
others. Stay alert and be clearheaded. (1 Thessalonians 5:5–6)

There is just something about sunshine that most people like.
Would you rather go for a walk on a sunny day or on a cloudy
day? Don't you enjoy an open, sun-filled room over a dark and dingy
room? Spiritually, you are a child of the light and Jesus is the light
giver. It is His light that represents life and all that is good.

Jesus said that His light came into the world but certain people
" 'loved the darkness more than the light, for their actions were evil.
All who do evil hate the light and refuse to go near it for fear their sins
will be exposed. But those who do what is right come to the light so
others can see that they are doing what God wants' " (John 3:19–21).

Truth is, darkness is all around you. Yet children of the light don't
belong to the darkness—the darkness of cheating, lying, stealing,
immoral thoughts and actions, etc. Yet today's Bible reading says
to "be on your guard" and "stay alert and be clearheaded." Darkness
wants to overtake the light. The light stays bright through praying,
absorbing God's Word, and fellowshipping with fellow believers.
That's the light you are called to walk in.

*My Prayer: I want to stay close to You and walk in the light
of Your ways. Help me persist in reading Your Word and
deepening my relationship with You. Keep me close to those
who love You and want to walk in the light of Your ways.
Thank You for making me a child of the light. Amen.*

Your Hope

My Bible Reading:

Don't forget that you Gentiles used to be outsiders. . . .
You lived in this world without God and without hope.
But now you have been united with Christ Jesus. Once you
were far away from God, but now you have been brought
near to him through the blood of Christ. (Ephesians 2:11–13)

What is hope? Hope is your expectations of a positive outcome. You want something to happen or be true and you think maybe it can happen or it just might be true. You hope that's the case. You are probably hoping to graduate, have enough money to go to college, and have a career. You might hope to deeply love someone, have a marriage that will last, and have a wonderful family. You may have a lot of hope for this life.

Truth is, without God there can be no expectation of a positive outcome in this life or of a meaningful life after this one. Your hope is "Christ in you, the hope of glory" (Colossians 1:27 NIV). Everything hinges on Him. Your trust is in Him. He is your source of true hope. Paul, inspired by the Holy Spirit, prayed "that God, the source of hope, will fill you completely with joy and peace because you trust in him. Then you will overflow with confident hope through the power of the Holy Spirit" (Romans 15:13). Your biblical worldview is one of hope because of Jesus.

My Prayer: Jesus, I do have dreams and hopes for my future. But I know my life is hopeless without You. Because I have trusted in You, I can truly have joy and peace about my future. Even if this short life on earth isn't the best I would hope for, I know I have an eternal home with You that will exceed my expectations. Thank You for giving me hope. And help me share my hope in You with someone today. Amen.

Confronting Others in a Nonjudgmental Way

My Bible Reading:

Jesus said, "Do not judge others, and you will not be judged. For you will be treated as you treat others. The standard you use in judging is the standard by which you will be judged." (Matthew 7:1-2)

Jesus said you're not to judge other people, right? Most people think everyone is his or her own judge and it's intolerant if someone judges another person. But that is not what scripture teaches and it wasn't what Jesus is saying.

In this passage Jesus is teaching about the Kingdom of God and how you should think and live with a Kingdom worldview. He established Himself as the Righteous King and that He and He alone is the final judge of everyone. But He isn't saying that you as one of His followers are not also to judge. The question is what standard you must use in order to judge in a godly way.

Truth is, when you accept God as the standard of righteousness and you are obeying God's standard yourself—you are equipped to speak the truth in love. God told the children of Israel, " 'Do not nurse hatred in your heart. . . . Confront people directly so you will not be held guilty for their sin. Do not seek revenge or bear a grudge. . .but love your neighbor as yourself' " (Leviticus 19:17-18). Jesus went on to say that if you use God's Word as the standard for right behavior and you're living up to that standard then " 'you will see well enough to deal with the speck [the wrong] in your friend's eye [life]' " (Matthew 7:5). God is pleased for you to confront others appropriately in a nonjudgmental way.

My Prayer: You are the righteous Judge and I want to always follow in Your ways. If I see my friends going down the wrong path, help me "speak the truth in love" (Ephesians 4:15) so they will not suffer the consequences of doing wrong. Help me be a good example of Your truth in front of my friends. I love You. Amen.

October 31

A Night of Deception

My Bible Reading:
Better to be poor and honest than to be dishonest and a fool.
(Proverbs 19:1)

On Halloween we dress up in costumes and go from house to house "trick or treating." Some like to dress in elaborate makeup and costumes so their friends cannot recognize them. Halloween for a lot of people is a fun night of innocent deception. But in real life, to engage in deception can cause real harm.

Truth is, hiding your life behind a mask of deception is never good. A little cheating or a few white lies may seem innocent at the time and no big deal. Yet the little things add up. Jesus said, " 'If you are faithful in the little things, you will be faithful in large ones. But if you are dishonest in little things, you won't be honest with greater responsibilities' " (Luke 16:10).

Life is a series of little acts and repeated small steps that add up to a way of living. Stay honest and faithful in the little things and you will be rewarded with a life of integrity and trust. Honesty is your best friend, and having the trust of others is a quality that will pay off in all your relationships.

My Prayer: You are a faithful and true God without any deception. Help me be a faithful and honest person even in all the little things of life. Let my life be an open book of transparency so others will find me worthy of their trust. You are such an exalted and trustworthy God. Help me honor You today through my honesty. Amen.

NOVEMBER

Real Community

Whose Church?

My Bible Reading:

Jesus asked His disciples: "Who do you say I am?" Simon Peter answered, "You are the Messiah, the Son of the living God." Jesus replied, "You are blessed, Simon son of John, because my Father in heaven has revealed this to you. You did not learn this from any human being. Now I say to you that you are Peter (which means 'rock') and upon this rock I will build my church, and all the powers of hell will not conquer it." (Matthew 16:15-18)

What kind of church do you attend? How big is your church and who started your church? All over the world churches have been founded by many people and groups. Who is the founder of your church?

Truth is, the founder of God's true church is Jesus Himself. He said He would build His church upon the declaration that He was the Messiah, the true Son of God who came to save the world from the slavery of sin. But when Jesus referred to His church, He wasn't talking about a building. The word He used in the Greek language was *ekklesia* which means a gathering of people. Jesus' church is a group of people who believe in Him as God's Son.

Some two thousand years before Jesus entered this world, God chose Abraham and his descendants as His people. And when Jesus announced He had a church—a gathering of people—it meant the children of Abraham and everyone else who accepted Him as the Christ. From that point on they were to be one body of believers. That ended up being one big church! Paul said, "This is God's plan: Both Gentiles and Jews who believe the Good News [about Jesus] share equally in the riches inherited by God's children. Both are part of the same body, and both enjoy the promise of blessings because they belong to Christ Jesus" (Ephesians 3:6).

My Prayer: Thank You, Jesus, that I belong to You and Your church. And it is thrilling to know that You chose a people so long ago and I'm part of that body of believers. Help me remember that church is about Your people believing in You, worshipping You, and being a witness to the world about You. Help me today to be a shining witness for You to those around me. Amen.

We Are One

My Bible Reading:
For there is one body and one Spirit, just as you have been called to one glorious hope for the future. There is one Lord, one faith, one baptism, one God and Father of all, who is over all, in all, and living through all. (Ephesians 4:4–6)

Do you have any brothers or sisters? How about aunts or uncles? Are you all the same or are you different? It's unlikely that all of you have the same hair color, look alike, share all the same views, or have the same personalities. You are all a little different, yet you share a common heritage.

Truth is, you and your Christian friends may attend different churches that have varying, distinctive styles of worship. Yet you all are still of one body and one Spirit because you all have the same Father. Different, but one. Distinct, yet unified. Jesus prayed that His followers from all walks of life would " 'experience such perfect unity that the world will know that you [Father] sent me and that you love them as much as you love me' " (John 17:23).

My Prayer: Thank You that all my Christian friends and I share the same spiritual heritage as members of Your great family. Help me focus more on what brings us together and less on what makes us different. You said the world would know us by how we, in unity, love one another. Let me show that love for my Christian brothers and sisters today. Amen.

November 3

Real Family

My Bible Reading:
See how very much our Father loves us, for he calls
us his children, and that is what we are! (1 John 3:1)

Parents and children, children and parents—that is family. But family is more than common ancestors. Family, real family, lovingly share life together. They are there to support you, encourage you, and lift you up when you're down. Family means people who care, listen, offer advice, and walk with you through life.

Truth is, those who know God as their Father have become your family. "Now all of us can come to the Father through the same Holy Spirit because of what Christ has done for us.... You are members of God's family" (Ephesians 2:18–19). "For all who are led by the Spirit of God are children of God" (Romans 8:14). You need a loyal and committed family of God. You need brothers and sisters in Christ to be there for you. And they need you. Together you can comfort one another, support one another, and become stronger, more loving followers of Jesus. Wise Solomon said, "As iron sharpens iron, so a friend sharpens a friend" (Proverbs 27:17). That's part of what family does.

My Prayer: Thank You for my Christian family. Help me be there for them. Let me lift them up when they need support and cheer them on when they need encouragement. Help me be there for a Christian family member today. Use me as a source of encouragement, support, comfort, or whatever he or she may need. I want to be a faithful member of Your family. Amen.

His Body

My Bible Reading:

The church is his body; it is made full and complete by Christ, who fills all things everywhere with himself. (Ephesians 1:23)

When you think of a body, you probably think of a physical body with a head, hands, feet, etc. So to say the church is Christ's body may seem a bit confusing. Because Jesus Himself said His church was the gathering of people who believed in Him as God's Son. Then which is it? Is the church Christ's body or is it His followers? Actually, it's a little of both.

Truth is, Jesus is the head of His body, the church, and you and all other Christ followers make up the other parts of His body. Paul explained that first "Christ is the head of the church," and at the same time, "He is the Savior of his body" (Ephesians 5:23). As head and Savior He leads His church. And each follower of Jesus is a part of His body (the church) and has a place in it. "Just as our bodies have many parts and each part has a special function, so it is with Christ's body. We are many parts of one body, and we all belong to each other" (Romans 12:4–5). That means you serve Jesus the head of His body and you serve other members of His body—your Christian family members. "This makes for harmony among the members, so that all the members care for each other" (1 Corinthians 12:25).

My Prayer: Thank You for being head of Your church and making me a special part of it. Help me care for other members of Your body—my Christian friends—even today. Let me show them we belong by finding out what they need and doing my best to meet those needs as I am able. You are the compassionate and loving head of Your church. I love You. Amen.

His Temple

My Bible Reading:
Together we are his house, built on the foundation of the apostles and the prophets. And the cornerstone is Christ Jesus himself. We are carefully joined together in him, becoming a holy temple for the Lord. Through him you Gentiles are also being made part of this dwelling where God lives by his Spirit. (Ephesians 2:20–22)

A long time ago King David's son Solomon built the great Temple of the Lord. The priests put the ark of the covenant, which contained the stone tablets of the Ten Commandments, in the Temple. Once that was done "the glorious presence of the LORD filled the Temple" (1 Kings 8:11).

When you think of a church building, you might think of it as the temple where God resides. It's like you go to church to worship God, because that's where He is—at church, right?

Truth is, you are God's church; you are His temple. He doesn't reside in a building; He resides in you. "Don't you realize that all of you together are the temple of God and that the Spirit of God lives in you? . . . For God's temple is holy, and you are that temple" (1 Corinthians 3:16–17). At one time God was present in an earthly temple, but once He sent His Holy Spirit, He took up residence in all those who trusted in Jesus as Savior. Now when you gather to worship, God is there because He is in each of His followers. Jesus said, " 'For where two or three gather together as my followers, I am there among them' " (Matthew 18:20).

My Prayer: It amazes me that You have chosen to make me Your temple. You show up at church because You are in Your followers who have come to worship You together. That is amazing! Help me remember that I am a walking church that others are watching. Let my life reflect a love and compassion toward others, just like Yours did. Amen.

His Bride

My Bible Reading:

Husbands, this means love your wives, just as Christ loved the church. He gave up his life for her to make her holy and clean, washed by the cleansing of God's word. He did this to present her to himself as a glorious church without a spot or wrinkle or any other blemish. (Ephesians 5:25-27)

Paul was telling husbands that they should love their brides as Jesus sacrificially loves the church. A husband and wife are to have an intimate love relationship just as Jesus has an intimate love relationship with His bride—the church.

Truth is, you are married spiritually to Jesus. Forget being male or female—this isn't about a human marriage. Jesus has a pure and holy love relationship with you. That intimate relationship is what He was referring to when He prayed to His Father that " 'they [Jesus followers] will be one [intimate], just as you and I are one' " (John 17:21).

When you think that you as the church are the bride of Christ, it really puts things into perspective. You want to please your one true love. You want to be faithful and true. That means being everything God wants you to be—loving, kind, gentle, and patient, not boastful, proud, rude, or demanding of your own way. Jesus died and rose again to have that kind of loving relationship with you and with all your fellow believers.

My Prayer: Thank You that You love me like a bride. In response, I want to love You with the same kind of sacrificial and caring love. As Your bride—Your church—let me show my love to You by loving and caring for those around me. Help me let someone know he or she is respected, loved, and cared for today. You are such a loving Savior. I want to be more like You. Amen.

His Agents

My Bible Reading:
You are a kingdom of priests, God's holy nation,
his very own possession. This is so you can show
others the goodness of God. (1 Peter 2:9)

You have practiced hard and long for years at your sport. Now your time has come and you're a winner. You look up at the scoreboard to confirm that you have just won Olympic gold. During the ceremony, a gold medal is placed around your neck, your country's flag is raised, and your national anthem is played. You are a proud representative or agent of your country.

Truth is, you are an agent of the Most High God who has the privilege and honor to "show others the goodness of God." "God has given us [his church] this task of reconciling people to him. . . . He gave us this wonderful message of reconciliation. So we are Christ's ambassadors [agents]" (2 Corinthians 5:18–20). The "message of reconciliation" is a message that people can have a relationship with God because of Jesus Christ. And that ancient message is best expressed through words that are backed up by a Christlike life. Paul said, "We try to live in such a way that no one will be hindered from finding the Lord by the way we act" (2 Corinthians 6:3 NLT).

My Prayer: Thank You for commissioning me as Your agent. It is an honor. And I want to make You proud by sharing Your message of salvation through a heart of love and concern for others. Help me lovingly point others to You today. Thank You for loving my friends through me. Amen.

His Multipliers

My Bible Reading:

You have heard me teach things that have been confirmed by many reliable witnesses. Now teach these truths to other trustworthy people who will be able to pass them on to others. (2 Timothy 2:2)

God created humans as complex beings. He made them with a circulatory system, a respiratory system, a nervous system, a digestive system, etc. And while all these systems help a person to sustain life, there is another system that is designed to multiply life. After God created humans He "blessed them and said, 'Be fruitful and multiply'" (Genesis 1:28). God gifted humans with a reproductive system that enabled them to reproduce other physical human beings.

Truth is, when God gave you spiritual life, He enabled you to reproduce spiritually. Jesus told his followers to "'go and make disciples of all the nations'" (Matthew 28:19). Spiritual reproduction is what characterized the new church Jesus had established. What started out with His twelve disciples turned into a multiplying church. "All the believers devoted themselves to the apostles' teaching, and to fellowship. . . . And each day the Lord added to their fellowship those who were being saved" (Acts 2:42, 47). Every follower of Jesus has the honor to participate in and be part of the spiritual multiplication process.

My Prayer: Thank You that someone took an interest in me to share how I could have a relationship with You. And thank You that someone has helped me grow in You. Help me pass that message on and be part of Your multiplying church. Give me wisdom and courage as I share Your saving message and teach others as I have been taught. I want to impact others with the same teachings and truths that have impacted me. Amen.

His Body Builders

My Bible Reading:
Train yourself to be godly. "Physical training is good,
but training for godliness is much better, promising benefits
in this life and in the life to come." (1 Timothy 4:7–8)

How many push-ups and sit-ups can you do? Do you do some jogging? Maybe you're into aerobics. Some type of physical training is good. Focusing on a healthy diet and physical exercise are important. How you treat your body now will pay off in the near term and as you grow older.

Truth is, while your physical health is important, your spiritual health is even more important. And the church is made up of God's body builders. Paul said that the leadership of the church is "to equip God's people to do his work and build up the church, the body of Christ" (Ephesians 4:12). And while knowing the teachings of the Bible and what you should and shouldn't do is part of being built up, it is learning to love as God loves that is the real body builder. "While knowledge may make us feel important, it is love that really builds up the church" (1 Corinthians 8:1).

My Prayer*: Thank You for giving me spiritual leaders who are teaching me and helping me build up my spiritual body. Keep my heart tender and teachable. And most importantly, help me know You more so I can love like You love and be compassionate and caring toward others. Express Your heart of love through me as I am thoughtful, kind, and caring to someone today. Amen.*

Shared Lives

My Bible Reading:
All the believers were united in heart and mind.
And they felt that what they owned was not their own,
so they shared everything they had. (Acts 4:32)

As you were growing up, were you taught to share? Was it easy for you to share your toys? Sharing with others doesn't come naturally for a lot of people. A sense of ownership and a feeling of possessiveness are universal. So sharing everything a person has with others is really uncommon.

Truth is, Jesus' church is a sharing bunch. In the early church, believers voluntarily "sold their property and possessions and shared the money with those in need" (Acts 2:45). But this heart attitude of sharing just wasn't about monetary things; it was the sharing in relationship and caring for each other emotionally. Paul put it this way: "We were like a mother feeding and caring for her own children. We loved you so much that we shared with you not only God's Good News but our own lives, too" (1 Thessalonians 2:7-8).

Sharing part of your life with others and others sharing their lives with you is what makes a group of Jesus followers so attractive to the outside world. This mutual exchange demonstrates a heart of care. It is giving emotional energy and time to encourage, support, comfort one another, etc. That's the kind of church that draws people to Christ.

My Prayer: Jesus, You have shared Your life with me. Help me share my life with others. Let me give of my time and energy to let my Christian brothers and sisters know I am there for them, especially when they are in need. Let me reflect the heart of Your true church so that people will be drawn to You. Amen.

Meeting Needs

My Bible Reading:
Do not let any unwholesome talk come out of your mouths, but
only what is helpful for building others up according to their needs,
that it may benefit those who listen. (Ephesians 4:29 NIV)

H ave you ever encountered someone who needed you emotionally,
but you didn't know what to say? Sometimes your friends may
be emotionally needy but you can't even identify what the need is, let
alone meet it.

Jesus said, "'As I have loved you, so you must love one another'"
(John 13:34 NIV). At least thirty-five times in the New Testament there
is this recurring word pattern of an action verb followed by the words
"one another." Followers of Jesus are to accept one another, support
one another, encourage one another, and comfort one another.

Truth is, by identifying the "one anothers" of scripture you identify
many of the relational needs that exist in you and your friends' lives.
And God is pleased that you meet some of these needs. Paul wrote,
"Our people must learn to do good by meeting the urgent needs of
others" (Titus 3:14).

God is your ultimate source for getting your needs met. But often
He is pleased to meet those needs through the loving heart of a friend.
And He is pleased to channel His need-meeting love through you to
your friends. Over the next couple of weeks your devotions will help
you discover what needs God is pleased to meet through you and
how to meet them in the lives of your friends.

---

*My Prayer: Thank You for being a need-meeting God. Help me be
Your instrument of support for my friends and family, meeting their
needs as You love them through me. I want to better learn how loving
people as You love me "build[s] others up according to their needs."
I want to be that kind of faithful member of Your church. Amen.*

The Need for Comfort

My Bible Reading:
"God blesses those who mourn, for they will be comforted."
(Matthew 5:4)

Have you ever had your feelings really hurt or had your heart broken? You don't have to live very long to suffer hurt and need comfort. You suffer emotional or relational hurt practically every week on some level, as do your friends. It is part of life. And that's why it's good to know how to both give and receive comfort.

Truth is, giving comfort begins with feeling the hurt with another. Scripture says "Mourn with those who mourn" (Romans 12:15 NIV). Another translation puts it, "If they are sad, share their sorrow" (Romans 12:15 NLT). Comfort isn't about trying to fix a problem, giving a pep talk, or offering advice. Pure and simple comfort is about sharing in the pain of a person. It sounds like "I'm so sorry this happened to you," or "This must be so difficult for you," or "I so hurt with you right now." And comfort could look like a tender hug or shared tears.

Comfort doesn't mean you understand everything a person is going through. Most of the time you can't. To give comfort you need to simply and lovingly identify with your friend's hurt and hurt with him or her. And when you do, God is involving you as a member of His church in a ministry of comfort.

My Prayer*: I have friends and family who at times need comfort. Help me feel their pain and express that I'm sorry they are going through the trouble they are experiencing. Help me identify with their hurt and be there for them. Let my words be words of comfort and let my heart weep with them. Thank You for being with me as I serve You in the ministry of comfort. Amen.*

He's There to Comfort You

My Bible Reading:
God said, "Sorrow and mourning will disappear,
and they will be filled with joy and gladness. 'I, yes I,
am the one who comforts you.' " (Isaiah 51:11–12)

Think of the last time you were emotionally hurting. You were feeling the heartache of a painful experience. You look to God and what does He say? "Oh don't feel too bad. It could've been a lot worse." Or "Hey, this is a teachable moment, so learn from it." Or does God say, "Don't be sad—the sun will come up tomorrow"? No, those aren't the words of a comforting God.

Truth is, during times of pain and heartache, God is not there to cheer you up, give you words of advice, or offer insights for living; He is there to comfort you. He is the God who weeps with you. He is the very source and origin of pure comfort. There is a time for advice and words of encouragement, but in times of pain, God is there to wrap His arms around you (figuratively speaking). He is there to let you know He hurts with you and will walk with you through it all. " 'Do not be afraid or discouraged, for the LORD will personally go ahead of you. He will be with you; he will neither fail you nor abandon you' " (Deuteronomy 31:8). "He [God] is the source of every mercy and the God who comforts [you]" (2 Corinthians 1:3).

My Prayer: Thank You for identifying with my hurts and being there for me to feel what I feel. Help me always turn to You as my source of comfort. And help me support my friends, to hurt with them when they are hurting. Lead me to someone today who might need some of Your comfort that You have given me. Amen.

The Need for Attention

My Bible Reading:
We have all been baptized into one body by one Spirit, and we all
share the same Spirit...so that all the members care for each other.
If one part suffers, all the parts suffer with it, and if one part
is honored, all the parts are glad. (1 Corinthians 12:13, 25-26)

Are you busy? Do you have a lot of things going on in your world?
It's easy to get caught up in all the busyness of life. And it may
seem that everyone around you is just as busy. What can happen
during all this busy activity is that you and those closest to you can
feel relationally neglected and alone.

Truth is, you have a deep need for attention and feeling cared for.
You feel cared for when someone enters your world to let you know
he or she cares what is going on in your life. The need for attention
can sound like, "Tell me about your day. I'm interested in what's
happening with you." That is what a real community of believers
does. Christians love and support each other. That is what family
and friends do—they care enough to enter each other's busy world.
People who care demonstrate "I'm here and want to know what you're
dealing with so I can 'Be happy with those who are happy, and weep
with those who weep' " (Romans 12:15).

*My Prayer: Thank You for giving me the need for attention.
When someone pays attention to me, it makes me feel wanted
and loved. Help me enter into someone's world today and let
that person know I care. Slow me down and deepen my sense of
caring for those around me. Amen.*

He Cares for You

My Bible Reading:

Jesus said, "Look at the birds. They don't plant or harvest or store food in barns, for your heavenly Father feeds them. And aren't you far more valuable to him than they are? . . . And why worry about your clothing? Look at the lilies of the field and how they grow. They don't work or make their clothing. . . . And if God cares so wonderfully for wildflowers that are here today and thrown into the fire tomorrow, he will certainly care for you." (Matthew 6:26, 28, 30)

Some people think God is some distant supernatural being who has created the universe and then left it alone. To them He is an impersonal God who really doesn't care what happens to humanity. In their view if any progress is made on this earth, it's fully in the hands of human beings.

Truth is, God truly cares for you. When sin separated humanity from God, He entered your world to die and rise again so you could have a relationship with Him forever. He has conquered sin and death so that one day you can live in a perfect world. That's caring!

Hopefully you get plenty to eat, have clothes on your back, and enjoy a home to live in. Sure, you may have it hard sometimes and uncaring people hurt you, but God still cares. King David wrote, "For the strength of the wicked will be shattered, but the LORD takes care of the godly" (Psalm 37:17).

My Prayer*: You are an almighty, powerful God who is infinitely above me, yet You care about me and the details of my life. That blows my mind! Thank You that You are such a caring God. Help me honor You by being thoughtful toward someone today. Let Your caring heart prompt me to be there for someone who needs caring attention. Thank You for being such a considerate God. Amen.*

The Need for Acceptance

My Bible Reading:
Accept each other just as Christ has accepted you
so that God will be given glory. (Romans 15:7)

What causes you to feel accepted by someone? You ace a test and your teacher gives you a thumbs-up. Does that make you feel really good? You score the final points to win a game and people cheer. Does that make you feel loved and accepted? You've worked hard at a job and you get paid well for it. Does that fill you with a feeling of acceptance?

Truth is, genuine acceptance isn't earned by your performance. True acceptance is given without condition; it embraces you for who you are, period. A real love for others does just that—it causes you to accept them for who they are. It overlooks their flaws and faults. "Continue to show deep love for each other," the Bible says, "for love covers a multitude of sins" (1 Peter 4:8).

You need acceptance, and so do your friends. Your friends need to know that regardless of their mistakes and imperfections, they are loved anyway. That's what your friends need and want. So do you—a Christlike acceptance that is given without condition. That is what Christ's body, the church, is intended to do—accept each other without condition.

My Prayer: Thank You for accepting me for who I am. That makes me feel I am valuable to You. Help me accept my friends and family like that. Fill me with Your love to accept those closest to me for who they are, not for what they do. Help me do that today. Amen.

November 17

He Accepts You, Period

My Bible Reading:
For since our friendship with God was restored by the death
of his Son while we were still his enemies, we will certainly
be saved through the life of his Son. (Romans 5:10)

What did you do to get God to forgive you of your sins and form a loving relationship with you? Did you crawl on your hands and knees through a pile of glass to prove you were really sorry for your sins? Did you perform a lot of good deeds to earn His acceptance of you? God surely needed some payment in advance to accept you, right?

Truth is, you were a sinner and enemy of God, yet Jesus died so you would live. That is the kind of acceptance He offers to you—an acceptance without any condition on your part. The religious leaders during Jesus' time brought to Him a woman who was caught in a sexual sin. They condemned her and were ready to stone her. But Jesus forgave her outright and said to her, "'Go and sin no more'" (John 8:11). Over and over again Jesus accepted people for who they were. In fact, He died for the entire human race while we were all still sinners.

All that Jesus asks of you and everyone else is to believe in Him as the sacrifice for sin and the Source of eternal life. He said, "'God sent his Son into the world not to judge the world, but to save the world through him. There is no judgment against anyone who believes in him'" (John 3:17–18). That is total acceptance without any requirements or conditions on anyone's part. That's the way God accepts you.

My Prayer: Thank You for accepting me without any performance on my part. You love me and died for me so I can have a relationship with You. I didn't have to earn Your love and acceptance, You gave it to me without condition. As a member of Your body, help me love and accept others just as You love and accept me. You are such a loving and majestic God! Amen.

The Need for Support

My Bible Reading:
Share each other's burdens, and in this way obey the law of Christ.
If you think you are too important to help someone, you are only
fooling yourself. You are not that important. (Galatians 6:2-3)

Sometimes life gets you down. You can feel stressed, loaded down,
and under great pressure. You can grit your teeth, buck up, and try
to bear it alone. But when you do, you fail to benefit from being loved
and cared for through the support of others.

Truth is, you need support. You need someone to come alongside you
to help lift your load and help carry your problem. You were designed
to need others and others to need you, and that often comes in the
form of sharing in one another's burdens. Scripture says, "When
God's people are in need, be ready to help them" (Romans 12:13).
Wise Solomon talked about the need for support when he said, "If
one person falls, the other can reach out and help. But someone who
falls alone is in real trouble" (Ecclesiastes 4:10).

Sometimes giving support to someone is easier than you receiving
it from others. It's not always easy to allow someone to give you the
help you need because you may feel you should be able to handle it
on your own. But when you resist that tendency and accept help from
a friend it deepens a sense of community with others. That's what
Jesus' church is called to do—to give and receive support from one
another.

---

*My Prayer: Help me be sensitive to those around me and help
them carry their load. And teach me to receive help graciously
from others when I need it. Thank You that You have formed
Your body, the church, to need and encourage one another.
It gives us a sense of togetherness. Thank You for that. Amen.*

He Supports You

My Bible Reading:
If I ride the wings of the morning, if I dwell by the farthest oceans, even there your hand will guide me, and your strength will support me. (Psalm 139:9–10)

Do you remember a time when you were young, when you tried to lift something but it was too heavy for you? If you were like a lot of little kids, when your mother, father, or someone else tried to help, you said, "No, I can do it." It's natural to want to do things in your own strength. But you weren't designed to carry every load on your own.

Truth is, your need of support comes from God Himself. He didn't create you as a totally independent person. He designed you to be interdependent on Him and others in the body of Christ. He wants you to call upon Him when the load in life gets too heavy. "The LORD always keeps his promises; he is gracious in all he does. The LORD helps the fallen and lifts those bent beneath their loads" (Psalm 145:13–14).

No matter where you are or what you're going through, Jesus is there with you. He wants you to know He's there to help carry your problem. And as you share your heart with Him, your relationship deepens.

My Prayer: Thank You for being my support. I know You are the almighty, powerful God who can do all things, but sometimes I may tend to think You aren't that interested in the details of my life. Help me remember You care about even the smallest details of my life. And help me call on You when life begins to get me down. You are such a caring and loving God who is always present. I love You. Amen.

The Benefits of Thanksgiving

My Bible Reading:
You have turned my mourning into joyful dancing. You have
taken away my clothes of mourning and clothed me with joy,
that I might sing praises to you and not be silent. O LORD my
God, I will give you thanks forever! (Psalm 30:11–12)

What do you like best about the Thanksgiving holiday? You have
a couple of days off from school and you probably eat a lot of
turkey. Do you like the white meat or maybe the drumstick? You may
enjoy cranberries, sweet potatoes or yams, pumpkin pie, or maybe
a special recipe from your family. There are a lot of benefits you get
on Thanksgiving. And there are many reasons to be thankful.

Truth is, there are real benefits to being thankful every day of
the year. Medical scientists have studied the social, physical, and
psychological benefits of gratitude. And they've found that practicing
thankfulness increases happiness and life satisfaction, reduces
anxiety and depression, strengthens the immune system, lowers
blood pressure, and helps you sleep better. The studies conclude
that when you become grateful, you develop better ways of coping
with difficulties and handling stress in life. Wise Solomon knew this
thousands of years ago. He wrote, "A cheerful heart is good medicine" (Proverbs 17:22). It's literally healthy to "give thanks to the LORD,
for he is good!" (Psalm 107:1).

---

*My Prayer: I have many things to be thankful for, including that I
benefit physically and emotionally by being thankful. You want me
to be grateful and You reward me for it when I practice it. Help me
practice it more often. I will tell someone this week of the many
things for which I am thankful. And I will start with You—I am so
thankful that You died for me, made me God's child, and have
given me eternal life in a relationship with You. Amen.*

An Attitude of Gratefulness

My Bible Reading:
O God, we give glory to you all day long and
constantly praise your name. (Psalm 44:8)

Expressing gratefulness isn't so much something you should do. It is more importantly a mindset—an attitude of thanksgiving. Being a thankful person with an ongoing attitude of gratefulness in life is something you have to cultivate. It doesn't always come naturally.

Truth is, there are ways to develop and to increase an attitude of gratitude. One way is to create a daily mental or written list of the things for which you are thankful. And then verbally express a few of them to someone. "This is the day the LORD has made," the scripture says. "We will rejoice and be glad in it" (Psalm 118:24).

Another way to cultivate an attitude of gratefulness is to lower your expectations. Expect fewer material things and then when you receive more, you will tend to be more thankful. Those who feel they deserve a lot are rarely thankful for what they do receive. Being a grateful person takes practice, but it pays off. We all would rather be around a grateful person than an ungrateful one.

My Prayer: I can give thanks to You all day long because You are so deserving of my praise. Help me cultivate a greater sense of gratitude. You have given me, my family, and my community so much. Thank You for being such a giving God. "Let all that I am praise the LORD; may I never forget the good things he does for me" (Psalm 103:2). Amen.

Thankful for. . . ?

My Bible Reading:
Give thanks to the LORD, for he is good!
His faithful love endures forever. (Psalm 136:1)

There are twenty-six verses in Psalm 136. Every one of them identifies what the children of Israel were to be thankful for and then repeats the refrain, *"His faithful love endures forever."* The idea was for God's people to sing what they were thankful for and be repeatedly reminded that God's faithful love toward them would last forever. Check out all thirty-six verses of Psalm 136 in your Bible.

Truth is, God's faithful love toward you will last forever too. So what are you truly thankful to God for? Take a deep breath, shut your eyes for five seconds, and think of some things for which you are thankful. You are alive! That's something to be thankful for. Think of all those who care for you, the privileges you have, and all the opportunities you have in life. "Give thanks for everything to God the Father in the name of our Lord Jesus Christ" (Ephesians 5:20).

Be thankful for everything and start listing out those things that immediately come to mind—life, breath, sight, hearing, touch, smell, taste, the ability to think, talk, walk, run, eat, sleep—the list goes on. Be thankful for even the tough things in life. Paul wrote, "We can rejoice, too, when we run into problems and trials, for we know that they help us develop endurance" (Romans 5:3). You have been blessed with so much—be thankful for it all.

My Prayer: *It is true that I have so much to be thankful for—everything! Help me praise You, not just on holidays, but every day for everything. Let my life be a daily praise to You and help me verbalize each day how much I am thankful to You for everything. Let me share some of the things I am thankful for with someone today. You are so worthy of all my praise. Amen.*

The Need for Encouragement

My Bible Reading:
Think of ways to encourage one another to outbursts
of love and good deeds. (Hebrews 10:24)

Have you ever been discouraged? There are times you may have lost hope through disappointments, rejections, or failures. Everyone gets discouraged at some time or another, so being discouraged from time to time is normal. But you don't want to stay there too long.

Truth is, you need others and others need you to dispel discouragement. We do this by providing hope, lifting the spirits of the discouraged, providing inspiration, and pointing someone toward a positive goal. That's what encouragement does. "So encourage each other and build each other up" (1 Thessalonians 5:11).

Encouragement can sound like, "I know things are tough right now, but I believe in you." Or, "Hey let's get out of here and get a bite to eat. And I'll even sing you a song." Encouragement offers a cheerful word, lightens things up—perhaps even with appropriate humor—anything that lifts the spirits of the discouraged. Music or a cheerful card can also inspire another and give him or her hope that things are going to get better. Your friends and family need encouragement and you can meet that need.

My Prayer: Lord, today there may be someone who needs a word
of encouragement. He or she may need some cheering up and hope
that things are going to get better. Lead me to that person and
let me be an encouragement and inspiration to him or her.
Give me wisdom and courage. Amen.

He's Your Encouragement

My Bible Reading:
God, You honor me by anointing my head with oil. My cup
overflows with blessings. Surely your goodness and unfailing
love will pursue me all the days of my life, and I will live in
the house of the LORD forever. (Psalm 23:5-6)

King David was a ruler and enjoyed a lot of good things. But he
also had enemies and experienced tough times. And when he
was discouraged he looked to God. What he saw was a heavenly
Father who cared, who honored him, who wanted to bless him, and
whose love would pursue him all his life. In the end God promised
that He would grant David eternal life to live with Him forever. That
is the God of encouragement.

Truth is, God is your source of encouragement too. He is the God
"who encourages those who are discouraged" (2 Corinthians 7:6).
Remember what Jesus said: " 'Don't let your hearts be troubled. Trust
in God, and trust also in me' " (John 14:1). He went on to say He was
leaving this earth to prepare a place for you and would send His Holy
Spirit to be with you now. And He concluded with, " 'When everything is ready, I will come and get you, so that you will always be with
me where I am' " (John 14:3).

There is no better source of encouragement than Jesus. He
believes in you, never gives up on you, and gives you hope for a
bright future with Him forever.

*My Prayer: Thank You that You are my source of encouragement. Your
goodness and unfailing love will be with me every day of my life. That
encourages me. And when this earthly life is over, my life with You will
begin and never, never end. Help me encourage someone today with
that encouraging truth. You are such an extraordinary God. Amen.*

November 25

The Need for Security

My Bible Reading:
The LORD is my light and my salvation—so why should I be afraid?
The LORD is my fortress, protecting me from danger,
so why should I tremble? (Psalm 27:1–2)

What do you feel like when your immediate needs for acceptance, attention, comfort, support, or encouragement are met? You feel satisfied, don't you? That's how you feel when your needs are currently being met. But you have another need that isn't met based on what is currently taking place in your life. However, that need is met by your having confidence in what's going to happen in the future.

Truth is, your need for security is met when you have the assurance that your physical, emotional, or spiritual needs will be met tomorrow, next week, next month, and next year. Someone gives you security when you are confident of his or her commitment to stand with you to provide for you and protect you. That removes the fear of uncertainty or danger. That kind of commitment is what scripture calls "perfect love." "As we live in God, our love grows more perfect.... Such love has no fear, because perfect love expels all fear" (1 John 4:17–18).

A perfect love removes the fear of loss or want in a person's life. When you let a friend know that no matter what, your relationship is solid, he or she feels secure. This is the kind of love that Christ's body—His church—is meant to express to its members.

My Prayer: Thank You for the people around me who have given me a sense of security. Help me enter someone's world today to meet his or her need for security. Guide me to give a person the sense that I will be there for the long haul as he or she goes through a difficult time. I want to be Your instrument, helping someone in need to feel safe and secure. Amen.

He's Your Security

My Bible Reading:

The LORD is my shepherd; I have all that I need. He lets me rest in green meadows; he leads me beside peaceful streams. (Psalm 23:1-2)

People can make each other feel secure, but not totally absolutely secure. For someone to make you feel secure in the absolute sense, that person would have to be in control of everything, know the future, and love you enough to always protect you and provide for you. That's a tall order for anyone to accomplish. In fact, no human can fill that role completely.

Truth is, the only one who can give you that absolute sense of security is God Himself. His power is absolute (Psalm 147:5); as Sovereign He is in total control of all things (Jeremiah 32:17); He knows the future (Isaiah 46:9-10); and He is " 'passionate about his relationship with you'" (Exodus 34:14). Placing your life and future in that kind of God can truly give you a sense of security. King David expressed his sense of security in God by saying, "I have all that I need." But he went on to add that even in the darkest hours of life he could rest secure in God. "Even when I walk through the darkest valley, I will not be afraid, for you are close beside me. Your rod and staff [that fend off danger] protect and comfort me" (Psalm 23:4).

My Prayer: Thank You that You are my absolute source of security. And while I believe that, when trouble comes and things get tough, I tend to feel insecure and a little fearful of the future. Remind me that even though life can be hard, You are always with me, and in the end, everything is going to turn out for my good and Your glory. You are a magnificent God! Amen.

The Need for Respect

My Bible Reading:
Show proper respect to everyone, love the family of
believers [the church], fear God, honor the emperor
[those in authority]. (1 Peter 2:17 NIV)

Have you felt respected lately? Your teacher pulls you aside to thank you for your input in class. "You made a valuable contribution to our discussion this morning," she says. Your grades were really up this semester and you got placed on the honor roll. You took a stand for a student who was being bullied. Your parents hear about it and say, "It took character and courage to do that. We're proud of you." In every instance, your teacher, your school, and your parents were honoring you—you were being respected.

Truth is, everyone has the need for respect. When you value other people, are polite, show kindness, or follow the instructions of those in authority—you show respect for them. Every human, no matter who he or she is, was created with dignity and worth and deserves respect. "Love each other with genuine affection," Paul wrote, "and take delight in honoring each other" (Romans 12:10).

We live in a time when people are disrespectful of others. Yet everyone wants to feel respected. So when the body of Christ—the church—shows "proper respect to everyone," people take notice and want to be part of a group like that. Showing respect honors God and builds up the church.

*My Prayer: Help me show respect to those around me. At
times people's attitudes and behavior may turn me off and my
disagreement with them may come through in a disrespectful way.
But please help me always be kind even with those who are unkind.
Let me show respect to other people regardless of who they are or
what they do. Help me be respectful to those around me today. Amen.*

He Respects You

My Bible Reading:

What is mankind that you are mindful of them, human beings that you care for them? You have made them a little lower than the angels and crowned them with glory and honor. (Psalm 8:4–5 NIV)

Think a minute of who you are and what you can do. You have a physical body that enables you to see, hear, walk, run, smell, touch, taste, and eat. And even if you are unable to accomplish all those things for some reason, God's "workmanship is marvelous" (Psalm 139:14). You experience sensations of joy, laughter, excitement, fulfillment, and satisfaction. You process words and thoughts and use a language that allows you to communicate with others. You are able to love others and allow others to love you. You are self-aware.

Truth is, God created you as a human being, just a little lower than heavenly beings. "God said, 'Let us make people in our image, to be like ourselves. They will be masters over all life'" (Genesis 1:26). God has honored you by making you in His image. He respects you as His creation. That means you have great value and worth as a living soul. And He honors you so much that He gives you a choice to love Him or not to love Him. As He told the children of Israel, "'Today I have given you the choice between life and death, between blessings and curses. . . . You can make this choice by loving the LORD your God'" (Deuteronomy 30:19–20). God respects you, values your personhood, and allows you the right to choose Him. God is the God of respect.

My Prayer: Thank You that You have given me inherent value by making me in Your image. How You honor me in that You, the infinite God, respect and love a finite being like me! Thank You that You didn't create me as a robot and just program me to love You. I have chosen to reach out to You in faith so You could give me life and the ability to love You for all eternity. Thank You for being such a loving and merciful God. Amen.

The Need for Approval

My Bible Reading:
So let's stop condemning each other.... If you
serve Christ with this attitude, you will please God,
and others will approve of you, too. (Romans 14:13, 18)

Do you care what people think of you? Is there something deep inside that wants others to be pleased with who you are and what you do? Then welcome to the human race. You have a need for approval. If you're human, you want others to express satisfaction with you as a person and demonstrate that they are pleased with you for who you are.

Truth is, God placed the need for approval within you, in part, so you would seek after Him in order to please Him. " 'You will seek me,' " God said, " 'and find me when you seek me with all your heart' " (Jeremiah 29:13 NIV). "Our purpose is to please God" (1 Thessalonians 2:4). That is why King David prayed, "May the words of my mouth and the meditation of my heart be pleasing to you" (Psalm 19:14). You were created to seek God and lovingly please Him. And as a member of Christ's body, you can meet the need for approval in someone's life by praising her for a quality she has or a giftedness she expresses. When you do, you help build up His church.

My Prayer: Thank You that You have instilled within me a heart to please You. And help me pass that on by expressing how pleased I am in someone today. Let me look for a quality in a person's life and let him or her know how much I appreciate it. Thank You that You are involving me in building up Your church. Amen.

You Are Salt and Light

My Bible Reading:

Jesus said, "You are the salt of the earth. But what good is salt if it has lost its flavor? Can you make it salty again? It will be thrown out and trampled underfoot as worthless. You are the light of the world. . . . Let your good deeds shine out for all to see, so that everyone will praise your heavenly Father." (Matthew 5:13–14, 16)

There are only a few times Jesus put these two words together— "You are." He said this to His followers—the church—"You are salt". . ."You are light." That is what Jesus' church is to be—salt and light to the world.

Salt is what gives flavor to food. Jesus used it to say that His church is what gives people a taste of what He is really like. You, as part of His church, are "Little Christs" walking around giving people a taste of Jesus. And that is when you also become an effective light that brings honor to God.

Truth is, as part of Jesus' church, you are truly an effective light for Him as you reflect Jesus in your life. That's why Jesus said, "Let your good deeds shine out for all to see." He wants His church to be like Him so His love can be felt and seen by others. That is what will attract your nonbelieving friends to your group of Christ followers.

My Prayer: My desire is to be "salt"—help me give people a true taste of what You are like. I want my life to shine out for You so it will honor You and bring others to You. Thank You that Your church is both "salt" and "light" to the world around me. Because of You, Your church lives to bring hope, love, and salvation to all who will believe in You as Savior. You are such an impressive God! Amen.

DECEMBER

Waiting for His Return

See You Later

My Bible Reading:

Just over five weeks after Jesus' resurrection, "He was taken up into a cloud while they [the disciples] were watching, and they could no longer see him. As they strained to see him rising into heaven, two white-robed men suddenly stood among them. 'Men of Galilee,' they said, 'why are you standing here staring into heaven? Jesus has been taken from you into heaven, but someday he will return from heaven in the same way you saw him go.'" (Acts 1:9–11)

Let's say you had a best friend for three years, but she is moving away. Your friend promises to be back in the area again soon. Yet you're going to miss her and all the good times you've had together. You are there as the car pulls away. You hear her say, "See you later," and you wave good-bye.

Truth is, as Jesus' disciples saw their Teacher and Savior ascend into heaven, they knew they would miss Him—a lot. He was their Messiah who was to establish the Kingdom of God on earth. He had healed the sick, raised the dead, and fed the people. Jesus' work didn't seem finished. That's why he told them, "I am leaving you with a gift—peace of mind and heart. And the peace I give is a gift the world cannot give. So don't be troubled or afraid. Remember what I told you: 'I am going away, but I will come back to you again'" (John 14:27–28). The reality was that Jesus' disciples and every follower of Jesus were to continue His mission while they waited for His return. And when He does return, He will establish His Kingdom on earth forever.

My Prayer: As I wait for Your return, it is obvious Your Kingdom has not yet been established in all the world. Sin and death are still here. So help me spread the word that You came to be a sacrifice for sin so that all who believe in You will have eternal life. And that one day You will return to finish the task that You began—to bring peace to all the earth. Amen.

The Great Restoration Project

My Bible Reading:
"He [God the Father] will again send you Jesus, your appointed
Messiah. For he must remain in heaven until the time for the
final restoration of all things, as God promised long ago
through his holy prophets." (Acts 3:20-21)

Have you ever been involved in restoring an old bike or an antique item, or in helping to redo a room with new paint, carpet, etc? To restore something is to bring it back to its original design or greatness. Almost everything around you deteriorates, rusts, or wears out. So in one way, you are in a constant state of restoring things.

Truth is, we live in a world that is totally imperfect. The physical world is imperfect, with disease, sickness, death, storms, and destruction. Human relationships fall apart creating tension, conflicts, war, and killing. But God spoke through the prophets long ago, " 'Look! I am creating new heavens and a new earth, and no one will even think about the old ones anymore' " (Isaiah 65:17).

Originally "God looked over all he had made, and he saw that it was very good!" (Genesis 1:31). But that perfect world with humans in perfect relationship with God was shattered by sin and death. God's great restoration project is to bring a perfect world back into being. "When Christ comes back, all his people will be raised [from the dead]. After that the end will come, when he will turn the Kingdom over to God the Father, having put down all enemies of every kind" (1 Corinthians 15:23-24). "He will judge the world with justice and rule the nations with fairness" (Psalm 9:8).

My Prayer: As I wait for Your return, I want to thank You for Your promise to restore this world to the kind of world You originally intended. Thank You that You will bring justice and fairness to an unjust and unfair world. Help me promote Your coming by demonstrating Your merciful justice and Your kind fairness in the life of someone today. Amen.

December 3

Going Up or Coming Down?

My Bible Reading:

In the vision that God gave him, John said, "I saw a new heaven and a new earth, for the old heaven and the old earth had disappeared.... And I saw the holy city, the new Jerusalem, coming down from God out of heaven like a bride beautifully dressed for her husband." (Revelation 21:1-2)

Exactly what is going to happen when Christ returns? Scripture gives us enough of a glimpse into the future of the world for us to understand that God's plan is to restore the earth, transforming it into to the perfect place where He will live with us forever. In John's vision it is described as "the holy city."

Truth is, everything in heaven and earth will be brought together under the rule of Jesus once He returns. "And this is the plan: At the right time he will bring everything together under the authority of Christ—everything in heaven and on earth" (Ephesians 1:10). That is what the prophets foretold. They quoted God as saying, " 'My dwelling place will be with them; I will be their God, and they will be my people' " (Ezekiel 37:27 NIV).

Right now, heaven and earth are separated. But when Jesus returns heaven and earth will merge like a marriage. It will be heaven on earth!

My Prayer: As I wait for Your return, let me say, You are a wonderful God with a wonderful plan. You will someday bring heaven and earth together. While I don't know when that will happen, it gives me a sense of anticipation and excitement that I will be part of it all when it does happen. In the meantime, I want to continue to help people know You and Your plan to give them eternal life. Amen.

His Home—Your Home

My Bible Reading:
"Look, God's home is now among his people!
He will live with them, and they will be his people.
God himself will be with them." (Revelation 21:3)

In the beginning God created the heaven, the earth, and humans to live in a beautiful garden. But more than that, God walked in the garden with them. That is what He wanted—He wanted to make His home their home. Yet their sin separated them from Him and God could no longer make His home with humans.

Truth is, when Jesus returns He will reestablish God's original plan and God will live with you and all the children of God forever. God said, "'I will walk among you; I will be your God'" (Leviticus 26:12). "'I will live with them and walk among them'" (2 Corinthians 6:16 NIV). He is going to live with us on the earth, a new earth that He has completely restored, transforming it into a perfect home for us for eternity.

You have God with you now in Spirit. In fact, He has taken up residence in you. Yet it's different when He makes His home on earth. At that point He will be living with us. Then wherever we go, we will enjoy the immediate presence of God. Now, you may at times have trouble feeling God's presence in your life. But then you will always experience the unhindered and direct relationship with your Lord.

My Prayer: As I wait for Your return, it is still a little hard to absorb the idea of Your living with me in a re-created world. I may not be able to understand it all now, but it's great to think that the loving Jesus who came and died for me wants to make His home my home. Thank You for that! I love You. Amen.

A New World

My Bible Reading:
He [God] will remove the cloud of gloom, the shadow of death
that hangs over the earth. He will swallow up death forever!
The Sovereign LORD will wipe away all tears. (Isaiah 25:7–8)

When you think about living in a heaven on earth, what do you imagine? Being really happy may come to mind. Getting along perfectly with friends and family is probably pretty high on your list. An absolutely perfect world sounds great, but is that really what it's going to be like?

Truth is, no one knows all the details of what the new world that God has planned will be like. But God's Word does give a little insight into what it will be like. Not only will Jesus be there, but "nothing evil will be allowed to enter, nor anyone who practices shameful idolatry and dishonesty—but only those whose names are written in the Lamb's Book of Life" (Revelation 21:27). "No longer will there be a curse upon anything" (Revelation 22:3). "The Son of God appeared for this purpose, to destroy the works of the devil" (1 John 3:8 NASB). What is certain is that God will "swallow up death forever" and He "will wipe away all tears" and no sin or wrongdoing will go on in this beautiful new world God has planned for you.

My Prayer: *As I wait for You to return, I want to thank You that You are going to re-create for me and for all who have trusted in You a place that is free of sin and death. I look forward to a world without conflict, fighting, hatred, jealousy, dishonesty, and every other kind of sin. You are a holy God who is making my eternal home a holy place. You are phenomenal! Amen.*

A Familiar World

My Bible Reading:
"For as the waters fill the sea, the earth will be filled with
an awareness of the glory of the LORD." (Habakkuk 2:14)

Have you ever been to a foreign country or in such a different place that it made you feel a little uncomfortable? If you felt that way, there probably weren't enough familiar things to make you feel comfortable. Some familiarity is necessary for you to feel at home in a place.

Truth is, when God's glory fills the new heaven and new earth, you will feel totally at home and at peace. Scripture refers to your eternal home as being a city (Hebrews 11:10, 16). Cities have buildings, streets, people, culture, arts, music, and all kinds of gatherings and activities. Scripture suggests the beauty and worth of what people made in His image will still enjoy when it says that for this city, "the kings of the earth will bring their splendor into it. . . . The glory and honor of the nations will be brought into it." (Revelation 21:24, 26 NIV) Other familiar and welcome things include a river of water, trees, and fruit (Revelation 22:1-2).

God never gave up on His original design of the Garden of Eden where He placed the first couple. He plans for you to enjoy perfect happiness and joy in a place that is familiar to you, yet without sin, pain, or death. That is your eternal future!

My Prayer: As I wait for You to return, let me thank You in advance that You will provide me a place where I will feel comfortable and at home forever. I look forward to Your return when You will make everything right and perfect. You are such a majestic God who loves me. I certainly love You. Amen.

December 7

A Forever World
_____

My Bible Reading:

No longer will there be a curse upon anything. For the throne
of God and of the Lamb will be there, and his servants will
worship him. . . . And there will be no night there—no need for
lamps or sun—for the Lord God will shine on them. And they
will reign forever and ever. (Revelation 22:3, 5)

How old is the house that you live in? If you live in a home that
was built over one hundred years ago, you probably consider
it an old home. And for it to be livable someone had to continually
make repairs and upgrade it. If not, it would have fallen into disrepair
a long time ago because nothing here on earth lasts forever.

Truth is, your new home in the new heaven and earth will last forever. There will be no curse on material things, so they won't wear out.
And more importantly, you won't wear out either. "For our dying bodies
must be transformed into bodies that will never die; our mortal bodies
must be transformed into immortal bodies" (1 Corinthians 15:53).

It's hard to imagine a perfect world without rust and decay, storms
and destruction, suffering and death. Yet that is precisely what you
can expect through all eternity because of Jesus' sacrificial death and
resurrection. You will live in a perfect forever world!

_____

*My Prayer: As I wait for Your return, I want to say that You are worthy of
my life of worship, not just in this life, but for all eternity. You are a loving
and merciful God who will change this decaying world and temporal
body into a life of joy with You forever. Thank You so much! Amen.*

What Then?

My Bible Reading:

"God blesses those who are humble, for they
will inherit the whole earth." (Matthew 5:5)

Have you ever inherited anything? Perhaps one of your grandparents passed away and left a special possession to you. You
may at some point inherit property or material things from your
parents. To inherit something comes with it a responsibility to care
for it and use it wisely.

Truth is, you will inherit the new earth. When God placed the first
couple in the Garden of Eden, He didn't just put them there to
vacation. He placed them there "to tend and care for it" (Genesis 2:15
NLT). You will have a responsibility in the new heaven and earth. Your
eternal inheritance will involve your doing things—not work you
don't enjoy—but a responsibility which will thrill you. Jesus gave an
illustration of what it will be like to enter into your eternal inheritance.
He said that the Master will say of His followers, "'Well done, good
and faithful servant! You have been faithful with a few things; I will
put you in charge of many things'" (Matthew 25:23 NIV).

Eternal life is much more than living in a perfect world. It is your
initiation into a whole new realm of meaning and significance of your
forever life. It will be a life of important responsibilities and fulfilling rewards.

*My Prayer: While I wait for Your return, I may not know all that You
have planned for me in the next life, but I want to continue to be faithful
in serving You here and now. Help me serve You by demonstrating care
and kindness to someone who needs to be encouraged, supported, or
comforted today. Help me show Your kind of love to others. Amen.*

December 9

Pure Joy

My Bible Reading:
Teach those who are rich in this world not to be proud and not to trust in their money, which is so unreliable. Their trust should be in God, who richly gives us all we need for our enjoyment. (1 Timothy 6:17)

Certain things in life have made you feel happy, right? You have experienced pleasure, been glad, felt delight, and at times were even thrilled and exhilarated. God created you to experience enjoyment even though you now live in a world of sin, pain, and suffering.

Truth is, Jesus came to save you from a world of sin and suffering and take you beyond earthly joy and give you an eternal life of pure joy. Jesus said, " 'I have told you this so that my joy may be in you and that your joy may be complete [in him]' " (John 15:11 NIV). While you can have a measure of joy now, Jesus intends for you to live in a constant state of joy in the next world. Once the Master says, " 'Well done,' " and puts " 'you in charge of many things,' " he will say, " 'Enter into the joy of your master' " (Matthew 25:23 NASB).

The joy we will experience is beyond our present comprehension. Whatever you will be involved in, rest assured it will bring you fulfillment, satisfaction, completion, gratification, a sense of reward, and the purest of joy beyond belief. That's heaven!

My Prayer: As I wait for Your return, I want my life to bring You joy right now. Thank You that You want me to experience Your kind of joy in this life and to know it in its purest sense forever. But I want to bring You joy by expressing one of the fruits of Your Spirit like patience, kindness, goodness, love, or gentleness toward someone today. Help me do that. Amen.

Let Heaven Fill Your Thoughts

My Bible Reading:
Since you have been raised to new life with Christ, set your sights on the realities of heaven, where Christ sits at God's right hand in the place of honor and power. Let heaven fill your thoughts. Do not think only about things down here on earth. (Colossians 3:1-2)

What are you going to think about today? You have subjects to study, school activities to think about, what you're going to eat, friends to meet after school, responding to texts, and the list goes on and on. Then there's the future to think about—a new or different car, college, a career, a love relationship, and maybe marriage. Life is full of thoughts.

Truth is, this life is short in comparison to eternity, and God wants your thoughts to include Him and make His Kingdom a priority in your life. Jesus said, " 'Don't store up treasures here on earth, where they can be eaten by moths and get rusty. . . . Store your treasures in heaven. . . . Wherever your treasure is, there your heart and thoughts will also be. . . . So I tell you, don't worry about everyday life—whether you have enough food, drink, and clothes. . . . Why be like the pagans who are so deeply concerned about these things? Your heavenly Father already knows all your needs, and he will give you all you need from day to day if you live for him and make the Kingdom of God your primary concern' " (Matthew 6:19-21, 25, 32-33). Letting heaven fill your thoughts is about keeping Jesus first in your life.

My Prayer: As I wait for Your return, I have a lot of earthly things to think about each day, but help me always keep You first in my thoughts and life. It's easy to get caught up in the details of my life. Yet You are the most important One in my life. "May all my thoughts be pleasing to [You], for I rejoice in the LORD" (Psalm 104:34). Amen.

He Gets Jealous

My Bible Reading:

If your aim is to enjoy this world, you can't be a friend
of God. What do you think the Scriptures mean when they
say that the Holy Spirit, whom God has placed within us,
jealously longs for us to be faithful? (James 4:4–5 NLT)

Jesus is returning to earth someday to restore it to its original
pristine order. And with all curses lifted it will be a wonderful
place to live with Him for all eternity. But Christians aren't to just sit
around pining away, just hoping for that day to come.

Truth is, while still living for Jesus in this world, you are to live
with your priorities, interest, and devotion focused in another world.
Jesus prayed that you and His other followers wouldn't be taken out
of the world, but that God would keep all of them "safe from the evil
one. They do not belong to this world any more than I do" (John
17:15–16). But when you get a little too focused on earthly things, God
gets jealous.

He jealously wants you to keep your heart and thoughts fixed on
Him. The reason? He knows that will keep your priorities in the right
place and allow you to live a life pleasing to Him. He wants you to
keep trusting in Him and living according to His ways for your own
good. King David understood this and wrote: "I reflect at night on
who you are, O LORD, and I obey your law because of this" (Psalm
119:55).

*My Prayer: As I wait for Your return, help me please You with my
attitude and actions. Thank You for jealously loving me and wanting
me to stay focused on You and Your return. You are my only hope of
eternal life in a world without sin and decay. You are an astonishing
God who has promised me an amazing future. Amen.*

Looking beyond Earth

My Bible Reading:
Regarding nonbelievers: "Their god is their appetite,
they brag about shameful things, and they think only about
this life here on earth. But we are citizens of heaven,
where the Lord Jesus Christ lives." (Philippians 3:19–20)

Do you look forward to grueling workouts and practices for sporting events or performances? How much thrill is there in disciplined practice and more practice? However, preparations for competitions and performances become meaningful when you look beyond the difficult practices and anticipate the result: victory!

Truth is, this life may include strenuous workouts that are painful, but faithful perseverance will pay off. "So be truly glad," Peter wrote. "There is wonderful joy ahead, even though you must endure many trials for a little while" (1 Peter 1:6). Those who don't have a relationship with Jesus look only at this life and what it can give them right now. But because you know Christ, you are a citizen of heaven. You are to look beyond this earth and all its suffering and anticipate great reward and victory. "What we suffer now is nothing compared to the glory he will reveal to us later.... [Because we] wait with eager hope for the day when God will give us our full rights as his adopted children, including the new bodies he has promised us" (Romans 8:18, 23).

My Prayer: As I wait for Your return, help me avoid just looking and thinking of this life here and what it can give me. I am a citizen of heaven, so help me keep in mind that what is done for You is what truly lasts. Lead me to do Your work today by being a shining light to those who need You. Amen.

In the Meantime

My Bible Reading:

We are looking forward to the new heavens and new earth he has promised, a world where everyone is right with God. And so, dear friends, while you are waiting for these things to happen, make every effort to live a pure and blameless life. (2 Peter 3:13–14)

L et's say you are going to an amusement park. What is the first thing you have to do before you get in? Stand in line and wait, right? It takes time for everyone to go through the turnstile to get into the park. Meanwhile you may chat with a friend, reply to texts, or just stare at the crowd.

Truth is, you're waiting your turn here on earth prior to Jesus' return when you and all His followers will inherit the new heaven and new earth. So what do you do in the meantime? Peter said, "Make every effort to live a pure and blameless life." And he went on to explain why. "And remember, the Lord is waiting [to return] so that people have time to be saved" (2 Peter 3:15).

While you are on earth, waiting for Jesus to return, God has a mission for you. He wants your pure and blameless life to be a witness to draw people to Him. He wants your life to reflect the image of Jesus so others will come to know Him as you do—as Savior and Lord. It is both an honor and privilege to share the truth with others that God offers eternal life through Jesus' death and resurrection.

My Prayer: As I wait for Your return, help me share Your message of salvation with those around me. Give me courage and strength to be Your witness to someone, even today, showing them that You are the only hope for the future. And thank You that You are coming again to give all Your followers a new world without sin and death. Amen.

What Pure and Blameless Looks Like

My Bible Reading:
I pray that your love will overflow more and more, and that you will keep on growing in knowledge and understanding. For I want you to understand what really matters, so that you may live pure and blameless lives until the day of Christ's return. (Philippians 1:9–10)

Live a pure and blameless life. That seems like an impossible task, doesn't it? A pure life sounds like perfection. A blameless life sounds like never doing anything wrong again. How is that kind of life even possible?

Truth is, a pure and blameless life is Christ living His righteous character through you. And you can live that kind of life as you allow Jesus' love to "overflow more and more" through you to others. Paul makes it clear: "It is not that we think we can do anything of lasting value by ourselves. Our only power and success come from God. . . . [So] as the Spirit of the Lord works within us, we become more and more like him and reflect his glory even more" (2 Corinthians 3:5, 18).

While you wait for Jesus' return, He said the most important thing His followers were to do was to " 'love the LORD your God with all your heart, all your soul, and all your mind. . . . [And] love your neighbor as yourself' " (Matthew 22:37, 39). As you put God first and grow to love Him more and more every day, His Spirit will empower you to love others with His kind of love. That's what a pure and blameless life looks like.

My Prayer: *As I wait for Your return, may Your Spirit work within me so that Your character of love will empower me to love others as I love myself. Thank You that I don't have to live a pure and blameless life in my own strength. Give me the strength to " 'do to others whatever [I] would like them to do to [me]' " (Matthew 7:12). Help me live that out today. Amen.*

The Instructions

My Bible Reading:
"The LORD is our God, the LORD alone. And you must love the LORD your God with all your heart, all your soul, and all your strength. And you must commit yourselves wholeheartedly to these command that I am giving you today." (Deuteronomy 6:4–6)

Over three thousand years ago something took place that had never happened before nor since. God personally gave Moses "two stone tablets inscribed with the terms of the covenant, written by the finger of God" (Exodus 31:18). In addition, God spoke aloud to the children of Israel. "He let you hear his voice from heaven," Moses said, "so he could instruct you" (Deuteronomy 4:36).

Truth is, what God gave that day was far more than a list of "dos" and "don'ts." It included ten commandments, or instructions, on how to love Him and others. They serve as God's guidelines for how a loving relationship with Him and with others actually is to work. Jesus said, " 'The entire law and all the demands of the prophets are based on these two commandments [to love God and one another]' " (Matthew 22:40).

The Ten Commandments that God wrote with His own finger are the very foundation to living a pure and blameless life while you wait for Jesus to return. The first four commandments give practical guidelines of how to love God. The next six commandments are practical instructions of how to love your neighbor. There will be ten devotions focused on those relational instructions throughout December.

My Prayer: As I wait for Your return, I want to thank You that You have given me clear instructions on how to love You and those around me by following the Ten Commandments. And thank You that You have given me Your Spirit that empowers me to follow Your instructions. You are a remarkable God! Amen.

The One and Only

My Bible Reading:
"You must not have any other god but me." (Deuteronomy 5:7)

What is a god? A person or thing becomes a god to someone when excessive attention and devotion are given to that person or thing. Or, it can be a nonhuman being or spirit assumed to be superhuman and to possess unusual power which someone would revere and/or fear. The first commandment says that the God of Abraham, Isaac, and Jacob is to be the only One that you are to worship and obey.

Truth is, there is no other true god, except God. The one true God said, "'You have been chosen to know me, believe in me, and understand that I alone am God. There is no other God—there never has been, and there never will be'" (Isaiah 43:10). This one and only God is eternal, holy, righteous, all-powerful, ever-present, unchanging, and all-knowing. The first step in having a relationship with God is in recognizing He is the One and only supreme God of the universe and there is no one else like Him.

He has chosen for you to know Him, believe in Him, and have a relationship with Him. He created you in His relational image for that very purpose. As the relational God of the Trinity (God the Father, God the Son, and God the Holy Spirit), He knows how relationships work and wants you to learn the true meaning and absolute joy of relationship, especially a relationship with only Him, a relationship which excludes all other gods.

My Prayer*: As I wait for Your return, You are my God, my only God. I believe there is no one like You. Thank You that You have chosen me to get to know You. I do long to know You better. I am humbled and amazed that You, being so mighty and all-powerful, desire for me to have a personal relationship with You. Help me deepen my relationship with You. Amen.*

Worship Only Me

My Bible Reading:
"You must not make for yourself an idol of any kind, or an
image of anything in the heavens or on the earth or in the sea.
You must not bow down to them to worship them, for I,
the Lᴏʀᴅ your God, am a jealous God who will not tolerate
your affection for any other gods." (Deuteronomy 5:8–9)

If you worship an image of God and not the person of God, you make God part of creation. And if you view God as something in creation, you end up worshipping creation rather than the Creator.

Truth is, God is transcendent, which means that He is unequaled and exists apart from the material universe and is not subject to its limitations. Jesus said, " 'God is Spirit, so those who worship him must worship in spirit and in truth' " (John 4:24). He wants you to recognize Him as the Creator, the Source of all things, and the Author and Judge of all that is right and wrong. It is God's character and nature that determines the standard of what is moral and right. To accept any other standard of right causes Him to be jealous. Because He knows that if you follow any other truth, it will be destructive to your relationships and cause you pain and suffering. Worshipping Him as the only way, the truth and the life leads to enduring happiness and joy in this life and in eternity.

My Prayer: As I wait for Your return, thank You for making it clear that You are my only true source of life and truth. You are above me and beyond me, yet You are able to relate to me and teach me Your ways. I worship You and only You. I love You. Amen.

Something about That Name

My Bible Reading:
"You must not misuse the name of the LORD your God."
(Deuteronomy 5:11)

When God sent Moses to lead the Hebrew people out of Egypt, he had a question for God: "They will ask me, 'What is his name?' Then what should I tell them?" (Exodus 3:13). Moses wanted to be able to somehow represent God correctly to the people of Israel, and to the Hebrews a name revealed a person's character and nature. So it was natural for Moses to want to tell his people who God was. "God replied to Moses, 'I AM WHO I AM. Say this to the people of Israel: I AM has sent me to you'" (Exodus 3:14).

Truth is, when you use the word *God,* referring to the God of the Bible, you are identifying the great I AM—the all-powerful, eternal, holy Being of the universe. He is who He is—the perfect and righteous Creator who holds the power of life and death in His hand. In fact, He is the One who "holds all creation together" (Colossians 1:17). That is why wise Solomon said, "The fear of the LORD is the beginning of knowledge" (Proverbs 1:7 NIV).

To carelessly, flippantly misuse God's name actually misrepresents the holy God that He is. It disrespects the very character and nature of God and displays a lack of respect and reverence for the awesome person of God. Misusing God's name in that manner can be done with words or in actions.

My Prayer: As I wait for Your return, let me always honor Your name by how I refer to You and how I reflect on You in my actions. You are my awe-inspiring Creator who has granted me life here and eternal life in the new world to come. Help me honor Your name by demonstrating Your nature of love and kindness to someone today. Amen.

December 19

A Special Day for a Special Person

My Bible Reading:
"Observe the Sabbath day by keeping it holy, as the
Lord your God has commanded you." (Deuteronomy 5:12)

Let's say you have a special person in your life. You really like this person—a lot. You write notes to each other. You smile at each other in class and as you pass through the hall. You chat during lunch, you text each other after school, and talk on the phone together. But that doesn't seem to be enough. You want some time to be together uninterrupted by other things. It would be great to enjoy each other's presence for a special day every week. A special day for that special person would allow you to deepen your relationship with each other.

Truth is, God wants to have a special day with you each week. He longs for you to know Him better and is pleased that you worship Him in prayers, singing, and studying His Word with other followers of Jesus. Scripture says, "Let us think of ways to motivate one another to acts of love and good works. And let us not neglect our meeting together, as some people do, but encourage one another, especially now that the day of his return is drawing near" (Hebrews 10:24-25). It's not that every day shouldn't be a day to love and worship God. But it is on one day every week that God wants you to enjoy a special day with Him.

My Prayer: As I wait for Your return, let me better focus on You, Your Word, and fellowship with other believers for at least one complete day each week. Help me make Your special day a holy day—a day set aside for You. Thank You that You love me and want to spend time with me. I want to spend more time with You too. Amen.

The Command with a Promise

My Bible Reading:
"Honor your father and mother, as the LORD
your God commanded you." (Deuteronomy 5:16)

Have you ever made the honor roll at school? Have you ever been honored with an award? That kind of honor comes from achieving something and it indicates you have performed really well. It's important to honor and respect others for the things they do. But that's not the kind of honor God is commanding you have for your parents.

Truth is, honor goes beyond respecting others for what they do. You are also to honor people for who they are and the position they hold. The fifth commandment says to honor your father and your mother. That respect, esteem, and honorable recognition is for who they are, not necessarily for what they have or have not done. And when you do show them respect for being your parents by obeying them, God says He'll reward you. "Children, obey your parents because you belong to the Lord, for this is the right thing to do. 'Honor your father and mother.' This is the first commandment with a promise: If you honor your father and mother, 'things will go well for you, and you will have a long life on the earth' " (Ephesians 6:1–3).

My Prayer: As I wait for Your return, help me show respect and honor to my parents by obeying them and loving them. I may not always feel they understand me, but I want to always respect them for who they are—the ones who brought me into this life, cared for me, and provided for me. Help me express that honor today by doing or saying something that would show that I honor them. Amen.

December 21

Hate Kills

___

My Bible Reading:
"You must not murder." (Deuteronomy 5:17)

Civilized countries have laws against murder. Title 18 of the US Code describes "murder" as "the unlawful killing of a human being with malice aforethought. [This] is murder in the first degree." It is universally accepted in civilized cultures that it's wrong to maliciously, intentionally, and hatefully cause harm to another person to the point of taking his or her life.

Truth is, God created humans with dignity and worth and wants everyone to respect each other—especially the lives of one another. Jesus made it clear that what makes taking another person's life so wrong comes from the malicious anger and hatred that is in one's heart. Hate kills. Jesus said, "You have heard that our ancestors were told, 'You must not murder. If you commit murder, you are subject to judgment.' But I say, if you are even angry with someone [hatred in your heart] you are subject to judgment" (Matthew 5:21–22).

The last six of the Ten Commandments, along with Jesus' teaching, focus on treating each other how you want to be treated. You want to be honored, so honor your parents; you don't want to be physically harmed or hated, so don't harm or hate another. " 'This is the essence,' " Jesus said, " 'of all that is taught in the law and the prophets' " (Matthew 7:12).

___

My Prayer*: As I wait for Your return, let me respect the human life of others so highly that I keep from hating even one person. Give me love for even those who may hate me. Help me, even today, show kindness toward someone who hasn't necessarily shown me kindness. Let me treat others the way I would like them to treat me. Amen.*

The Beauty of Purity

My Bible Reading:
"You must not commit adultery." (Deuteronomy 5:18)

Have you ever had a candy bar that stated on the wrapper that it was "pure milk chocolate"? How about a jar of honey? Some labels read "Pure Honey—no artificial sweeteners." Purity of chocolate or honey means there is no foreign substance in it to contaminate it; therefore it is unadulterated.

Truth is, when a man and woman marry, their love and sexual relationship are to be kept purely between them and unadulterated. When the relationship is kept pure, the two people grow deeper and closer together. That's the beauty of purity. And that's why God instructs you to not adulterate a relationship with sex outside of marriage. The Bible says, "Marriage should be honored by all, and the marriage bed kept pure" (Hebrews 13:4 NIV). "God's will is for you to be holy, so stay away from sexual sin. Then each of you will control his own body and live in holiness and honor—not in lustful passion. . . . God has called us to live holy lives, not impure lives" (1 Thessalonians 4:3–5, 7). When you abstain from sex until marriage, you are keeping that future relationship pure.

My Prayer: As I wait for Your return, help me honor marriage by keeping myself sexually pure until I decide to lovingly commit myself to someone for a lifelong married relationship. You want me to enjoy the deep and close relationship that faithfulness and purity can bring. And if failures in this area have taken place, I'm glad that Your forgiveness is available to create in me a pure heart for a clean start. You are such a merciful and loving God. Amen.

An Amazing Visitor

My Bible Reading:
The angel "Gabriel appeared to her [Mary] and said, 'Greetings, favored woman! The Lord is with you!' Confused and disturbed, Mary tried to think what the angel could mean. 'Don't be afraid, Mary,' the angel told her, 'for you have found favor with God! You will conceive and give birth to a son, and you will name him Jesus.' " (Luke 1:28-31)

How many times have you been visited by an angel? Imagine how you would respond if an angelic being appeared to you and announced, " 'The Lord is with you!' " You would probably be startled and puzzled too. It would be a pretty big deal for an angel to appear to you.

Truth is, it was a pretty big deal to Mary as well, because the angel told her, "He will be very great and will be called the Son of the Most High. The Lord God will give him the throne of his ancestor David. And he will reign over Israel forever; his Kingdom will never end!' " (Luke 1:32-33).

Two thousand years ago, an amazing visitor delivered an amazing announcement. That is what this Christmas season is all about: the announcement of the Messiah who came and will eventually set up a glorious Kingdom that will never end! He will one day bring peace to all the earth!

My Prayer: As I wait for Your return, I will remember the amazing visitor to Mary who identified You as the One who would reign eternally over Israel and all who are born of God. Thank You for coming to die so that I could live with You forever. And thank You that You are coming again to complete the Christmas story. You are going to give me and all Your followers a forever home here on a new earth. Help me spread this amazing story! Amen.

An Amazing Birth

My Bible Reading:
"Look! The virgin will conceive a child!
She will give birth to a son, and they will call him Immanuel,
which means 'God is with us.'" (Matthew 1:23)

Christmas Eve! Tomorrow you are probably going to give and receive gifts in celebration of Jesus' birth. But that first Christmas Eve, the night before Jesus' birth, was so different in a very significant way. It's true that Joseph and Mary had come to Bethlehem to register for a census ordered by the Roman Empire. And all the places to stay were full, so they had to stay in a stable overnight. But that wasn't the big deal.

Truth is, what was about to happen was the most amazing birth of all time! A young woman was about to give birth to a baby who was fully human and fully God! Scripture says, "'The child within her [Mary] was conceived by the Holy Spirit'" (Matthew 1:20). This child's father was not Joseph, Mary's husband. This child's Father was God Himself, making Jesus God's Son. What was about to happen had never happened before.

Many years earlier, God had revealed Himself to Moses in a burning bush and on Mount Sinai in the form of fire. But to see God in all His glory would be too much. God told Moses, "'No one may see me and live'" (Exodus 33:20). Scripture says, "He lives in light so brilliant that no human can approach him" (1 Timothy 6:16). But on that first Christmas Day, God would come to live among us in human form so that He could become the God-man. God would now be approachable. It was to be an incredibly amazing birth!

My Prayer*: As I wait for Your return, I will always be amazed that You left Your home in heaven and were born as a baby in Bethlehem over two thousand years ago. You grew to a man, died for my sins, rose again, and ascended into heaven. Because I have trusted in You, I have the promise of eternal life when You return and give me a new heaven and a new earth. Thank You for Your amazing birth! Amen.*

December 25

An Amazing Good News Celebration

My Bible Reading:
"That night there were shepherds staying in the fields nearby, guarding their flocks of sheep. Suddenly, an angel of the Lord appeared among them, and the radiance of the Lord's glory surrounded them. They were terrified, but the angel reassured them. 'Don't be afraid!' he said. 'I bring you good news that will bring great joy to all people. The Savior—yes, the Messiah, the Lord—has been born today in Bethlehem, the city of David! And you will recognize him by this sign: You will find a baby wrapped snugly in strips of cloth, lying in a manger.'

"Suddenly, the angel was joined by a vast host of others—the armies of heaven—praising God and saying, 'Glory to God in highest heaven, and peace on earth to those with whom God is pleased.' When the angels had returned to heaven, the shepherds said to each other, 'Let's go to Bethlehem! Let's see this thing that has happened, which the Lord has told us about.' They hurried to the village and found Mary and Joseph. And there was the baby, lying in the manger. After seeing him, the shepherds told everyone what had happened and what the angel had said to them about this child. All who heard the shepherds' story were astonished. . . . The shepherds went back to their flocks, glorifying and praising God. . . ." (Luke 2:8–20)

Truth is, today you are celebrating the "good news that will bring great joy to all people." Christmas is a time to rejoice that "the Savior—yes, the Messiah, the Lord—has been born." It is a time to give thanks that Jesus has given His life and been resurrected so that all who receive Him will be granted eternal life. That is news worth celebrating!

My Prayer: As I wait for Your return, like the shepherds, I will praise God for sending You as the Savior of the world. And I will forever thank You for being my personal Savior. That is the greatest and best gift I could ever receive on this Christmas Day—the gift of Jesus as my Savior and Lord. Amen.

The Meaning of Christmas

My Bible Reading:
John saw Jesus in a vision and wrote: "His face was like the sun in all its brilliance. When I saw him, I fell at his feet as if I were dead. But he laid his right hand on me and said, 'Don't be afraid! I am the First and the Last. I am the living one. I died, but look—I am alive forever and ever!... [And] Yes, I am coming soon!'" (Revelation 1:16–18; 22:20)

Christmas is a holiday celebrated by billions of people all over the world each year. It commemorates a birthday that people have recognized for centuries. Thousands of Christmas songs are sung annually. Stores and homes are decorated in festive lights and tinsel. The holiday is supposed to honor and celebrate the birth of Jesus Christ.

Truth is, the true meaning of Christmas goes beyond the birth of Jesus. His purpose for entering this world was to offer Himself as a sacrifice for sin "'so that everyone who believes in him will not perish but have eternal life'" (John 3:16). And that eternal life cannot truly take place without both Christ rising from the grave (which He has) and then returning to earth again so that God will give "his Son authority over all things, [so that he] will be utterly supreme over everything everywhere" (1 Corinthians 15:28). Christmas celebrates Jesus' first coming so that you and all His followers can look forward to His second coming.

My Prayer: As I wait for Your return, let me never forget why You came to earth. The Christmas holiday is great—the decorations, the music, the time with family and friends—but help me always to remember why You came and that You are coming back to bring peace to all the earth. Amen.

As the Christmas Tree Is Put Away

My Bible Reading:
The Word [Jesus] gave life to everything that was created,
and his life brought light to everyone. The light shines in the
darkness, and the darkness can never extinguish it. (John 1:4–5)

Do you help put up and take down a Christmas tree each year? Some say that back in the 1500s, an influential German Christian leader (Martin Luther) started the tradition of the Christmas tree. It is said that he was struck by the beauty of a forest of starlit fir trees and brought one indoors to decorate it with candles for his children. The idea is that Christ is the light that shines in the darkness and the evergreen tree represents the life He gives us forever.

Truth is, Jesus is your light that will never go out. He said, " 'I have come as a light to shine in this dark world, so that all who put their trust in me will no longer remain in the dark' " (John 12:46). And there is a tree that lasts forever in the new heaven and new earth. John saw this in his vision. The water of life flowed from God's throne and "on each side of the river grew a tree of life" (Revelation 22:2). So as you put away your Christmas tree, remember the light of Jesus and His tree of life that will last forever. As a child of God you are destined for an eternal place. "And there will be no night there—no need for lamps or sun—for the Lord God will shine on them. And they will reign forever and ever" (Revelation 22:5).

My Prayer: As I wait for Your return, help me share with those around me that You are the Christmas light of the world that will never go out. And when people trust in You, they are granted life forever. That is a wonderful message from the everlasting God. Help me spread that message today and all next year. Amen.

Takers

My Bible Reading:
"You must not steal." (Deuteronomy 5:19)

One of the highlights of the Christmas season is the giving of gifts. Jesus loved the world and gave His life. His followers are to give His kind of love to others. That's why from the very beginning God gave His instructions to be a giver, not a taker.

Truth is, when God said not to steal from others, He was saying you must respect both people and their possessions by not taking what doesn't belong to you. One of the foundational principles in developing healthy relationships is respecting certain boundaries of others. God set up a boundary of possessions and said that boundary was to be honored and respected.

To take from another without permission is another way of saying you have a right to your own way, whether you've earned it or not. That reflects a selfishness that violates others and destroys relationships. "Don't be selfish," the Bible says. "Don't look out only for your own interests, but take an interest in others too" (Philippians 2:3-4). God gave us this commandment to teach us that honoring what another has actually builds a trust and respect in relationships.

My Prayer: As I wait for Your return, let me be a shining witness for You by respecting others and what they own. Help me avoid an attitude of entitlement—which is the view that people owe me. Rather, let me earn what I get and honor what others get by not selfishly taking what doesn't belong to me. You are a God of fairness and justice. Thank You for that. Help me live unselfishly today. Amen.

Honesty Is the Best Policy

My Bible Reading:
"You must not testify falsely against
your neighbor." (Deuteronomy 5:20)

Have you ever had someone lie about you? How did you or would you feel toward someone who intentionally told an untruth about you? You shouldn't resent or hate that person, but that would certainly create a barrier to a friendship, wouldn't it?

Truth is, dishonesty breaks down relationships. God wants you to build strong, healthy relationships and that is one of the main reasons He says not to lie against your neighbor. "The LORD detests lying lips, but he delights in those who tell the truth" (Proverbs 12:22).

If you tell the truth all the time, people who know you can believe you all the time. But if you tell the truth just some of the time, people who know you can't trust you any of the time. That's how dishonesty works; it undermines trust in a relationship. Honesty, on the other hand, deepens friendships by demonstrating loyalty and trust. Honesty truly is the best policy. "Many will say they are loyal friends, but who can find one who is truly reliable? The godly walk with integrity" (Proverbs 20:6–7).

My Prayer*: As I wait for Your return, help me live a life of honesty. I want to be trusted by my parents and friends. Let me begin this coming new year committed to being fully honest and truthful to all those around me. Thank You that You have given me these guidelines to build healthy relationships in life. You are a loving God who cares about my relationships. Amen.*

Greedy

My Bible Reading:

"You must not covet your neighbor's wife. You must not covet your neighbor's house or land, male or female servant, ox or donkey, or anything else that belongs to your neighbor." (Deuteronomy 5:21)

Y‍ou see a friend's car, a piece of jewelry or an outfit someone is wearing and you'd like to have it—or one like it. Is that coveting something from another person? Is that wrong?

Truth is, when God instructs you not to covet what other people have, He is telling you not to selfishly desire things, or be greedy or envious of what others have. This commandment addresses the desire of the heart. God doesn't want you to hunger after the things of this world. "Don't be greedy, for a greedy person is an idolater, worshiping the things of this world" (Colossians 3:5). The problem with those who covet, are greedy, and are envious is that they are never satisfied. The more they covet, the more they want. "Their god is their appetite," Paul said, "and they think only about this life here on earth. But we are citizens of heaven. . . . And we are eagerly waiting for him to return as our Savior" (Philippians 3:19–20).

Instead of hungering for the things of this earth, Jesus wants His followers to " 'hunger and thirst for righteousness, for they shall be satisfied' " (Matthew 5:6 NASB). Hungering for Jesus and His ways is what truly satisfies.

My Prayer: As I wait for Your return, help me keep my heart focused on You and what You want for me. I know You and Your ways will bring me true joy and satisfaction in life. I want to learn more of You in this coming year as I study Your Word. Give me a greater hunger for You. You complete me. I love You. Amen.

Forever Grateful

My Bible Reading:
"Worthy is the Lamb, who was slain, to receive power and
wealth and wisdom and strength and honor and glory
and praise. . .for ever and ever!" (Revelation 5:12–13 NIV)

A s you close out this year, think of this: Where would you and this
entire world be if God was not a God of love and mercy? What if
God had not responded to the first couple's sin by sending His Son as
a sacrifice to be able to forgive sin? The first couple and every person
born into the human race would be forever lost!

Truth is, God has shown us love and mercy. Some three thousand
years ago King David wrote, "The unfailing love of the LORD fills
the earth" (Psalm 33:5). "For your unfailing love is higher than the
heavens. Your faithfulness reaches to the clouds. Be exalted, O God,
above the highest heavens" (Psalm 108:4–5). A thousand years later
the apostle Paul wrote, "We praise God for the glorious grace he has
poured out on us who belong to his dear Son" (Ephesians 1:6).

Down through the ages, people have been praising God for
redeeming them. And throughout the ages of eternity you and every
redeemed person will continue to be forever grateful for His love
and mercy. As this year ends, it is an excellent time to express your
personal gratitude to God, for He is worthy of your praise. Praise Him!

---

*My Prayer: As I wait for Your return, I want to express how incredibly
grateful I am that You have shown me mercy. You died a terrible
death that I might live. You are coming again to rid the world of
sin and death. And I will be able to live in a perfect world with You
forever. I love You now and will love You through all eternity. Amen.*